Advance Praise for *Play*
A Family Guy (Reluc

"Bob Brody's *Playing Catch with Strangers* is a gem. Brody spent years honing his craft as a hard-working newspaper and magazine reporter. He has a reporter's eye for detail and ear for a good story coupled with a writerly heart. This collection is filled with insights, wit, pithy observations, common sense and neighborly decency. This delightful and thought-provoking memoir proves that Brody has developed into a master of the short essay."
—Dan Rather, former CBS-TV anchor

"Bob Brody is a modern-day E.B. White who writes about everyday life with clarity, honesty and humor. He has a light touch and a piercing intelligence that floats above the swamp gas of most contemporary literature. He is a delight to read."
—Bob Guccione, Jr., former editor of *Spin* and *Discover* magazines

"In this winning memoir, Bob Brody wears his heart on both sleeves, along with a chip on both shoulders. He's every inch a diehard New Yorker, equally tender and tough. Give the guy credit: he gets stabbed five weeks after moving into the city, but sticks around for the next 41 years."
—Nicholas Pileggi, author of *Goodfellas*

"A good man, Bob Brody is also an observant one. Nothing escapes his vision. Growing up with deaf parents, he learned to listen hard to the world around him, and this poignant memoir is the result."
—Phillip Lopate, author of *My Mother's Tale*, editor of *The Art of the Personal Essay*

"Brody offers us ringside seats to an engrossing journey through his life with unflinching honesty and quirky charm. *Playing Catch with Strangers* is full of wonder, regrets, and ultimately love."
—Danielle Ofri, MD, author of *What Patients Say, What Doctors Hear* and editor-in-chief of *Bellevue Literary Review*

"Bob Brody's work is poignant, heartfelt, always good natured and earnestly funny. In a world swollen with snark, it's refreshing every now and then to sit down with a writer so sincere." **—Joshua Greenman, opinion editor of *The New York Daily News***

"In *Playing Catch with Strangers*, Bob Brody honors his parents for confronting the struggles of being deaf—back when society still saw deafness largely as a stigma—and pays tribute to his father for ultimately becoming a hero to the deaf community nationwide." **—Robin Feder, executive director, Central Institute for the Deaf**

"Bob Brody writes about family, friends, life and love in mesmerizing and meaningful prose. Every essay engages and teaches. Every essay shines a new light on the heart and the soul."   **—Maureen Mackey, former features editor of *Reader's Digest***

"A family memoir always heartfelt and occasionally harrowing and hilarious. A New York baby boomer lays his life on the line about love sought, lost and regained."
—Judy Mandel, author of *Replacement Child: A Memoir*

"If you like to laugh or cry, but don't get around to big, satisfying emotions as much as you'd like -- rejoice! (in between laughing and crying, that is). Bob Brody is here!"
—Lenore Skenazy, author of *Free-Range Kids: Giving Our Children the Freedom We Had Without Going Nuts with Worry*

"Bob Brody's essays provide a visceral experience. Readers become 11-year-olds, stretching the days of summer to their furthest edges; they become grown children, standing outside the home of a parent they haven't seen in ages, anxiously wondering if the door will open. As his long-time editor at *Newsday*, I was grateful when Bob's submissions showed up in my inbox. I knew I was in for a great read that would resonate deeply with our audience, while shedding a little more light on those universal human conditions: nostalgia, yearning, love and loss."
—Alleen Barber, former editor of the opinion section of *Newsday*

"There is a reason Bob Brody's writing has been featured in many top publications: He has a sharp eye for life and his prose is powered by beautifully disciplined emotion. Here is a fine writer worth your time."
—Skip Bayless, former ESPN anchor and author of *The Boys* and *Hell-bent*

"Bob Brody writes about issues that matter -- work and family, courage and cowardice, how we hurt those we're closest to, and how we reconcile with them -- with a touch as light as a Zen painter's brush. He navigates the thickets of everyday life with the sharp eye of a jungle explorer, discovering nuggets of wisdom under coffee-shop napkins, on sidewalks in Queens, and in the wallet of his sleeping father. These essays are smart, moving, compassionate, and often laugh-out-loud funny."
—Kenneth Miller, contributing editor at *Reader's Digest* and former senior editor of *People* magazine

"I can't imagine a better Sunday morning than having the kids entertain themselves, nursing a cup of coffee and settling down to pore over Bob Brody's essays."
—Jill Smokler, author of *Confessions Of A Scary Mommy*

"What makes Bob Brody remarkable is his commitment to fully, and courageously, observing his relationships. Where he discovers cracks, he shines a light. He is able to get us to look at his life—and therefore at our own -- more closely than before."
> —**Patty Chang Anker, author of** *Some Nerve: Lessons Learned While Becoming Brave*

"In his essays, Bob Brody believes in getting personal. Whether the topic is family, friends, life in New York City or pickup basketball, he shares these intimate experiences with all his heart. And we come away feeling both a little more understanding and much more alive."
> —**Howard Dickman, former deputy editorial features editor of** *The Wall Street Journal*

"Brody helps us see ourselves more clearly by using the tools of a great journalist to tell deeply personal stories. By sharing his unflinching view of the man in the mirror, he tells us something about what makes us tick. By exposing his fears and vulnerabilities, he makes us feel stronger. Savoring Bob Brody's life lessons is like spending time with a true friend."   —**Robert Davis, former reporter at** *USA Today*

"*Playing Catch With Strangers* gets you right in your heart and soul. Bob Brody's memoir is about the sorts of struggles so many of us face with our families. It will bring you to laughter and tears, often at the same time."
> —**Tania Grossinger, author of** *Memoir of an Independent Woman: An Unconventional Life Well Lived* **and** *Growing Up At Grossinger's*

"Bob Brody writes about friends, family and bygone times with grace, compassion and a simplicity that is deceptive, given that his essays capture so beautifully the profound truths that touch upon us all."
> —**Neal Hirschfeld, co-author of** *Dancing With The Devil, Detective* **and** *Homicide Cop* **and former** *Daily News* **reporter**

"With genial prose and thoughtful insights, Bob Brody reminds us not only what is important in life, but that we're all in this together. *Playing Catch With Strangers* is wondrous commentary told wonderfully."
> —**Clem Richardson, former human-interest columnist for the** *New York Daily News*

Playing Catch with Strangers:
A Family Guy (Reluctantly)
Comes of Age

Playing Catch
with Strangers:

A Family Guy (Reluctantly)
Comes of Age

Bob Brody

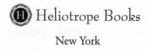 Heliotrope Books

New York

Credits

Many of the chapters are adapted from essays that originally appeared in the following publications: *The New York Times, The Atlantic, The Washington Post, The Wall Street Journal, Esquire, USA Today, The Daily News, Newsday, Newsweek, Reader's Digest, The International Herald Tribune, The Los Angeles Times, Forbes, The San Francisco Chronicle, The Smithsonian, The Record, The Newark Star Ledger, Glamour, 50 Plus, The St. Louis Post Dispatch, The Forward, Jewish Week, Chicken Soup For The Soul, National Public Radio, The New York Sun, The New Haven Register, AM-New York, The Queens Chronicle, CNBC.com, The Huffington Post, The Daily Caller, Brevity, The ASJA Monthly,* and the blog letterstomykids.org.

Heliotrope Books LLC
heliotropebooks@gmail.com

Cover design by Naomi Rosenblatt with AJ&J Design

For Nettie

Author

Bob Brody, an executive and essayist, lives in New York City.
He and his wife Elvira have two children, Michael and Caroline.

Photo by Aaron Showalter

Table of Contents

Home Boy

To Be Heard

In my earliest memories, at perhaps age three or four, I'm talking with my mother face-to-face. I'm trying to tell her something, though I forget what. Maybe I'm hungry. Maybe my stomach hurts from drinking too much soda. Maybe I'm in the mood to play a game of make-believe. But my mother, her eyebrows lowered in puzzlement, nods her head from side to side. She's having trouble making out my words.

Say it again, she says. So I say it again. Move your lips more, she says. So I move my lips more. Speak more slowly, she says. So I speak more slowly. Sometimes I fail again. But I keep trying to get it right. And eventually I break through. Now she will make me lunch or give me Pepto-Bismol or join in a session of hide-and-seek.

So went my early boyhood on Radburn Road in Fair Lawn, New Jersey. Year after year, I struggled to get my mother to understand my speech. She's deaf, profoundly so, stricken with spinal meningitis soon after her first birthday. She never heard me cry as a baby. She's never heard my voice nor a single word I've ever said.

Back then, she instructed me in how to speak with her so she could pick up my words. She trained me to regulate my speech, its pace and its rhythm, to shatter the barrier between my vocal cords and her broken ears. She had to read my lips to understand me, to listen with her eyes, so I needed to shape my mouth perfectly. I had to articulate every syllable, enabling her, for example, to tell an "b" from a "p."

I tried hard because I had the most powerful of incentives. I wanted to please my mother.

I had my work cut out for me. Sometimes, as I repeated the same sentence two or three times, she managed to be patient. But often she gave in to frustration, scolding me with a hiss. It could be intimidating. As a result, we lost so much in translation.

Why did it have to be so hard for us simply to talk to each other? Each of us felt walled off, marooned within ourselves. I grew up wondering whether the world would prove likewise deaf to me.

Far, Far Away

The five-year-old boy who would become my father in 21 years stood on a platform in Newark Penn Station with his mother and father waiting for the train that would soon take him away from all he had ever known and loved. Unable to afford to join him for the trip, they both leaned over to kiss him on the forehead. It was September, 1931.

Irwin Lee Brody handed the conductor his ticket and boarded the train under the care of a porter assigned to him. He looked out the window at his parents waving goodbye to him and he waved back. The train chugged out of the station, whistle hooting, billowing steam with a hiss. His parents grew smaller, receding in the distance, back into the past, until gone from sight, just a memory.

He was leaving home and alone now and in for a long ride, headed 868 miles away. None of the strangers on the train knew his name or where he lived or where he was going or, for that matter, his most defining physical characteristic—that he was severely hard of hearing, all but deaf. Because his mother gave birth to him while she had German measles, Irwin Lee Brody was born with nerve deafness and able to discern only about 10% of all sounds. He had difficulty making himself understood when he spoke, and an equally hard time understanding anyone who talked to him. None knew how his hearing loss frustrated his family, but most of all him.

The train entered Pennsylvania, rumbling through Harrisburg and Pittsburgh. The boy saw all the houses relegated to the outskirts of town, near the railroad tracks, all the plants and factories, industrial America forlorn and forsaken in the fresh depths of the Great Depression. He understood only that he was going away, but had no idea for how long and what might come of it.

On went the train, on into Ohio and through Columbus, on into Indiana and through Indianapolis, on into Illinois and through Springfield, and finally into Missouri. Hour after hour, the train rattled through big cities and woebegone small towns, one in four Americans jobless. The boy heard next to nothing, none of the rattling or the conversations around him, all of it just a bottomless silence to him. Then he arrived at Union Station in St. Louis, where a staffer met him and drove him to his new home away from home, the Central Institute for the Deaf.

The Campaign

The girl who became my mother fell ill with spinal meningitis six days after her first birthday, in the summer of 1929, and almost died. The disease left her stricken with permanent nerve deafness. She would never again hear a chick peep or rain splattering on a lake or the voices of her mother and father and brother.

She was the first-born, and my grandparents were shocked and heartbroken at the diagnosis of deafness. They felt overwhelmed at the prospect of raising a deaf child. In those days, the deaf were still ridiculed as freaks.

At age three, my mother was sent to the Lexington School for the Deaf. After my grandfather dropped her off at school, she would scream in fear so loudly that he could hear her several blocks away. He never got over the sad sounds of those screams.

My mother remembers the frustration of trying to make herself understood at home. She learned to speak properly and read lips well, but the best of lip-readers might understand only 35 percent of what is said. She felt inferior to the other children in the neighborhood. They called her deaf-and-dumb, and never played with her. At home, she went into tantrums and broke whatever was handy. I've seen pictures of my mother as a girl. In many, she looks hidden away inside herself, as if deafness were a prison.

My grandmother began a campaign to make her daughter feel equal to other children. She held birthday parties so my mother could become popular. She arranged weekly piano lessons for two years, until my mother could play a Strauss waltz without a mistake. She taught her words. With the most unstinting love, my grandmother tried to make her daughter feel like other, hearing children—and in that respect, help her escape to freedom.

Oralism—the philosophy that the deaf should learn, above all else, to communicate with the voice, not hands—prevailed then. And so my grandparents never learned sign language, in the hope that my mother could get along without it. For a long time, I suspected that they tried to deny to themselves the undeniable—that their daughter was deaf, that she would probably always be deaf.

Her deafness ultimately spun a web of special hardships that entangled everyone who ever loved her.

A Miracle In St. Louis

There, at the Central Institute for the Deaf, the staff taught Lee Brody how to make the most of what little hearing he possessed. They showed him how to read and how to listen—we all learn to talk by listening—and also how to speak, but without using sign language. They taught him, in effect, how to hear and—above all, this being the central mandate—how to function more or less the same as a hearing person.

The school was different from most schools, just as the children were different from most children. My father would hold a mirror in front of his own mouth in class to see how his lips, teeth and tongue should move to produce certain sounds. He would place his fingertips on his own cheek or throat, and sometimes on those of the teacher, to feel the vibrations that accompanied those sounds. He would wear headphones connected to an "amplification box" and watch a teacher speak into a microphone to observe how certain sounds corresponded with certain movements of her mouth.

Back then, the deaf were still walled in by the ignorance and prejudice of the hearing. After all, the few words they knew were poorly pronounced in hollow voices without melody. They misunderstood the hearing and were themselves hard to understand. For centuries, the deaf lived in shame in the face of unrelenting hostility. They were ridiculed as freaks and turned into outcasts. They were routinely barred from taking on even the simplest of jobs. All too many were wrongly diagnosed as mentally retarded and left to languish, utterly forgotten, in state institutions.

Still, The Central Institute for the Deaf was founded on an overriding principle— namely, that every child in attendance, though afflicted with the invisible disability of permanent hearing loss, should be regarded, and treated, not as a deaf child but simply as a child. In most respects, then, life there was much the same as at any other boarding school. My father would take classes in history, math and science. He would join other students for family-style meals at a round table. He might have performed in a theatrical production and danced to music at the annual prom and played the occasional dormitory prank.

There he stayed for the next 10 years, going home to visit his parents and two sisters only once or twice a year on holidays. There, in the face of a society that regarded the deaf largely as dumb—several doctors originally diagnosed him as retarded—he paid close attention to his teachers and studied hard.

He returned home to Newark sounding, as he spoke, exactly like any hearing person, and attended Weequahic High School, the only deaf student there. He always sat in the first row in his classes, the better to follow the teacher. He lived with his parents and two sisters, Zelda and Gayle, on the second floor of a small house on Leslie Street in the Weequahic section of Newark.

He was bright and, by all accounts, also absent-minded, a daydreamer, his head in the clouds, demonstrating a scientific, creative turn of mind. From the start, he liked to tinker, first with telegraph machines. He also experimented with a chemistry set in a homemade basement laboratory, once causing a minor explosion that sent plumes of fumes spiraling through the house. He could take apart almost anything, whether a clock or a washing machine, and put it back together again, only better than before.

His first invention, as a teenager, was an alarm clock rigged to shine a bright light in his face.

He was among the first students with hearing loss ever accepted at Washington University, where he took more notes than the other students, intent on recording every detail, the better to refer back later. His ambition was to become a doctor and specialize in the care of the deaf.

But that never happened. Two years later, his mentor broke the news to him that he stood no chance of ever getting into medical school. He was having difficulty learning German, then a language required of all medical students. He also faced competition from all the returning World War II veterans on the G.I. Bill also eyeing medical school, plus the extra challenge of admission quotas set for Jews. Disappointed and likely devastated, my father returned to New Jersey to transfer to Rutgers University, among the few with hearing loss ever accepted there, too, and graduated with a degree in psychology.

Head Over Heels

The 23-year-old man who became my father in two years was in the Bronx climbing up a fire escape. He was there on an afternoon in 1950 to surprise the 21-year-old woman who would become my mother.

They'd met in a banquet room in a midtown hotel at a social event for deaf people a few months earlier, and started dating. My father had spotted my mother—an Elizabeth Taylor lookalike—and turned to a friend.

"That's the girl I'm going to marry someday," my father told him.

Now my father had driven 25 miles from Newark for an unexpected visit to the apartment building on the Grand Concourse where my mother lived on the fourth floor with her parents and younger brother, Leonard.

Only no one answered the doorbell. My mother was home, but unable to hear the ringing.

So my father finally hoisted himself up the fire escape, climbed up to the fourth floor, pulled open a window and stepped in.

My mother was apparently unaccustomed to visitors, much less male suitors, entering into her home through the window.

"What are you doing here?" she asked.

"I wanted to see you. I missed you."

"Oh."

"I just wanted to see you."

Today, he could have simply texted her. The deaf community can connect with each other—even engage in the rituals of courtship—through the same devices and social media channels as the hearing do.

All those years ago, my father could have given up. He could have stopped ringing and returned to Newark. He could have been pegged as a burglar during his aerial act and arrested. He could have fallen to the sidewalk.

My mother could have called him crazy and kicked him out, never to date him again.

Instead, a few months later, my mother and father became engaged. The next year, they were married in Manhattan and honeymooned in the Catskills, at the Concord Hotel. They rented a one-bedroom apartment on Sheridan Avenue in the Bronx.

Nine months later, I was born, and 20 months later came my sister. My parents moved to the suburbs of New Jersey and stayed married for 35 years.

He took a risk with that surprise visit. Maybe his determination and daring made all the difference to my mother. Maybe seeing him there at the window, so stubborn and smitten, convinced her that he was indeed the guy for her. Maybe, after he told her he just wanted to see her, she finally understood just how much.

Cries Unheard

My mother and father had met at a social club for the deaf in Manhattan. Hard of hearing, my father wore a hearing aid that, then as later, enabled him to hear most sounds and speak almost perfectly. He'd gone to a regular high school, so he knew no sign language and spoke too quickly for my mother to understand. My mother reminded him again and again, with only the most gradual success, to speak slowly for her.

Over the next year, my parents went out together—parties, bowling, ice skating, horseback riding, movies—and dating evolved into serious courtship. They married in 1951.

Nine months later, at age 23, my mother gave birth to me—and in so doing, lost most of what little hearing she had left. As a result, my mother never heard me cry as a baby.

My grandmother was frightened about that. So my father, ever the handyman, clipped a standard microphone over my crib and connected it to bare light bulbs in the master bedroom, the living room, the kitchen and the bathroom in our apartment in the Bronx, a makeshift sound alarm system to capture my crying in the middle of the night. Every time I cried, the bulbs flashed, telling my mother that I was wet or hungry or wanted to be held, translating my cries into light. Seeing the bulbs flash, my mother said years later, was just like hearing me cry.

Still, my mother never heard me. She still had no idea how my cries sounded, whether loud or soft, wailing or whimpering, pianissimo or staccato. And so this central connection between any mother and child—the ability to interpret this most primal of signals, that of a baby crying—was missing between me and my mother.

In my earliest memory of my mother—as in her earliest memory of *her* mother—I'm struggling to get through to her in simple conversation. I would face her directly, so she could read my lips, and try to speak slowly and move my lips enough.

But she misunderstood me more often than not. Sometimes I spoke too fast, without moving my lips enough, and had to repeat myself, trying hard to pronounce every word crisply.

The Go-Between

I began to make phone calls for my mother at the age of three, acting as her voice and ears. She would tell me what to say and I would let her know how the other person responded. Mainly she asked me to convey news and plan meetings with her mother or other relatives, or with her deaf friends who had hearing children, like me, old enough to handle phone calls.

As I grew older, I spoke on her behalf with strangers on neighborhood errands as well. I ordered her meals in restaurants and spoke on her behalf to post-office clerks and department-store salespeople. May I have some stamps? Do you accept these coupons? Does this blouse come in a smaller size? In turn, I would tell my mother how they answered.

She tried in vain to make out what our relatives said around the table at family gatherings on holidays. She would turn her head right and left, looking from one talking face to another, to try to follow the conversation by reading lips and facial expressions alone. My uncles and aunts and cousins, all of whom could hear normally, seldom included my mother in conversations, even though she could speak clearly. She would tug on my sleeve or tap my shoulder to ask me to interpret.

My job was to build a bridge between her and the hearing world. I never complained. She was my mother. She needed my help. What would she do without me? I tried to see my role of translator as just another household chore, like throwing my dirty socks in the hamper.

At times the job of liaison gave me a feeling of singular importance. Only I, on behalf of my mother, could call an aunt to schedule a Sunday dinner, or a friend to set up a trip to the mall.

Sometimes, though, I minded such chores—and for good reason.

Even when my sister Linda, two years younger than I, reached age four or five, my mother still asked me to handle most of her phone calls. She understood me better because I spoke more clearly than my sister. In a sense, my mother trained me so well for the job that she saw no need to replace me. I was also more willing to help than my sister, who went so far as to avoid a conversation with my mother because the process of communication was so slow, so draining. Linda kept to herself, detached from my mother's demands.

We often felt we took care of our mother almost as much as she took care of us. I often felt cheated of my independence—and, to an extent, of my childhood itself. The calls amounted merely to five minutes here and there, but to me they seemed to last *hours*. And it seemed that whenever I wanted to play softball in the park or join my friends at the soda fountain in my town, my mother needed me for "just one more call" to the dentist or the beauty parlor. Eventually, she seemed almost as much my responsibility as I was hers.

What kept me from complaining was that I always felt sorry for her. Sorry she would never hear my voice, or how Barbra Streisand sings, or a car screeching around the corner, honking at her crossing the street. It somehow seemed unfair that I could hear.

Prince Robert

My Nana would do anything for me, and often did.

Look at my grandson. Just look at him. Is he the most beautiful grandson you ever saw? He's mine, you know. All mine. Yes, I'm his grandmother, his Nana, and he's my grandchild, the very first.

That's how it was with my Nana, the only Nana who ever really mattered to me. That's what she said and that's how she thought.

In my earliest memories as a boy, my Nana would make me anything I wanted to eat, at any time, without any question or hesitation.

I'll make him French Toast and coffee with a lot of milk and sugar and I'll let him stay up later than his parents do and watch whatever he wants on TV.

Throughout my life, even well into adulthood, Nana would look to feed me. When I took my first apartment in Manhattan, on East 7th Street between Avenues A and B, she would give me food to take home. Brisket, stuffed cabbage, the plumpest, juiciest shrimp, tuna salad made with her own hands (complete with carrots and raisins), homemade chopped liver, macaroons, and on and on.

In my every visit to her apartment, she would offer me something to eat, a snack, a sandwich, a nosh, something, anything. Her drive to feed me was primal, instinctive and all-powerful. Sometimes I would agree to eat something she offered just because I felt I should, and because it was easier than saying no, because to say no would disappoint her and leave me feeling guilty.

Her desire to feed me, to see me eat and grow sated and strong as a result, expressed itself as a force of nature, like a strong wind that bends everything in its path.

Ah, but her wish to see me happy went well beyond food.

Prince Robert: The Sequel

Look at my grandson. He's so smart. That's why he's bored in school and never does his homework and gets such poor grades. He's so clever.

So my Nana believed.

That's why he's always making wonderful observations at museums and in restaurants and wherever I take him. He's so sensitive, too sensitive. That's why he talks back to teachers and gets in trouble and everything bothers him and he feels hurt and angry half the time. Look at him and listen to him and marvel at him.

All hail, Prince Robert!

Nana took me everywhere in Manhattan, as my own parents never had. I would stay overnight with my grandparents, often for a few days during school vacation, and every day Nana would take me on some adventure in the great city.

As a boy, especially one growing up in the suburbs, I saw the city as all hustle and roar, as a movie that was all action without letup, something to see and hear at every turn. Nana took me to the Statue of Liberty, the Empire State Building, Radio City Music Hall (for movies yet!), the New York Historical Society (where I pored over newspapers from the Revolutionary War), Central Park, a toy store on the Upper East Side called Rappaports, Schrafft's (for ice cream sodas), Chock Full of Nuts, Saks Fifth Avenue, Barney's (where Barney himself once took care of us) and who knows where else.

All our adventures centered on Manhattan. I rarely saw her outside it. She came to be synonymous with it, its representative, its most loyal advocate and tour guide.

He's the smartest, most beautiful, most sensitive grandson in history.

He can do no wrong and he never will. He's my grandson, after all, so how could he? It's genetically impossible. Moses had nothing on him. He's perfection itself. He's everything to me. He's my second chance, a child who's neither deaf nor wildly disobedient, so unlike my daughter and son, a chance to start over, a clean slate.

In later years, she would remind me of a remark I apparently made at the Guggenheim Museum (yet another cultural landmark she took me to). We were there looking at some modern painting, maybe a product of Abstract Expressionism. And I said, according to her, "If you turn it upside down, it will look the same."

Everything he does is right. Even everything he does wrong is right. Every word he writes is brilliant. He's going to accomplish something big.

She would do anything for me, my Nana. She listened to me at length and heard my words as my parents never could.

Dilemma

Embarrassing as it is to admit, I was self-conscious about my mother. She may speak too loudly, in a hollow, tuneless voice, because she has no idea how she sounds. Some hearing people, on listening to her speak, would squint in curiosity and confusion, as if she were an exotic, alien creature. Others, trying to penetrate her deafness, would talk to her more loudly than necessary.

I introduced my mother to all the friends I brought home, even though I might not have always wanted to. Some friends hesitated at first to speak to her. I remember one kid, visiting our home for the first time, who asked me, point blank, why my mother sounded so funny. Once, a hospital nurse asked me whether my mother was addressing her in Italian.

When my parents used sign language in public—conversing without speaking, hands gliding and swooping, dancing a ballet, fingers shaped into words to illustrate the silence—passers-by would stare.

As it happened, our house was a magnet for deaf friends my mother had known since childhood. I would go to sleep upstairs while they talked all night in the living room. The voices of the deaf made for a strange cacophony, and every once in a while I would hear my mother laughing over the din. I sensed how warm, how much at home, she felt in deaf company.

My own sense of hearing became fine-tuned, and I turned out to be more listener than talker, as if hearing for my mother by proxy, an unconscious act meant to compensate, somehow balancing out the universe.

I wanted so much for my mother to hear that I entertained a long-running fantasy: she was only pretending to be deaf. The underlying logic of her charade, to my mind, was that she told everyone she was deaf, even acted and sounded deaf, just so people would cooperate with her. I clung to the hope that someday she'd announce to us that she could hear after all, that she had only wanted to test us. We'd all gasp in shock to find out that for years she'd heard every word ever said behind her back.

I sometimes pretended that I, too, was deaf. I would watch television with the sound turned off and try to follow the action. I would go to a playground with my hands cupped over my ears to block out the sound and observe the surroundings.

I was trying, if only temporarily, to make life as difficult for myself as I imagined it to be for my mother. My experiments in empathy left me feeling like a disconnected tape recorder, trapped in silence. Sound was a dimension of existence I was unprepared to live without.

My pity even materialized in my dreams. I once had a nightmare in which I saw my mother without ears. She was clutching the sides of her head in horror, as if she had suddenly discovered her ears missing. At that very moment, I heard my mother scream from the master bedroom. It made me wonder if she was having the same nightmare, as if I had somehow passed it on to her.

I secretly prayed that doctors would discover how to transfer hearing from the non-deaf to the deaf, as if transplanting a kidney or transfusing blood. I felt compelled to decide in advance what I would do if such a miraculous procedure came to pass and I were called on to help. Would I volunteer to make the sacrifice for her? Would I give my mother all my hearing? Half? None? I lay in bed at night groping for an answer.

I never settled on a choice; I never had to.

The Boys Of Alden Terrace

Every Sunday afternoon, with something like clockwork regularity, we boys all gathered at Paul Solomon's house. Me, Don, Andy, Carl, Steve, sometimes Mike and Larry. We had to be 12, 13, 14 years old, all of us living on the same block or two, in the same kinds of split-level houses built in the 1950s, going to the same school.

We watched either pro football or pro basketball, on the only color TV in the neighborhood, the football field suddenly lush green, the basketball court suddenly a golden hue. It might be the Green Bay Packers against the Dallas Cowboys, both teams then dominant, or the Los Angeles Lakers versus the Boston Celtics, also powerhouses.

After the games, we would all put on our overcoats and caps and go outside to play touch football in the street in front of Paul's house. Our field went from telephone pole to telephone pole, probably about 50 yards, with the sidelines marked by the curbs on either side. Sometimes a car or two would be parked out on the street (most stayed in driveways) and we had to play around those (though sometimes we accidentally collided into one going out for a pass).

We played two-on-two or three-on-three, depending on how many guys showed up, and we went at it all afternoon, oblivious of time and responsibility and the world at large, our minds intent on the next pass, the next catch, scoring the next touchdown.

Paul, the biggest and strongest then, played the best (he would later be the only one of us to join the high school football team). He had the calm air of the superior athlete, and usually played quarterback.

Don, my best friend, a lefty, could run fast, and so could Andy.

Me, I could throw and catch pretty well, always equipped with better arms than legs.

Only now, though, do I realize how odd it was for us to play football in the street. We lived in the suburbs, after all, with a grassy, sloping park barely 100 yards away. Maybe it was because the street gave us readymade end zones and boundaries, whereas in the park we would have had to create our own demarcations.

Or maybe it had to do with where our parents came from, New York City, mostly the Bronx. In the city, you played mainly in the street, close to the apartment you called home. So maybe we played in the street as some kind of unconscious carryover from our old neighborhoods, an unacknowledged inheritance from our parents.

At any rate, those games represented a special moment in my life. We all came together, me and my chums, to play ball. We huddled and called our plays, our buttonhooks and down-and-outs and our going-longs, and played football all through the January and February afternoons.

Nothing else going on in the world mattered and, as far as we could tell, nothing else ever would. All that counted was to be out there playing a game in the cold with your friends. We came together almost magnetically, gravitationally, without even a phone call first, to test ourselves against each other, to see who would win, to mimic everything we saw the Packers and the Cowboys do on TV.

We all knew each other so well, knew each other's mothers and fathers and brothers and sisters, had gone to each other's houses. We took the same classes, had the same teachers. We all loved to play—that was the real common denominator on those winter days. We all wanted to excel as athletes.

I never had anything like that again, a band of friends with whom you could kid around and burp and fart. Never again would I feel so close to other males, in friendships that ran so deep, so unquestioning. I never even came close, neither in college nor at any office.

It was the circumstances that made it possible, I suppose, the time and place and our proximity to each other, all of us the same age. We had something special, irreplaceable, a closeness.

But at least I had that once, and sometimes once can be enough.

It might have to be.

Prince Robert: Once More Around The Block

Without my Nana—her care, her guidance, her very presence—I might well have grown up feeling altogether alone, isolated, shunned, unloved.

Much of what I have turned out to be—for good and for ill—I am because of her. She gave me her all from the very start, even wheeling me around the Bronx as a baby. Through her, probably as much as anyone, I learned to speak and behave, learned manners and diction and appreciation of history and culture and Manhattan itself.

She saw so much in me, maybe a second chance to be the right kind of mother. She saw in me a child who could hear her, as her first child, my mother, never could. She saw in me, too, a child largely obedient, respectful, appreciative, compliant, descriptions all most likely inapplicable to her second child, my Uncle Leonard.

She must have seen me, even, as a kind of opportunity for redemption, for success where she felt she had previously failed.

In short, she had her reasons for treating me as well as she did, reasons that probably had more to do with her than with me.

Oh, and here's yet another reason, perhaps the most important of all. She might have blamed herself for my mother being deaf, and so she might have held herself responsible for her deaf daughter's son as well.

She probably saw me as a child who could never get from my parents everything she could give me, neither the attention nor the culture nor the guidance. By the same token, just as she always made me feel special— secure, loved—so must taking care of me have made *her* feel special, even vaguely heroic, a stature she no doubt savored.

That's how it felt with her. She hovered, my guardian angel, my Greek chorus, my personal cheerleading squad. She pulled out all the stops, showered me with compliments and peptalks, assured me I could accomplish anything. I was the chosen one. I could walk on water.

Every child should be so lucky. Every child deserves extravagant attention and unwavering love, someone who would do anything for you, and often did. It meant the world to me back then. Every boy should grow up feeling, at least now and then, just like a prince.

Held Aloft In His Arms

My father never held me in his arms as a baby. At least that's what my Nana once told me.

I'm unsure why my maternal grandmother disclosed this detail to me, and mentioned it so matter-of-factly at that, as if oblivious to its implications. No doubt she had some underlying agenda.

I had no clue whether it was true. It could have just been a rumor she picked up somewhere.

Maybe my father, then all of 25 years old and new to babies—you came along first, almost two years before your sister—felt uncomfortable holding a baby in his arms, even his own son. Maybe his own father, for whom he arrived first as well, before two sisters, never held him as a baby, either, and thus set a template for the next generation to follow.

Maybe, too, my father worried he would hold me wrong or drop me, and so decided to play it safe, keeping his hands off. Maybe, given the times—this was the 1950s, after all—he believed holding a child, even his own, to be a chore unfit for a father, somehow unmanly, better for a mother, or any woman for that matter. That's just how fathers acted then, or were supposed to act anyway, at least in public.

Then again, maybe the story goes differently. Maybe, during my first year alive, my Nana just never saw my father hold me. She might have just missed the event. And maybe my mother never saw it, either, and so assumed it to be true. And told my Nana, who then decided to tell me. So do rumors start, despite the utter absence of evidence.

Maybe, in reality, there in that one-bedroom apartment in the Bronx, my father held me only when no one was around, when he knew no one would be looking. Maybe, in fact, he waited until my Nana left the room, and only then, without anyone there to tell him otherwise, much less a bossy, nosy mother-in-law, would he hold me in his arms. Maybe that's what happened.

It could, perhaps, have happened late at night, while your mother slept and after your Nanna went home. My father would sneak over to my crib and gaze at me, marveling at the creature he helped create. Then, unable to resist the experience any longer, with his curiosity finally getting the best of him, wanting to find out what it felt like, he would gingerly pick me up and cradle me in his arms.

It could just be that your father sought to be alone with you, his baby boy, flesh of his flesh, in order to perform this most intimate of acts. Given complete privacy at last, he would finally feel free to do as he wished. He would cuddle me in his muscular arms and bring my face close to his, close enough to feel my breath on his skin, and coo and pucker his lips until I smiled and stroke my cheek and whisper that he loved me, loved me with all his heart, loved me forever and ever, no matter what anyone said.

So I've believed all along. To be sure, whatever the era, men are always men. But so, too, whichever cultural norms might prevail at the moment, are fathers always fathers.

Hooked On Hoops

You're all of 10 years old. A fifth grader in suburban New Jersey. Four-foot-eight, 70 pounds. And you've recently started playing basketball.

Your father put up the hoop over your driveway. The bright orange rim, at the regulation height ten feet, seems impossibly high to you. You bend your knees and bring the ball back to your right ear and aim for the basket. You tend to shoot air balls.

It's all new to you, this sport. Over the next 10 years, you play in games with other, generally bigger kids. You're always the worst player out there—the weakest, the slowest, the most timid. That explains why you're always picked last. You feel left out, useless, inferior.

You pretend, as you practice the game alone on an empty court, that you're playing for the New York Knicks in Madison Square Garden. The clock is always running down to the final seconds in the last quarter with the score tied. You have the ball, your teammates expecting you to bring victory.

In the classroom at school, while teachers are trying to teach you something, you draw make-believe basketball games in your notebook. You scrawl lines to represent the ball itself being dribbled, passed, shot and rebounded from one end of the court to the other.

At night, just before you go to sleep, you imagine yourself shooting the ball. Jump shots. Hooks. Turnaround fadeaways. Layups. In your dreams, you get the ball in the basket—swish! swish! swish!—over and over again.

Why you play, why you care so much, you really have no idea.

The Second Disability

All along, my grandmother hovered over my mother. She drove to our apartment almost every day. She cooked for us. She took my mother shopping. She brought meat from the butcher and hired a maid, and she tried to tell my mother how to raise me.

My mother, feeling inadequate as a wife, mother, and homemaker, endured long, deep depressions. She slept late. She punished me for no good reason. She argued violently with my father in defense of my grandmother.

Even as an adult, my mother remained a child. My grandmother, in trying to give her daughter a sense of competence, unwittingly made her feel helpless. I've since realized that the tendency for parents to be protective of their children can be heightened in the event of a disability. Some parents help a deaf child too much, some too little—few, just enough.

My grandmother may well have typified mothers of disabled children in that she was too attentive, too helpful and ultimately, too loving. She was also, quite possibly, the one who suffered most from the deafness in our family. As she later admitted, she felt guilty that my mother ever became deaf. She was forever haunted by the suspicion that she could have—should have—prevented her daughter from going deaf at all.

And so she accidentally gave my mother a second handicap: dependence.

My Height: A Short Story

It was probably right around the age of 12 that I started to worry about winding up too short. All my friends were taller, some probably as much as six inches taller, and most of my classmates, too, male and female alike.

I'd already taken an interest in sports, in playing baseball and basketball and football, and I wanted to excel, but being shorter than my competitors seemed no advantage. I'd also taken a blooming interest in girls, in how much prettier they are than boys, and being short was no big plus there, either.

The event that really brought home my height difference with my contemporaries was my bar mitzvah. As it happened, I had a triple bar mitzvah, because we three were all born around the same time.

One guy, named Mike, was already almost six feet tall. The other, named Ross, was a husky five-six. And then there was me, barely five feet tall and maybe—maybe—100 pounds.

You can see the photos in my bar mitzvah album, Mike looming like a skyscraper, then Ross, then me, lowslung as Manhattan's West Village.

OK, so set aside for a moment such considerations as childhood self-consciousness (if you can in good conscience actually do so).Forget that except perhaps socially my height really made no difference. What really bothered me now was the worry that I might always be short.

I thought I might never grow any taller.

And I remember expressing my worry to my Nana.

"I'm so short," I said. "Why am I so short? Am I never going to get any taller?"

And my Nana always reassured me that I would get taller, that I would eventually catch up with my friends, that I might even attain greater height than they.

I tried to believe her. But I suspected she was merely telling me what she felt she needed to tell me, what I should hear, rather than the truth.

I would have to see for myself. I would have to see it in the mirror and in the clothes I wore getting too small.

Well, my Nana turned out to be telling me the truth. In the next two years, I probably added about four inches, reaching maybe five-four, 120 pounds, by age 15. And over the next two years, the pattern largely held true, with me gaining another five inches or so, making it to about five-nine, 140 or 150.

And even after I got my driver's license, at 17, I picked up another inch, arriving at my final destination of five-ten-and-a-half.

But in all the years since then—and it's now more than four whole decades, I've learned some lessons about height.

For starters, I never quite outgrew the feeling of being short. And so I always find myself rooting for the shortest basketball players. It thrilled me that in 1986 the NBA slam-dunk contest champion was won by five-six Spud Webb (and later by five-nine New York Knick Nate Robinson).

And I often found the shortest players both the best teammates and the toughest opponents on the basketball court. I'd rather go up against a taller player almost any day. In my experience, shorter players always have more to prove—after all, they're short—and what's more, they *know* they have more to prove.

As a result, they play harder. They run faster and longer, fueled by extra incentive. They also tend to be quicker.

Tall players, on the other hand, know they have less to prove. Sometimes it's as if being tall all by itself is enough to do the job. In general, taller players tend to try less, take the game for granted, even play lazy. I almost never worry about going up against taller players.

No, it's the shorter players you have to watch out for. It's the shortest players I always find the toughest to stop.

Workaholic

My father always worked.

Day after day and night after night, he came home mainly to eat and sleep, the first quickly, the second loudly, snoring away. He was always on the go, here and gone, but more gone than here, no sooner here than gone again, always going, going, gone.

Even while briefly at home, he remained remote from us. Often, unless he puttered in the garage, he went down to the recliner in his den and, exhausted from working all the time, napped.

First, he worked in real estate, managing office and residential buildings, working alongside and under his parents for 15 years. He collected rents and oversaw maintenance and paid the superintendents, often putting in 18 hours a day. But his job frustrated him. He was drawn to technology and the possibilities of innovation. He kept inventing, ever devoted to research and development.

As a little boy, I grew up feeling wronged.

Back then, in the 1950s and 1960s, my father acted as fathers were expected to act. He worked. That's the lesson fathers had learned from the fathers who came before—to be all business.

But that's something of a red herring. Lee Brody had another motive for being a workaholic, another rationale. He had a debt to his own father that needed to be repaid.

Around 1914, his father, Harry Brody, came to the United States, to Newark, New Jersey, from Austria at the age of 12, to live with an aunt and uncle he had never met. He arrived alone, an émigré with no money and barely any education, unable to speak more than a little English.

Later, he ran a blue-collar tavern in Newark, working seven days a week and coming home only to eat and sleep. He saved almost every penny he earned—enough, eventually, to bring his mother, father and six brothers and sisters to America.

In the depths of the Great Depression, he financed an expensive special education for his son, sending him on an odyssey of his own. His parents had decided to put his education first and family second. Tuition plus room and board for him during those ten years cost him more than later putting all three of his children through college. Year after year, his wife, Anna, wore the same dress, unable to afford a new one.

Surely the decision to send him away came hard. Surely my grandparents felt as heartbroken as he.

My father talked little with me about his experiences in St. Louis. He never spoke a word against his parents for sending a five-year-old boy 800 miles away for 10 years, never told me what he felt like being so far away from his parents and two sisters for so long at so young an age. All he would say, and then only briefly, was that he was grateful—grateful to his parents for sending him, grateful to his teachers for teaching him, grateful for getting the opportunity to better himself.

He left me to imagine how lonely he must have felt, how homesick and bewildered and abandoned.

For years I condemned my grandparents for shipping him off. First, I figured, the kid lost his hearing, then his family and home, too. The decision to send him away addressed one disability but created a second one.

Because his parents dispatched him, he never learned how to be a member of a family, neither as a son nor as a brother, husband nor father. How could he? And so I held a grudge against my grandparents, a chip on my shoulder that grew bigger every year.

Boyhood, Airborne

We're 14 years old—me, Kevin, and Eric. The August day is hot, probably 85 degrees, the air almost tropical. Cicadas hum away rhythmically. We wear polo shirts and shorts and baseball caps and Keds sneakers. As we go deeper into the woods, we watch our step on the tangled brush underfoot. Kevin leads us on. Only he knows where we're going, and why, and when we'll get there.

As parks went, Dunkerhook Park had all the usual amenities -- swings and seesaws and slides, picnic tables and benches, a gravel parking lot. But it also had a section where we had never ventured before -- the woods beyond, with the stream curling alongside the path, and the secret Kevin had promised to share with us.

You never knew with Kevin. He was always kidding around, making wisecracks, putting you on. He would tap your right shoulder from behind you, even though he would be over on your left, and make you look right, with no one there. Or he would point to your belly button asking what might be wrong with it, and as you looked down, flick his index finger on your nose. He always got the better of the taller, beefier, Eric, who remained good-natured and easygoing, every insult rolling off his back, a trusty sidekick whom he more or less led around by the nose. Now, without our having any reason to trust Kevin in the least, we had entered these woods and left ourselves entirely in his hands.

Within minutes we're about half a mile into Dunkerhook Park. We hear no sounds except those of sparrows warbling and chipmunks scurrying through the leaves and the ever-present stream gurgling alongside us, below the banks. It's even hotter now, over 90 degrees, the glare from the sun turning the sky into a white haze. No whisper of a breeze comes along to stir the leaves in the trees. Our shorts and shirts stick to our skin. As the cicadas buzz louder, we move ever-slower, as if trudging through molasses. We feel far away from everyone and everything, our homes, our rooms, our parents, our schools, our other friends, all out of sight and beyond earshot.

We go through spells of friendship, me, Kevin, and Eric. We like to kid around and hold burping contests and try to light farts. More seriously, we play basketball and wonder about girls. We're close for a while, then less close, even no longer particularly close at all, but then we come back together, close all over again, if never quite the very best of friends then friends just the same. And now our on-again-off-again kind of friendship is taking a new turn. Now Kevin the master mischief maker is luring us ever-farther into this foreign frontier, all on the pretext that Eric and I will find the experience immensely entertaining.

Maybe Kevin is right. Maybe whatever he's brought us here to show us will actually be the genuine article -- a cave with some Indian drawings, or an abandoned 1956 Chevy Impala with the chrome tail fins all rusted out, or three cute girls our age or older, or a dead bum who wound up wasted on cheap whiskey.

In high school you and your friends pull a trick you had pulled in junior high, taking a shortcut to class every day. To get to Fair Lawn High School from your house, you would ordinarily take a left on Fair Lawn Avenue, another left onto Plaza Road, then a right onto Berdan Avenue. All 90-degree turns. Instead, all the same friends as before—Don and Andy and Paul and Carl Steve, and sometimes Mike and Larry; we always traveled as a tribe—take Saddle River Road.

You cut across Daly Field, near a factory and the gravel hill next to the local ambulance corps headquarters where you tried your first cigarette a year or so earlier, coughing the whole time, unable to inhale with any degree of success. There, in the shadow of an overpass for Route 17, with cars and trucks surging loudly overhead, we approach the railroad tracks for New Jersey Transit that ran through town.

We always want a train to come, of course. We know a train, whether a commuter or freight line, is bound to come along at some time, either from the East or West, but we have no idea when.

Usually no train comes, and that's highly disappointing. We always look down the tracks in both directions, straining to spot some telltale sign of its imminent arrival, a plume of steam spouting into the sky. We listen, too, because invariably we hear the train before we see it. We listen for that unmistakable clickety-clacking, the rattle of metal wheels grating against metal rails like bone against bone, a whistle wailing its woebegone warning.

Sometimes, though, a train shows up. It roars past us at 50 or 60 miles an hour, car after shuddering, wobbling car, barreling thunderously along the railroad tracks. To you, the train seems more creature than machine, less vehicle than beast—so fast and large and powerful, able to crush anything in its path in an instant.

"There," Kevin says. "There it is."

"Where?" Eric asks." Where is it?"

"Right *there*," Kevin says, pointing emphatically straight ahead.

To our left, about 20 feet away, we see it. The stream that ran parallel to the trail we took has deepened and widened, the banks steeper here, and transformed itself into a makeshift pool, still and lake-like. There it is, all right. A swimming hole is better than any of the other scenarios I imagined, miles better than a cave or some old car or a dead body or even three cute girls our age or older. No contest.

Our ringleader has come through, erasing our worst suspicions.

Just then, though, the swimming hole goes itself one better. A tall sycamore that juts out over the water from the bank on the other side, its trunk cantilevered at a 45-degree angle, has a rope dangling from it. The rope hangs long and thick from the lowest, sturdiest branch, about 10 feet off the ground, with a knot at the end, a knot evidently designed to serve as a handle. Some venturesome early pioneers to this spot, maybe other 14-year-olds, had rigged the rope to the branch just so, sensing the possibilities.

The trains that come down the railroad tracks in our hometown inspire us to experiment with games of our own invention. We lay twigs across the rails just to see the wood crunch and splinter in a heartbeat. We chuck rocks at the cars rushing past just to see the projectiles bounce right off, inflicting no harm. Andy dares Steve to go stand as close as possible to the passing train, only for Steve then to take his chances, holding himself still and stiff a mere few feet from the speeding leviathan as we all watch breathless.

Such a cut-up, that Andy.

He also dares us to wait until the train is only yards away to dart across the tracks right in front of it, just for the thrill of finding out how close we can cut it. Again, only Steve takes up the challenge, executing this bravura feat and coming within an inch of losing his life in front of his best friends.

One day we notice a dead raccoon laying across the slats on the tracks. Its back and neck are snapped askew, its teeth bared for the last time, its eyes bulging out as if from the shock of its own death. Clearly, the train has run it over. We gape at the raccoon for a while, our mouths hung open in a stupor of disbelief. None of us say anything. We poke it with a stick a few times just to make sure it's dead. We've never seen anything dead before, at least never in real life, only on TV. Certainly we've never seen anything killed by a train.

You waste no time getting yourselves started at the swimming hole, you and Kevin and Eric. You strip off your shirt, shorts, socks and sneakers, leaving only your briefs on. You clutch with both arms the trunk of the sycamore that hovers over the bank and shimmy up. Bark bites into the skin on your bare chest as you clamber higher, your nostrils flaring so wide you can fully whiff the lush, fertile woods around us.

All you know is now. Now is all you have on your mind. The tree, the rope, the water below. The stillness and the swelter have lulled you into a trance. Nothing else exists. Nothing else going on in the world matters and maybe nothing else ever will. The day has come to a standstill, as if it will never end, as if nothing will ever end, as if you have all day, all the time in the world. You will be in the eighth grade for the rest of your life and everyone you know and love will live forever.

Now you yank the rope back toward yourself and hold tight and launch yourself away from the tree, swinging out into the open air. You swing hard and fast out over the swimming hole, thrusting so suddenly and suspending gravity with such reassurance that you feel your heart thrum in your ears. You swoop out high over the water, then higher still. Then, at the peak of your ascent, you let go of the rope—look, Ma, no hands!—and leap, flinging yourself, taking flight. Then, only a second or two later, you drop, drop sooner and faster than you expect to drop, giving in to gravity now, plummeting in a flat-out free-fall. Then you splash down feet-first, the water so cool and welcoming, embracing you, and plunge underwater, sinking lower and lower until your toes touch the bottom and you feel the mud there, the chill, velvety mud squishy between your toes like some uninvited alien substance declaring its presence, and float to the surface starved for air, gasping, and blink in the shimmering summer sunlight. The sun refracts through the droplets of water on your eyelashes, the world around you—the woods, the sky—suddenly a rainbow kaleidoscope.

Whoa.

You went a little wild at the swimming hole in Dunkerhook Park in 1966, on a summer afternoon that gleams in memory as good as gold. You and Kevin and Eric went airborne, competing to see who could swing the highest, propel himself the farthest and create the biggest splash. You made like Tarzan and the Flying Wallendas and your favorite American astronauts, freeing yourselves from terra firma, weightless in your defiance of gravity.

You could have hurt yourself at the swimming hole of course, just as you could have hurt yourself taking shortcuts through the marsh and trespassing across the railroad tracks. None of you ever bothered to measure how deep the water went until you decided to dive in. You could have snapped your ankles or cracked your skull. Someone could have drowned.

But that never happened. You were all boys then, and you were doing what boys do. You scouted around to get the lay of the land and claimed your turf and charted your own course, ruling out conventional routes. You trailed away from the streets and sidewalks, going off the grid and toward the marsh, the railroad tracks, the swimming hole. You played with an abandon absolute and uncompromising. Play was your full-time job, accident and injury beyond your imagining. No taboo intimidated you. You slipped away from it all, into the beckoning unknown, carefree and heedless, without any guarantee of survival, and lost yourself where no one could find you. You all hurtled yourselves into swimming holes and played chicken with oncoming trains. Your parents never knew about your escapades. You never told anyone because no one else had to know. You were a 14-year-old boy, and nothing could ever hurt you.

Never again can you recall yourself behaving with quite that degree of abandon— nor with its essential companion, spontaneity. To your surprise, you grew up. Soon enough, then, you would be 15 years old, and later 20, and eventually you would turn 30, and then in a blink you would arrive at 40 and 50, and then, almost before you knew it, you would even start to push 60. *Whoa*, indeed. Middle age would force you to migrate from childhood.

Your hometown would change. One night the fire department would burn down the old, unoccupied barn the next block over. The older sister of a classmate would be found shot to death, the first homicide in town in decades, and the murderer would never be found. A flood would wash out the old narrow stone bridge to Dunkerhook Park. The marsh would be turned into townhouses called Parkview Place. Tractors and bulldozers would plow over some of the last traces of the rural.

To your astonishment, your life would change, too. The dead raccoon you found on the railroad tracks one day taught you a lesson. It reminded you in no uncertain terms what a train could do to you, too. From then on you learned to be a little afraid. You learned responsibility, too. You learned to stop taking risks and play it safe. Your newfound caution coalesced into a habit and you started to suffer from hardening of the attitudes. Before any decision you weighed every variable, performing a benefit-risk analysis. You grew domestic, tamed, bled dry of all daring.

Oh, you've swung on other ropes since then, of course. Marriage. Children. Jobs. A new career at age 39. As an adult, you keep taking leaps of faith.

And every once in a while, you still pull a little stunt. You tiptoe along a street curb as if balancing on a tightrope, or you climb on a seesaw and teeter away, pretending to be surfing. You hop onto the back of a shopping cart and propel it, scooterlike, down an empty aisle, riding shotgun, or—if you feel really frisky and acrobatic—you leapfrog over a parking meter. In those rare, brief, moments, you imagine yourself to be a boy again, back in Fair Lawn, back in 1966, back with your friends. In those moments, if only then, you're forever 14. You're once more roaming free, a daredevil reborn. You're airborne again.

Answering His Calling

Still, even without going to medical school, my father never lost his ambition to be of service to the deaf community. And in 1969, he got his big idea literally by accident. He went hunting by himself and slipped on a rock and hurt his back. Barely able to move and unable to call anyone for help, he took seven hours to crawl to his car. Ironically, the deaf never could use the telephone—a device invented by a teacher of the deaf expressly so his students could learn speech. The traumatic episode gave him a revolutionary idea—to establish a network that enabled the deaf to communicate by phone with one another and everyone else for the first time.

He would enable the hearing-impaired population to communicate with each other and anyone else over standard phone lines without ever having to speak or hear.

Toward that end, he stored, adapted and distributed teletypewriters, or TTYs, with specially constructed modems that operated over ordinary phone lines. He turned a closet in our den into his office, complete with a flip-out desk, and founded a non-profit organization, New York-New

Jersey Teletypewriters for the Deaf. Anyone suffering from hearing loss could then dial up anyone else by phone to type messages on scrolling paper and hold a conversation without ever having to speak or hear.

At first, the TTYs he stored, refurbished and delivered cropped up only regionally. Then he rented a warehouse in Hackensack, and soon distribution went nationwide. The devices materialized in homes, schools, hospitals, libraries, airports, local police precincts, fire and ambulance stations, federal agencies, the U.S. Senate, even the White House. Largely through him, deaf and hard-of-hearing Americans established a network, creating access to a large-scale communications lifeline that enabled anyone with a hearing impairment to communicate independently—and instantly—over any distance. They could "hear"—and in turn, make themselves heard—at last.

The TTY enterprise took over his life for 28 years, and thus mine as well.

My father went on to be hailed as a hero. The deaf community honored him with awards for his public service. Bell Telephone accepted him to the Telephone Pioneers of America, only the 29th member since Alexander Graham Bell in 1911. He once received a letter on White House stationary—congratulations on his accomplishments from President Ronald Reagan. After he died in 1997, The Stevens Institute of Technology held a memorial service for him and 500 people showed up to pay tribute. Gallaudet University, in Washington, D.C., the world's only higher education institution for the deaf, named a scholarship after him.

Almost certainly he would have accomplished none of that without the education he received at The Central Institute for The Deaf.

Drummer Boy In A Boy Band

I'm playing my drums in a band in our basement. Bob Lawrence is on lead guitar and Bob Hernandez on bass. Three guys named Bob.

Maybe we're practicing "Wipeout" by the Ventures or "Twist and Shout" by the Beatles. I'm pounding out some standard rock beat on my four-piece Ludwig drum set—

snare drum, small and large tom-toms, bass, ride and crash cymbals, high-hat. The other Bobs are twanging away on all the right chords.

I'm feeling pretty cool behind my drums, the next Ringo Starr (he also played Ludwig). I'm probably tilting my head right and left once in a while as Ringo used to do. We're all feeling pretty cool playing our instruments there in the basement, our music— if you can call it that—sounding all the louder for being contained in this underground space.

We're musicians now, or at least wannabe musicians, and we're trying to get the right sound down, and the right look, too. It's largely a matter of mimicry, less so artistic inspiration.

Of course I do want to make music here. I'm doing my little rolls here and fills there, backing the guitars with my beat, giving the songs an accent now and then.

And oh, I'm in heaven. Playing the drums, getting behind all the equipment as if climbing into the cockpit of some fighter jet, is as cool as a job gets. Your whole body goes into it, your left hand flicking the snare, your right hand teasing the ride cymbal, your left foot tapping on the high hat and your right foot pressing the pedal to the bass drum. It's a physical, athletic act, calling for masterly coordination and a precise sense of rhythm.

Of course I'm still picking up my skills here, still new to the drums. I have some raw ability, pretty good hand speed and a knack for tempo, but hardly anything approaching real technique. But hey, I'm 13 years old here. It's 1965 and everyone is listening to the Beatles and the Beach Boys and the Rolling Stones, and I'm in a band, and back then, with all the great music coming out, nothing could be cooler than to be in a band.

We're absolutely of the moment, we are.

And we've got the potential to be pretty decent. Bob and Bob are serious guitar players, trained guitarists, fresh from lessons and able to read music. They can play rock and pop and even a little blues.

Hernandez is particularly fluent. He would practice for hours a day, his blond hair dangling over his face as he watched his own fingers pluck at the frets. He would pretend to be Segovia on his acoustic, and pull off a pretty fair impersonation at that.

We were going to practice hard, our band. We were going to play all the popular songs. We were going to get gigs eventually, too, first locally, at weddings and bar mitzvahs, then at clubs in the city, the more grotto-like the better, and then we'd go national and international.

If the Beatles could do it, we could.

I'd break into a solo in the middle of some number, pumping my arms all over my drum set, and the spotlight would hit me, and the crowd would go nuts. That's the dream you dream as you play drums with your band in the basement in 1965. You're going to be cool at last! All the girls are going to like you! You'll never have to worry about anything ever again!

Our first rehearsal as a band went well, all of us excited just to come together, our individual sounds joining to make a collective sound. We thought we sounded all right. We rehearsed again about a week later, and then again about a week after that. Some friends caught our rehearsals and told us we sounded good.

Step aside, Dave Clark Five! Here we come! Forget about the Kinks and the Animals. The Jersey suburbs were going to produce the latest music sensation. Down in our basement, as the three Bobs practiced, a phenomenon would soon emerge.

Except then we stopped.

We never rehearsed again.

Maybe one of us caught a cold, or we had creative differences, or we stopped believing in our genius, but whatever happened—maybe someday the reason will come back to me across the decades while I sleep—we were a band no more.

Disbanded.

But that's cool, too. Yes, I would have liked to go on, to take it further, to see how far we could have gone, to really give it a good shot. We'll never know what might have come of sticking with it.

Maybe something.

Probably nothing.

But at least we had our little moment. And sometimes that's all any of us ever get.

Mr. Too Cool For School

I pretty much never really actually wanted so very much to go to school.

School was away from home, where I had my own room, right near the kitchen and the bathroom and the den with the new TV.

School was in a building really long and tall, with stairwells and an auditorium and a boiler room.

School had all those other little kids, too, boys and girls, cute and less than cute, all coming out in the halls at the bell to go here and go there.

School had all those teachers, too, who got to tell you what to do, whether you could go to the bathroom and had to do homework or take a test.

Worst of all, I guess, worse even than how far from home school took me and all the strangers in the halls and the bossy teachers, was that school was where you had to stay put. You had to stay in your seat and listen and learn and some day you would suddenly walk out the door all smart and educated.

And here was the problem for me. I never really wanted to sit and listen. (I've never changed all that much since then, either, have I?).

No, I would look out the window and daydream about playing baseball and, later on, maybe when I got to be about 12 or 13, I started to pay attention to those intriguing creatures called girls.

In school, I always pretty much wanted to be somewhere else so I could be doing something else. I wanted to be out playing baseball or stickball with my friends or watching some monster movie on TV or maybe in the park climbing a tree higher and higher until the branches grew too short and thin.

And all the while, as I sat in class, a prisoner, bored, seeing no point in this activity, the teachers would be talking, talking, talking, and I would once again find myself utterly incapable of the one act expected of me, namely listening.

No, I never wanted to listen to anyone, because to me listening meant obedience and feeling beholden, and I preferred my freedom and independence, the freedom to imagine my life as I saw fit, and the independence to live it as I saw fit, too.

And now we get to the real problem here. I was too young for school, too immature, completely unprepared for its demands, too undisciplined. I should have started school at maybe 18.

I say 18 because that's when I went to college and started to like school.

Suddenly, without ever quite realizing why, I found myself able to listen to my professors.

Suddenly I saw school as a place where I could go with other students to learn stuff, including how to think.

Suddenly I recognized that I could go from being a rather hapless, hopeless high school student—graduating, it still pains me to acknowledge, maybe 600th in a class of 700—to someone rather serious, maybe even a touch scholarly.

Of course I loved the classes in Literature and had a really good teacher of Shakespeare who grew animated and acted out scenes. But I also came to like History and Psychology, too. And naturally my grades improved, to about a "B" average, and so did my self-respect and pride. And I'm really glad it all changed like that.

From then on I've always felt like a student, curious, ready even to sit still and listen, at least once in a while.

And it all probably had a lot to do with me becoming a writer and a journalist, because reporters ask questions and listen to the answers and find out stuff to tell the world. And when it comes to a job, to making a living, that's all I've ever wanted to do.

It took me a long time to see that life itself is the best school.

The Tony Gargano Fan Club

When I was 13 years old, I belonged to a clean-cut clique called the Rah-Rahs. In accordance with its dress code, I typically wore madras shirts, crew-neck sweaters, chinos with cuffs, white sweat socks and either penny loafers or, if really out to impress the girls, brown-and-white saddle shoes.

I followed the party line of the Rah-Rahs all through seventh grade. I steered clear of beer. I expressed my awakening sexuality only at officially sanctioned neighborhood makeout parties. We considered ourselves insiders, qualified as cool.

Secretly, though, I admired our opposite number, known as the Boppers or Hoods, especially one Tony Gargano. As far as I was concerned, Tony had the market on cool cornered.

If he slouched at his desk in class, the teacher would order him to sit up straight, but he would just roll his eyes. He had long, greased-up black hair combed straight back, except for a single curlique forelock that dangled strategically over his eyebrows.

For a while there I wanted to be Tony.

Back in 1966, after all, I had never quite cut it as the quintessence of cool. I wore thick black glasses and my hair frizzed in humidity. Besides that, I was shorter and skinnier than almost all of my male contemporaries. Plus, I seemed to feel too much. I would always let you see me sweat. Everything about me ran counter to cool.

Mr. Uncool.

I would stand in front of the bathroom mirror, trying, with a profound sense of futility, to torture my renegade curls into a facsimile of the same hairstyle.

So with shoes. Tony wore these pointy black suede lace-ups with two-inch heels. I went to a local shoe store to get a similar pair, only to discover, crestfallen, that my feet were still two sizes too small for that style.

I watched the Boppers hang loose at curbsides around town, Tony snorting cigarette smoke through his nostrils, flicking the played-out butts across the street without looking. He went out with a girl who teased her hair and wore heavy eye-liner. I quietly yearned, with an ache in my chest, to defect from the Rah-Rahs to the Hoods.

Going Full-Tilt Bozo

Always I've wanted to make people laugh. I made silly faces in class to break up my fellow students. I pretended to trip on the sidewalk or walk into trees to amuse my friends.

One day in high school I found out my classmates had voted me Class Clown (male division) for 1970. Somehow it came to be decided that I would be photographed for the school yearbook holding a bottle of whisky. That was before I knew my mother was an alcoholic, or I might someday be.

One night, years earlier, I had a party for friends at our house, my parents out for the night. I had to be maybe 15. My friends hung out in our living room while I would emerge from my bedroom at the head of the stairs to do my act.

Each time I came out I might affect a British accent or lumber out like a hunchback—I loved doing Quasimodo—or just talk in a silly, high-pitched voice a la Jerry Lewis. For a while there, I broke everyone up, no one more than my friend Larry, who always laughed hardest and considered me a king of comedy, so much so he would laugh even in anticipation of my pulling something funny.

So it went all through my boyhood and on into adulthood, me always answering the impulse to go for a laugh. I might be introduced to girls as a guy with a sense of humor.

I've maintained my reputation to a degree, but my stabs at comedy have changed, evolving from vaudevillian slapstick to something more cerebral, more laced now with wit and wordplay than physical antics. I'll always feel like a clown at heart, and have always fantasized about going to clown college—yes, Ringling Brothers has one—for a magazine assignment.

But I've also had to watch my step.

The funny business that goes over well in eighth grade will often come across as out of place in a job at an office. So I've learned to temper my sense of humor, to hold it back and deploy it only at strategic moments.

In my earliest memories, I'm trying to make my mother laugh, anything to get her to forget her deafness, to render it irrelevant, to enable me to forget, too, that she could never hear me, or hear anything else in life for that matter.

Make mommy laugh, my mandate went.

My humor thus seems born of this, the central sadness of my life.

Once with others, my mischief had less to do with spreading sunshine, really, than with making me feel less ill at ease and even somewhat important. If I can get someone to laugh, it makes me feel, even to this day, less uncertain, less awkward and alienated, more in control somehow. I'm unable to help myself and am totally at the mercy of this whim.

As it turns out, I've always seen my sense of humor as both blessing and curse. Sometimes my fooling around has backfired big-time—landed me in detention, wound up insulting others, led to my being branded unserious, a wise guy.

Truth be told, anyone who can see the humor in life takes the world quite seriously. Cracking a joke is just a risk you run. Some will laugh, others will just stare. It's touch and go, a catch-as-catch-can proposition, just like most everything else.

We all went to a diner with my father in New Jersey once. For some reason he decided that dinner was the ideal occasion for him to give all of us an explicit description of brain surgery. We're all there in a booth enjoying our food and he's telling us how the skull has to be sawed open, even demonstrating with his hands the act of cutting. He might even have made some reference to drilling.

He went on in this vein, evidently utterly clueless of the likely effect on anyone with an interest in uninterrupted digestion.

As I recall, I winced with disgust, waved my hand to indicate all of us eating, and said, "Dad, do you think you could give us a break?"

My father paused and you could see him in that instant recognizing the incongruity of it all—incongruity, by the way, so often being absolutely essential to comedy—this explicit narrative on cranial surgery during our family dinner.

Suddenly he exploded with laughter, bending forward in his seat, laughing harder and louder than ever before. All of us laughed right along with him, and the meal went better from then on, the food going down just right.

Sometimes humor works its magic. It's a sprinkling of fairy dust.

Lapped

I'm running around the oval running track near the water tower that looms over the football field at Fair Lawn High School on a Saturday afternoon in November 1969. I'm 17 years old, competing in the mile in my first track meet and running as hard as I know how.

We're barely a lap into the race, one-fourth the distance to be covered on the quarter-mile track, and already I'm lagging behind the six or seven other runners. I'm pumping my arms and legs with all the force I can muster, gasping, groaning, grunting, yet the farther we run, the farther behind I fall.

I'd joined my high school track team the year before, right after the Olympics in Mexico City, inspired by the American Olympian Jim Ryun. A great miler, striding so sleekly along, and I wanted to run the mile, too.

Maybe, I figured, if I ran fast enough, it would rescue me from the asthma I had suffered since adolescence. Maybe, too, I would be more popular with girls, grow hair on my chest and get into Harvard. Maybe my parents would stop being deaf.

I went to track practice every afternoon after school. We ran drills, practiced fast starts and fast finishes, covered different distances at different paces, doing the 100-yard dash, the 220, the 440, the half-mile, the mile, the two-mile.

Every Friday came the drill I found toughest of all: one 440-yard-run after another, either six or seven in a row, going full-tilt, with only a minute to rest in between. One day, exhausted to the point of nausea, panting myself breathless, I bent over under the stands, my stomach in violent upheaval, and puked my guts out.

Sometimes, such as then, I felt like quitting the team. But soon I discovered myself running faster, feeling stronger, breathing better, and that kept me going. I still ran slower than anyone on the team. Clearly, I would never be much good, much less win or place in any meets.

But I kept practicing in the off season, running around the block surrounding our house, always timing myself with a stopwatch. My sessions awakened a vaguely gladiatorial spirit in me, motivating me enough to return in my senior year.

Week after week I drilled with our team, and week after week I watched from the field as my colleagues went head to head against the local competition on the track. I was left out of the action, feeling every inch a failure.

The coach of the track team, a hard case with a crew cut, never asked me to run in those meets, understandably so, and I never asked him to let me. So any time our milers went up against rivals from another town, I watched, wishing I could participate, knowing full well I probably never would.

Then came the last track event of the season. It would be now or never. So I asked the coach to let me run in the mile.

"No," he said. "Sorry." He was quite decent about it all, sounding downright sympathetic, but it was still a "no."

"Please," I said. "It's my last chance."

The coach looked down at the ground, as if my begging embarrassed him.

"OK," he said.

And now I'm in the race, losing ground with every step. The other runners are 200 yards ahead of me, already around the last curve as I approach the back stretch, then 250 yards, then 300. We go into the last lap now, my lungs screaming from the exertion, my legs leaden, my panting growing ragged, and I hear footsteps behind me.

No.

The runner in the lead passes me.

Lapped. I got lapped. Lapped by the winning runner. Lapped in an event that had only four laps in the first place. Lapped in public, right in front of the whole school. Lapped in the only track meet the coach ever let me run in, and then only because I had begged him.

I finished the race—my time: 5:56, about 90 seconds slower than the three top finishers—feeling utterly humiliated. Nobody is supposed to get lapped in the mile, and nobody ever does, but somehow I had proved an exception to the rule. The winner had completed four laps before I could even log three. I had wanted to see how I would do, and now I had seen it in the most vivid terms possible.

But humiliation has its uses. It can be harnessed as motivation. After graduating, I committed myself to staying fit, mainly through pick-up basketball. Years later, now well into my 40s, I went to a local track and timed myself in the mile.

Surely, I could beat 5:56, I reasoned, a milestone so mediocre even someone my age could do better. Let me now put in perspective just how mediocre. Decent marathoners average faster miles over 23 times that distance.

If I succeeded, I might redeem myself, at least in my own eyes. It might wash away the shame of my long-ago defeat. I might finally feel, out on that race track, something like a winner.

I clocked 6:21. And in the years since, I've forced myself to try again sporadically, in a crusade nothing less than quixotic, but could never do better than 6:35 or 6:40.

But I still have something to prove, if only to myself. So someday, I'll be ready to go that extra mile. Maybe my legs will still have enough left to get me to the finish line on time.

Everyone deserves another last chance.

My Five Minutes As A Member Of The Temptations

On a Saturday night in May of 1970, my friends Larry, Eric, and I, each of us then 17 years old, performed in the annual talent show of Fair Lawn High School in Bergen County, New Jersey. We chose to do an act that came naturally to us. We three upper-middle-class Jewish white boys, just months away from going off to college, impersonated the Temptations, the all-black Motown musical group, lip-syncing the lyrics in our rendition of the now-classic song "Cloud Nine."

We had practiced our routine for weeks in my shag-carpeted bedroom, its walls then decorated with large posters of Raquel Welch, Sophia Loren and Paul Newman, in the post-WWII split-level colonial house that I shared with my parents and sister. We played the album that contained "Cloud Nine" again and again on my Panasonic turntable as we choreographed our dance moves. Larry took the lead, deciding who would play which member of the Temps and how long we would rehearse and even the steps we would do. Eric and I, much his inferiors both athletically and academically— and glad simply to be aboard for this ambitious musical enterprise—complied readily with his every command.

Though the three of us had markedly different personalities—Larry serious to the point of driven, Eric easygoing bordering on lax and I somewhere in between—we had in common something powerful, just a notch below our diehard habit of playing pickup basketball. What brought us together was our love of soul music, and most particularly the soul music that came out of the justly fabled locale known as Motown.

Of course, we loved other kinds of music, too—the Beatles and The Rolling Stones and the Beach Boys, Led Zeppelin and Jimi Hendrix and Bob Dylan. But soul music came equipped with a unique agenda. For as much as we loved listening to it and singing along to it, we most of all loved dancing to it. And the soul music from Motown Records, rhythm and blues tinged with gospel, made us want to dance as nothing ever had before.

By then we knew about Motown, of course. We had bought the records, seen its stars on "Ed Sullivan" and "American Bandstand," danced to its tunes at all our school dances, and that special sound had seeped under our skin. Smokey Robinson and The Miracles, The Supremes, The Four Tops, Martha and the Vandellas, Stevie Wonder, Gladys Knight and the Pips, the Isley Brothers, Junior Walker and The All-Stars, Marvin Gaye and his heavenly honeyed wail—it spoke to us on a level all but molecular. "You've Really Got A Hold On Me," "Baby, I Need Your Loving," "Dancing In The Street," "Please Mr. Postman," "Reach Out, I'll Be There," "I Second That Emotion," "Love Child," For Once In My Life," "Never Can Say Goodbye"—such tunes from the

Motown catalogue mainlined themselves into our bloodstreams.

But perched at the peak of the Motown hierarchy were the mighty Temptations. The five young men from Detroit who made up the group debuted in 1962 and broke through in 1964 with "The Way You Do The Things You Do." Along came other hits— "Beauty Is Only Skin Deep," "Get Ready," and "My Girl." "Cloud Nine" had come out as a single in 1968, the Temps venturing away from romantic ballads and into what came to be called psychedelic soul, landing Motown its first Grammy Award for Best Rhythm and Blues Group performance. More than anything, we loved how the Temptations danced, how they shimmied and sashayed, and perfected a signature move known as "The Temptation Walk." Eventually, with no fewer than 43 top 10 hits over 25 years, the Temptations would evolve, despite some musical chairs among its members, into the most successful rhythm and blues group ever.

Out we bopped onto the stage of our high school auditorium for our big number, then, strutting in front of the footlights and hundreds of spectators, our families, friends, neighbors and classmates. And streaming over the public address system came the guitar riff with the wah-wah pedal that signaled the overture of "Cloud Nine." And for the next three minutes and 27 seconds, Larry was lead singer David Ruffin, Eric baritone Paul Williams, and I Eddie Kendricks, he of the creamy tenor falsetto.

We performed onstage just as we had practiced. We mouthed the words in sync to the lyrics of the first stanza—all about a guy raised in the slums, in a one-bedroom shack, along with 10 other children, and hardly ever enough food to go around. To the thrumming bass line, the pounding congas and the blasting horns, we, too, shimmied and sashayed. As we fake-sang—all about the lazy father who "disrespected" his wife and treated his kids "like dirt"—we clapped and swayed our hips and pranced and twirled, a glide to our stride. We walked the Temptation Walk.

Yes, we had the patented Temptations moves down cold, or at least lukewarm. And all along, even though our grasp of hardship in general and poverty in particular was highly suspect —we each occupied our own bedrooms, never lacked for food and had fathers gainfully employed who treated us and our mothers reasonably well—we nonetheless bobbed our heads peacock-style, super-cool dudes keeping it real, as if we somehow now embodied the very essence of Motown soul.

And then, about halfway through, I stepped out front for my solo as Eddie Kendricks, the group's co-founder. "And every man, every man, has to be free," I "sang" in an ever-ascending falsetto, the word "free" elongated into four syllables, my hands flung aloft, fingers fluttering, as if in holy-roller, glory-hallelujah prayer.

It was ours, that moment, all ours. I had finally verified my longstanding suspicion, once and for all, that I, too, had soul.

But then the audience, to a person, exploded in laughter. About 30 seconds later, I stepped forward again to offer the refrain, "I wanna say I love the life I live/And I'm gonna live the life I love," and laughter again erupted. It stunned me with its tidal-wave force, and I was unsure what to make of it.

The music of Motown speaks to me today no less than it did then. The music we love as teenagers tends to stay with us, carving a groove in our neural pathways. For decades, I've relied on Motown to get me through my exercise routine during New York winters. I'll put on the headset of my Sony Walkman and listen to the tunes as I walk up and down the stairwell in our 22-story building for 30 to 60 minutes. Sweating and panting, I often stop to re-enact those same dance moves. Fellow tenants navigating the stairwell purely for transportation purposes will spot me doing my stuff and feel an urge to call security. But hey, it's just me, a 60-plus father of two still getting high on Motown.

Only years later would I come to understand certain details about that night so long ago. For starters, back then we remained clueless about the meaning of the lyrics to "Cloud Nine." We assumed the song was about feeling good. Consider: "I'm doing fine / Up here on cloud nine / Listen one more time / I'm doing fine / Up here on cloud nine."

Eventually, I recognized that "Cloud Nine" was actually a strong dose of social commentary, a warning about drug addiction, presumably heroin in particular. After all, the song is about a man who left home looking for a job he never found and wound up "depressed and downhearted" and then "took" to cloud nine. That's where he found himself "riding high" and "free as a bird" and "a million miles from reality" in a "world of love and harmony." The song we naively considered so celebratory was actually a cry of ecstatic anguish. And it was this anti-drug message we unwittingly delivered that night to a white suburban audience most likely as ignorant as we.

Years later, too, I would see that talent show in context. In 1970, race relations in America still qualified as incendiary. We performed our act only two years after the assassination of Martin Luther King Jr., only four years after the founding of the Black Panthers, and only five years after the signing of the Voting Rights Act into law. The riots in Watts and Newark remained likewise still fresh in memory. In 1970, the Miss America pageant had its first black contestant. Our country was still in the thick of the Civil Rights Movement.

Our suburban town of Fair Lawn, New Jersey, 11 miles from the George Washington Bridge, was a Caucasian enclave, its population mostly the children of

European immigrants -- Jews, Italians, Germans, Poles, Czechs—many of whom had migrated from the Bronx and Brooklyn. The only black person I knew as a child was Marie Esposito, our maid, who came to our house once a week by bus from Paterson, a predominantly black town just across the Passaic River, to scrub our floors, dust our furniture, and babysit me and my sister.

Against this backdrop, then, Larry and Eric and I had performed pretending to be black entertainers. We three white upper-middle-class Jewish boys suffered then from what could be diagnosed as a mild to moderate form of black envy. To us, certain blacks had a certain kind of cool—talked cool, walked cool, acted cool, sang cool, danced cool —and we, too, wanted with all our hearts to be cool. And so dancing to the rhythm and blues of Motown was our humble attempt to do that. Call it a symbolic act of support and solidarity—how we sought, at least from within our safe suburban cocoon, to get down with the brothers and sisters. It also made us forerunners of the generation of black wannabes who would come along 30 years later, likewise afflicted with a strain of black envy, to go all ghetto and help propel hip hop.

But in retrospect I realize that the stunt we pulled masquerading as The Temptations could be interpreted as mockery. In May, 1970, it's conceivable that what we had intended as innocent tribute could be misunderstood as satire, even as downright insulting.

After all, we had no familiarity with tough times. We had clean streets and pretty much no crime and good schools and both our parents around for the long haul and fireworks at the municipal pool on the Fourth of July. In terms of struggle, I occasionally got detention for flicking spitballs in class. My idea of The Man, against whom the oppressed back then invariably found themselves pitted, was the junior high school principal, who once suspended me from class for a day for talking too much in homeroom.

Maybe that's why the audience laughed so hard at my little solo turn. Maybe the sight of a skinny white bespectacled upper-middle-class suburban Jewish teenager, complete with frizzy "Jewfro," my face and dance moves so earnest, looking to channel the spirit of a broken-hearted young black man from the housing projects of the Detroit ghetto, all while lip-syncing a voice so flamingly, flamboyantly falsetto—well, maybe it came off as absurd.

In May of 1994, 24 years after the talent show, an incident brought me full circle back to Motown. I was at Ellis Island, in the Great Hall, attending a dinner ceremony for an organization formed to preserve diversity in America and pay homage to the immigrant experience. Over the years, the group had conferred its award on six U.S. presidents and numerous Pulitzer Prize winners, among others, not to mention Bob

Hope, Muhammad Ali, Henry Kissinger and Frank Sinatra.

I was on duty there—in a black tux, no less—as a newly hired vice president of Howard J. Rubenstein Associates, a New York City public relations firm. My job that night was essentially to escort Norman Brokaw, chairman of the William Morris Agency, a client who also happened to be an honoree. Brokaw, who had started his career in the agency's storied mailroom, wound up representing the likes of Marilyn Monroe, whom he reputedly discovered, as well as Barbara Stanwyck and Clint Eastwood.

About halfway through dinner I left our table to take a stroll around the premises. As I turned a corner, there, coming toward me, flanked by associates, was Berry Gordy, Jr. I recognized him right away—the baby face that carried a hint of bulldog pugnacity. *The* Berry Gordy, Jr., a.k.a. Mr. Motown. He had founded Motown Records in 1959. He had discovered Smokey Robinson and The Miracles. He had signed Mary Wells, Marvin Gaye, The Four Tops, Gladys Knight and the Pips, Martha and the Vandellas, Stevie Wonder, the Jackson Five and, yes, the mighty Temptations. He was the mastermind who had engineered the music that had kept me high from boyhood on. And now I was in a public place all of 10 feet away from him.

"Hello, Mr. Gordy," I said with my hand extended.

"Hello," he replied, and shook my hand.

"You're responsible for a lot of great music," I said.

"Thank you," he responded with a smile, slightly bowing his head.

I could have said more. I wanted to say more. I could have told him about how Larry and Eric and I had simulated The Temptations performing "Cloud Nine" at our high school talent show in 1970. And how we had just wanted to be cool. And how we had meant it as a tribute. And how my little solo as Eddie Henricks drew a big laugh. And how I for one had never, in all the years since, quite cracked the code for cool.

I could have told him, too, how deeply I loved the music of Motown, how much soul music spoke to me, how I danced to it while going up and down the stairwell in our apartment building, getting high on its funky fumes.

But somewhere along the line, my capacity for common sense, all too infrequently deployed, kicked in, and I thought better of it. I had gotten the opportunity to pay my respects to Berry Gordy, Jr., alighting briefly on my own version of cloud nine, and realized I should leave it at that. What I had told him he no doubt already knew. Everything I left unsaid he probably knew, too.

The Bridge

For years all through my boyhood, my father drove our family over the George Washington Bridge. Almost always we were going from our house in Fair Lawn to visit my maternal grandparents, the Shefts, at 79th Street and Second Avenue, and always we took the George Washington Bridge.

It would be the four of us, my sister and I in the back seat, headed in for Passover or Thanksgiving or just a Sunday dinner. The bridge was tall and long and wide, all steel and cables suspended over the Hudson River. And as we crossed, I always looked to the right, toward the south, because there, spread out along the horizon, lay the towers of Manhattan.

We lived in a town of maybe 35,000 in Bergen County, where almost everyone had a house and was white and had some money, and on weekend mornings you heard all the lawnmowers going. So the George Washington Bridge came to mean something special. It connected us to a different universe, another dimension.

For here in Manhattan, as I learned as a young boy, was everything I saw in the movies and read about in books. Here, I knew, were the Wall Street tycoons and the ladies who lunch, the Broadway theaters and all those yellow cabs streaming through the night. That bridge, with its structure so muscular, those cables like tendons in the arms, linked my past and present to what would become my future.

I had no idea back then, at the age of 6 or 10 or 14, that Manhattan would remain my destination. Then again, maybe I suspected it. Certainly I always felt a gravitational pull toward that skyline. Certainly so much that I came to love was there.

Little did I realize, back then, that I would at the age of 23 move there and work there and meet Elvira there. And it was the George Washington Bridge that transported me to the rest of my life, that conveyed me all those years, in the 1950s and 1960s, from my old home to my new one.

Going Independent

Mugged

A stranger in a woolen cap is racing down the hall toward me with a raised hunting knife that seems to grow longer and sharper by the second. I am carrying two supermarket bags stuffed with groceries and a heavy Sunday newspaper, about to fish out my keys and open the door to my home.

It is just before noon, July 5, 1975, warm and sunny. Just five weeks earlier, I had left Jersey to move into my first New York City apartment, a $150-a-month studio on East 7th and Avenue A.

"Gimme all your money," the stranger grunts. He is black, about 6-foot-1 and 175 pounds, with a prominent jaw and glaring eyes. He points the knife to my chest. It is about 10 inches long, dull gray and hooked at the tip.

I hand over all my cash: three singles and change.

"Let's go inside," the stranger commands. I have visions of plunder and death—and then I refuse.

"Gimme the keys," he snarls, wagging the knife.

"You're not getting into my apartment," I say.

The stranger's eyes bulge. I want desperately to escape, but I am cornered at the end of a hall less than six feet wide. I glance down toward the 12 other apartments on the floor, but all the doors are closed, all the rooms silent. If I yell, he may kill me.

"Better not try nothing," the stranger warns.

He reaches for my pocket to get the keys. I abruptly turn sideways, lifting my elbow to block his arm.

Then I am stabbed in the chest. The knife cuts into a spot two inches below my right pectoral, close to the heart. It feels as if a faucet inside me has opened and begun to drip. Warm blood spreads across my shirt.

"You cut me," I tell him.

"You want more?" he threatens.

I give the stranger my keys.

Inside he takes a towel from my bathroom and instructs me to press it against my chest. In doctorly fashion, he diagnoses my knife wound as superficial, reassuring me I will be "all right." Then, for a reason I can never fathom (to justify his crime?), he tells me he is a veteran of the Vietnam War.

I make it a point to study his features as he moves silently among my belongings, appraising the merchandise, declining to take my typewriter because I "probably need it for business." He ties my hands behind my back with a bathroom sash: I am warned to remain still for at least five minutes after he leaves.

Suddenly I am alone again, minus a television, a radio, a clock, a watch and a suitcase. And several pints of blood.

Two cops from the Ninth Precinct drive me past Tompkins Square Park and toward East 14th Street. We are going after a mugger with a bulging suitcase. But the manhunt is soon called off. I am dizzy and soaked with sweat. Worse still, it is hard for me to breathe, since I feel as if my lungs are being wrung. So we head for Bellevue.

In the emergency room, a young doctor wipes away the blood and smiles weakly. He has obviously seen much worse.

A minor hemorrhage has caused my right lung to collapse. After expert treatment, I am wheeled over to an intensive-care unit and left alone. Later I will enter the trauma ward and hear the screaming of an ex-convict with a bullet in his stomach.

Two weeks later, as I recover at home, the two Lower East Side detectives who are handling my case show me a black-and-white snapshot.

"This the guy?" one detective asks.

I look at the picture closely. It is unmistakably the same guy who stabbed me.

"We got him at Rikers on a forced entry," the other detective says. "He was shooting $60 to $100 a day into his arm."

"Listen," the first one interrupts, "we'll want you downtown for a lineup. But it may take a week or two. Understand? We'll call you first."

I am patience incarnate.

A lineup is arranged. I go to the East Fifth Street Precinct for a ride to the Criminal Courts Building at 100 Centre Street. But the detectives are elsewhere,

As it turns out, they are attending a funeral. Two days earlier, a dope dealer had murdered two cops on East Fifth Street and Avenue A. The lineup is cancelled.

Another lineup is arranged. Again I go to the precinct, and again the lineup is cancelled. The defense attorney refuses to release a suspect from prison until a judge so orders. Issuance of the court order is guaranteed to take several more weeks.

A third lineup is arranged, and falls through. Guards at the House of Detention on Rikers Island cannot locate the prisoner. The two detectives matter-of-factly call this a common foul-up.

Meanwhile, the pink scar on my chest is fading and my right lung is billowing freely. I see people in my neighborhood who resemble the suspect. At this point, I am not even sure the cops have the right guy.

My patience has metamorphosed into disbelief. I am frustrated and angry. My sense of right and wrong is wounded. I am being made a victim twice.

Finally, more than four months after the crime, a lineup is conducted in Room 738 of the Criminal Courts Building. I watch through a one-way mirror in the next room.

With me are an assistant district attorney and the suspect's lawyer.

The city's prosecutor pulls down a wall panel, draws a black curtain around me and turns off the lights. Through a window I see six black men on a bench facing me. I hear faint instructions.

One man stands and walks towards the mirror, stops and turns to the right, then to the left. He returns to the bench.

The other five men follow the same procedure, each with an idiosyncratic interpretation. One smiles and cocks his head. A different one scowls menacingly, as if to joke. Still another keeps his head turned sideways and his eyes averted, hurrying along. Four of them are clean shaven and two are wearing bushy beards. The stranger who stabbed me was beardless.

The lineup has become a whodunit, I feel like a dumb panelist on "I've Got a Secret." It is time for finger-pointing.

The panel is shut and the curtains opened. When the lights return, the glare makes me blink. The assistant D.A. is holding up a clipboard, his pencil poised to record my momentous utterance.

"Have you seen any of these men?" he asks. "Don't worry, there's no need to rush."

I realize it is pointless to deliberate. I mumble my answer:

"I honestly don't recognize any of them."

The defense attorney grins and lets out a sigh, then leaves to pass the news to the one who held the knife so long ago.

My Last First Date

I'm evidence Cupid still exists. You know Cupid. Cute little guy from Roman mythology, son of the gods Venus and Mars. Winged, carries a bow and arrows, top matchmaker in history.

Well, my Cupid happened to be a guy from New Jersey named Carmine, an Al Pacino look-alike -- short, stocky, with thick hair and eyes like a beagle puppy. Cupid-like, really.

I got to know Carmine soon after I moved into a studio apartment in Manhattan, at 160 square feet possibly the city's smallest. He lived on the floor below me with his girlfriend Diane, a native of Lindenhurst.

One Friday night, Carmine knocked on my door and woke me from a nap. "Come out with us tonight," he said. "Me and Diane and her girlfriend, Elvira."

Groggy and in no mood to socialize, much less go on a blind date with another couple, I declined. My exact words: "Nah."

"Oh, come on," Carmine said, as if my decision were demonstrably ridiculous. "We'll have fun."

I had no reason to question this claim. Carmine knew more about fun than I ever would. I once saw him grab a vertical pole in a subway car and hoist himself sideways, acrobatically, all without seeming self-conscious. My idea of a good time on a Saturday night, on the other hand, might involve watching an old movie on television until three in the morning.

So I changed my mind -- or, rather, Carmine changed it for me—and out we went on our double date.

We hit a restaurant in New York City's Little Italy, Puglia's on Hester Street. Fettucine, garlic bread, house wine, red-and-white checkered tablecloths, the whole nine yards. A waiter nicknamed Mr. Spoons played spoons percussively on his lap as a floor show.

Immediately I'm taken with Elvira. She's 23, adorable, Italian, from Williamsburg, Brooklyn, with bangs and doe-like brown eyes. But she's also smart and, if only because she consented to go out with me, she's got a good and generous heart. Naturally, she makes me nervous.

So I do what a guy in that situation might do—I clam up, too jittery to say anything. I also drink too much red wine, the house red—much too much—all without eating.

Afterwards, we head back uptown, to the apartment building in the Flatiron neighborhood where I live on the third floor and her Diane and Carmen on the first. We're all saying goodnight, and then Elvira and I are alone.

"Would you like to come up?" I ask, feeling pretty frisky.

"No, thank you," she says gently.

"Are you sure?"

"Yes. I'm going to stay here tonight, with my friends."

And then I say something I never should have said. Something that I find it hard to believe I said. Something that I'm still sorry and embarrassed and ashamed I said.

"What are you," I say, "a lesbian or something?"

Now, you're welcome to chalk up this remark to all the red wine I had drunk, or to this being 1976, or to rank immaturity, or to a guy being a guy, taking the only recourse left to his manly pride after seeing his advance rebuffed -- questioning a woman about her sexual preferences -- or just garden-variety idiocy. Or all of the above.

Whatever my motivation, I know instantly I've made a major mistake. Surely Elvira will now react in kind. She'll slap my face or call me rude or walk away or challenge me to do something anatomically impossible to myself. Or all of the above. No matter what happens, I suspect, I will somehow have to pay the consequences.

But no. She neither blinks nor flinches nor balks. Instead, she laughs it off and looks me right in the eyes.

"You've had too much to drink," Elvira says to me. "It's late at night and you have no idea what you're saying. So let's just ignore it and wish each other good night."

Well, I think as we part company, that is certainly going to be that. Under no circumstances will I ever get to see this girl again. I've blown it. Our first date is going to be our last.

But that, too, proves untrue. I call Elvira the next day to apologize, and she accepts. I then invite her out again, and she takes me up on that, too.

Now, what if Carmine had never invited me out that night? What if he had failed to convince me to meet Elvira? His knock on my door that night, rousing me from a nap, turned out to be my Great Awakening.

Even so, my romance with Elvira almost ended before it began -- one blind date, over and out, all thanks to a comment that showed my judgment to be highly suspect at best.

Talk about close calls. It haunts me to realize all the opportunities we would have missed, the love never gained, the wedding never held, the children never born.

I used to think this story was all about me, about my desperately obnoxious remark. But again, I've turned out to be off-base. This story is about Elvira, about her response and how she cut me some slack.

Luckily, she gave me that second chance. She saw something redeemable in me, whatever it might be, and bet the house. And I've made it my business ever since then to try to live up to her belief.

So let me raise a glass to all the Carmines out there, those independent third parties flying around, cherub-like and shooting golden arrows into the lucky victims. My friend sensed the possibilities of bringing us together and cared enough to take the time to do it. Thanks to him, nature took its course.

The Tabloid Kid

My first real full-time job after college turned out to be just about the best imaginable. All I really wanted to do for a living after finishing college was go work as a reporter on a newspaper.

So I wrote letters and sent resumes to about 70 newspapers around the country, including, of course, New York City. Nothing—no interest, no interviews and still no job.

I'd looked for a job for about a year, though admittedly none too hard. And I'd gotten a few small freelance reporting assignments, mainly doing a three-part series about then newly developed Roosevelt Island for a weekly newspaper called *The Manhattan East* (my first article fetched me all of $15, then I got a raise to a princely $20).

I was living on East 7th Street between First Avenue and Avenue A, in a $150-a-month studio apartment, and the bar mitzvah savings I was living on were just about gone. I'd graduated from college a whole year earlier and still had yet to get any kind of career going, let alone a journalistic or literary one.

Then one day I saw a job ad in the paper and went in for an interview. It was a new weekly community newspaper, the *Eastside Courier*, that covered Manhattan's East Side from 14th to 79th Streets. And I got the gig.

I remember one moment afterwards particularly well. I walked out of the building on Park Avenue South and 17th Street and a light snow was coming down, the streets thinly coated with white. I looked up at the sky, just to watch the flakes falling, and happened to turn my eyes straight into the glare of a street lamp. I was already excited about getting my first real job, an adult job, ecstatic about going to work at a real newspaper and making $175 a week being a reporter. I was looking forward to telling my family and friends and everyone being proud of me, all those doubts about whether I could even find a job finally laid to rest.

And because of my angle of vision at that moment, the light from the streetlamp refracted through the shower of snow, and I saw a kaleidoscope of colors, a whole rainbow. I squinted in disbelief at the spectacle, my eyelashes wet with snow, and the prism effect became exaggerated, the rainbow colors shooting out in bright spokes. It was quite a moment, full of fate, and I was giddy, just deliriously happy, about this important step, much needed, toward becoming a grown-up (though full membership in that organization was still probably about 10 years ahead).

That Monday I started at my desk. The editor was Bill, who was mostly Irish but part Cherokee and had hair down to his shoulders, maybe 10 years my senior, married to an Israeli woman and living in a hotel on Gramercy Park with a new baby. A good guy,

Bill, with a sharp editorial eye and a sense of humor and appreciation of my reporting abilities.

The publisher was Richard, only two years older than I, a former *Daily News* reporter, a rich suburban kid from Tenafly, New Jersey, who got the startup funds from his father.

The other reporter there was Shelley, a gum-chewing, wise-cracking blond from Long Island who acted just like the Rosalind Russell character in "His Gal Friday," all sharp elbows and crusty patter.

And so for the next year I was a big-city reporter on a small newspaper, and it felt like I got to do just about everything you can do on a newspaper.

Every week I went to the local police precinct to get the lowdown on the latest crimes in the neighborhood.

I went to local community board meetings to hear about efforts to put up new buildings and otherwise alter the cityscape.

I attended press conferences held by State Senators and City Council members and, once, a congressman named Ed Koch, whom I briefly met and who of course then went on to become Mayor New York City for 12 years.

I covered a murder in a union office suspected of being a mob hit, and fires and political feuds and all kinds of scandals and controversies.

I reviewed movies, plays, books and restaurants, and for a while there I even had my own column, called "Deadline," that presumed to be humorous.

I wrote everything from articles to headlines and photo captions, edited pieces contributed by freelancers, and even did some layout and paste-up. Every week the paper came off the press and I held it in my hands with the kind of pride you feel only once in your life, right at the start of your career, a pride fresh and pure and free of precedent or taint. You know you're finally getting going. I was covering the city and learning the city and loving the surprises that lurked around any corner, because on any newspaper you never know what the news is going to be the next day.

So what if it was a small paper, with only about 50,000 readers, and free. So what that I was making only $9,000 a year. To a kid who wanted nothing more than to be a reporter for a newspaper, it was everything I might have expected, and then some. It was home. It was heaven. It was the best background possible for everything that came after.

I'm so glad I got that job, so grateful, because it would turn out to be my only stint on staff at a newspaper. But I would go on to freelance for many newspapers for many years. That first job meant the world to me. It's yet further proof of the axiom that sometimes it's better to be lucky than smart.

All the Time in the World: Saturday Night in FlatIron, 1977

She's coming over to my apartment, this young woman from Brooklyn. I'm living on East 23rd Street, in the city's smallest apartment, all of 160 square feet, and it's Saturday night.

It's 1977, early spring, and we just started going out six months earlier. We clicked right away, the second date soon after the first, and so on. Jimmy Carter is president, Hugh Carey governor and Ed Koch the new mayor. The city is in lousy shape, crime high, the streets dirty, jobs hard to find.

But that's all a distant backdrop for us. She's in my doorway now, looking cute, as she tends to do, and out we go. We go east toward Park Avenue South and hang a right on Third Avenue. In those days, Third Avenue had the action, the restaurants, the bars, everyone out on Saturday night.

We're holding hands now, her hand feeling so warm tucked into mine. We stop off at a pizza place we liked, thin crust and all, maybe two slices each. We're doing the town on a shoestring. We'd spent our first New Year's Eve lingering for three hours over a five-course dinner complete with a cabaret singer on piano.

We go to eat and talk a little, nothing serious on our agenda. Maybe I'm telling her how I hated Hebrew school, or she's letting me in on life with nuns at Catholic school, and maybe we imagine what would have happened if we had traded places.

She eats like a lady, no tomato sauce dripping onto her cheek, and it's all so easy. She's easy to talk to, easy to listen to, easy to be with. We each feel no need to be anything other than who we are, and being ourselves seems to fit the bill all around.

She's more than cute and smart and funny, too. She's steady, mature. She never raises her voice or gets hysterical. We're still busy discovering each other, feeling it all out, and it's feeling comfortable. It's feeling right.

Now Third Avenue has grown thick with pedestrians as night comes on. We go down toward Union Square Park, but stay out of it, the better to avoid the drug dealers. We head back uptown and go into a Bagel Nosh to pick up some tire-sized bagels.

It's all as easy as it gets, a guy from the Bronx and a girl from Brooklyn out on a Saturday night in Manhattan. Everything feels new. We're new to each other. Our careers are new. The city itself seems to have a certain innocence tonight, still a few months away from the Big Blackout and the Summer of Son of Sam.

We're back on 23rd Street now, passing the magnificent Metropolitan Life Building all lit up. We take a bench in Madison Square Park, but only briefly, because the drug dealers are out here, too.

Otherwise, though, the city is ours, and that's because we're young and everything is ahead of us, our pasts containing little more than our childhoods. She has such a sweet smile and she makes me laugh more than any girl I've known, and nothing else matters. I feel good around her, better, smarter, more successful than I've ever felt before.

Neither of us knows whether we have a future together. We're still in suspense, nothing a given yet. We're making it all up as we go along, heavily vested in the moment, no plans on our minds beyond tonight.

We're back in my apartment now. Soon we'll watch *Saturday Night Live*. We'll catch Chevy and Dan and Bill and John and Gilda and Jane and Loraine in the act, and we'll laugh together. Life is good, still pretty carefree, still light on obligations. All is promise and possibility. We have no idea what's coming.

Elvira and I will keep going out together, seeing no one else. That November, we'll move in together in Forest Hills, and within eight months we'll get engaged, and the following year we'll be married. Within a decade, the rest of us will arrive, first Michael and then Caroline, completing us forever.

But for now all that's still ahead. Right now it's only the spring of 1977, on a Saturday night in Flatiron, and nobody's in a hurry to get anywhere. We still have at least 40 Valentine's Days in front of us. We still have all the time in the world.

Competing with Cool

Even as a kid, I had a talent for getting ticked off in athletic competition. No occasion was too trivial for a tantrum, whether I was striking out, dropping a pass, or blowing a lay-up. In my more reserved moments, I had the decency to blame such failures on myself. But I also had a knack for discerning obscure causes that ranged from lucky curveballs and errant winds to lazy teammates and uncooperative backboards. In retrospect, it was uncanny how seldom I was at fault.

Of course, all my fuming and cursing were bad news when it came to the caliber of my play. The more upset I became at my shortcomings, the worse I performed. I swung at bad pitches, forced jump shots from well beyond my range, double-faulted ad nauseam. Distracted from the business at hand, my concentration in smithereens, I could usually count on my game to self-destruct.

In short, I had no cool.

Now that I'm an adult, poise is still hardly my specialty. Some years ago, a guy guarding me in basketball was hacking at my arms every time I took a shot and was climbing over my back for rebounds. After one especially nasty foul—I remember feeling to make sure my head was still attached—I shoved him to the court. He laid off me from then on, but no matter—I was so ashamed of my violence that my game was hopelessly undermined for the night.

And so it has gone my whole life. Under competitive pressure I have all the composure of an unfed Doberman. My anger gets so far out of hand that whatever skills I possess are seriously hampered. Only years later would I realize that playing with poise is essential to a top-notch performance in any sport.

Some athletes are naturally blessed with glacial equanimity. The best display of athletic self-control I ever witnessed took place in a long-ago NBA play-off game. Walt Frazier of the New York Knicks was outclassing his opponent, Phil Chenier of the Baltimore Bullets. At one point, as Frazier was dribbling the ball up the court, Chenier felt so stymied that he smacked him on the back of the head. Frazier never so much as flinched, much less cried foul. And, to cap it off, he went one-on-one on every shot.

Say what you will, that man was *born* cool.

My tip for today: it's perfectly okay to get angry in competition as long as you can channel your anger in the right direction.

This I once discovered in a two-on-two basketball game. The guy I was covering drove for the basket, jumped straight into me, and clipped me in the jaw with his outstretched elbow, scoring on the shot. You can bet I was not tickled by this raw aggression. But to call an offensive foul in schoolyard basketball is to risk being branded a candy-ass.

Besides, I decided retribution would be infinitely more rewarding. So I went into a fever of concentration. The next time he dribbled the ball toward me, I lunged forward, as if going for a steal. He was faked out by the move, forced to stop dribbling and clutch the ball. Then I pulled off a trick I had never done in all my years of playing basketball.

Like a pickpocket, I simply plucked the ball from his hands and scored on a lay-up. The guy was so flabbergasted that he quit the game and left the court with hardly a word. I guess he had no cool.

Antoinette

I went out of the subway with my girlfriend Elvira, passed the White Castle and approached the three-story walk-up. Elvira pressed the buzzer and we were let in and started to climb the crooked, creaking steps. The whole building tilted to the right, as if it belonged in Pisa or had one drink too many.

And then from the top of the steps came this thunderous voice.

"That you, Vira Ann? You said you would be here a half hour ago."

"Sorry, Mom. Subway. Stuck."

"I worried something went wrong. You know how I worry, Vira Ann."

So it went for the whole climb, the voice calling down to us from the third floor, Elvira calling back. The voice asking if it was still raining and Elvira saying no, and the voice asking was she sure. The voice narrating our entire ascent, Zeus-like.

I came to Williamsburg, Brooklyn with Elvira to meet her mother for the first time. It was 1976. I'd gone out with Elvira for a few months and we were pretty well sold on each other. She'd told me about her mother, of course, but now I was about to find out for myself.

I reached the top floor and there, framed in the doorway to her one-bedroom apartment, dressed in a sleeveless house dress, was a handsome woman of 56. Warm brown eyes, a noble Neapolitan nose, graying hair frizzed high and a smile almost saintly.

Her name was Antoinette. Antoinette Chirichella. But everyone knew her as Nettie.

I said I was glad to meet her, but the truth is I was unsure.

Say Hello To The Chirichellas: When Jews and Italians Marry

It was a long time ago, probably 1976, before my adult life got going, and Elvira and I were taking a stroll around her neighborhood in Williamsburg. It was drizzling out, but neither of us seemed to mind much—it was as if being together kept us dry.

And then I heard Elvira call out, "Grandpa." And I looked over to where she called and there he was, her grandfather, Nicholas, or Nick, skinny as a stick, his face gaunt and shriveled, standing in a doorway in the rain.

He looked old, really old (I was only 24 then, so half the world came across as old), and as he said hello, I saw he was missing some of his teeth.

Elvira introduced us, we shook hands, and he seemed pleasant enough. It was my first time meeting anyone in Elvira's family other than her mother, and it was jarring. All I could think was that her grandfather was nothing like either of mine—nothing, even, that squares with my concept of a grandfather.

It had to do with him standing in the doorway in the rain. I tried to imagine anyone in my family standing in a doorway in the rain, but no such image would come forth.

Oh, make no mistake: Nicholas Chirichella turned out to be a decent guy, and always treated me well. He was quiet, though with a colorful tongue, and a good grandfather and father as far as I knew.

It's just that he was . . . different.

Different from my family—and different as everyone in Elvira's family was different from my family.

At one point we took Nettie to visit my grandparents the Shefts in their Upper East Side apartment, maybe on Thanksgiving. If I recall right, Nettie was reluctant to go, feeling uncomfortable about it, even nervous, maybe worried about feeling out of place. Somehow we must have convinced her the visit would turn out fine.

And on the whole it did. She looked around my grandparents' handsomely appointed apartment, with the thick carpeting and heavy drapes and gleaming old-wood furniture, and I imagined her thinking she had entered another universe. She spoke very little, quite uncharacteristic of her, and only when someone, my grandmother Gertrude or my Uncle Leonard, said something to her. And when she did speak, she spoke a little differently from the usual, her diction just a touch crisper.

Everyone got along well, but the room definitely was fraught with anxiety, both guest and hosts uneasy with each other, unsure what to say or ask.

Yes, deep down we're all people, all presumably the same. But was my grandfather going to ask Nettie about her stock portfolio? Was Nettie going to ask him where he bought his mozzarella? I doubted it. A gulf loomed between our families, all but impossible to breach (though Elvira and I managed to do it all right).

We were Jewish and she was Italian.

We were rich and she was poor.

So this divide spanned class, money, culture and religion.

And so it went at our wedding.

Over here you had my Aunt Zelda from West Orange, elegant and beautiful, and over there Aunt Nettie's sister Carmela, earthy and volcanic and loud.

Over here you had my Uncle Mark, inheritor of an insurance company, and over there Elvira's Uncle Nick, who once tried out for the New York Giants (the baseball team that once played at the Polo Grounds in the Bronx, before it moved to San Francisco) and fixed elevators for a living.

I could go on about this clash of cultures, about how seriously I took it at the time and how funny it seems in hindsight, but for now I'll finish with Nettie's first visit with my family that night. I remember feeling protective of her, alive to any potential insult.

But most of all, I remember being proud of her, proud of how she carried herself, proud of how she represented her family, proud of how she demonstrated, to anyone willing to notice, that she was just as good as they—and maybe, just maybe, a whole lot better.

Hooked On Hoops: Part 2

You're 20 years of age now. Five-foot-ten, 150 pounds. A sophomore in college in the heart of Boston, living in a dorm room. You take up cigarettes, a sure sign of maturity, and put away two packs a day.

You have good hands, strong but "soft," but your feet need work and so does the rest of you. In the last two years, you've practiced basketball regularly, playing more frequently than ever. You keep in mind, to motivate yourself, how you tried out for the junior high school basketball team at age 15, only to get cut in the last round.

In the last two years, you've played basketball more than ever, really practiced hard. All you want out of life, if you leave aside a regular girlfriend and better grades and a respectable literary career, is to get better at basketball. To get good enough to hold your own and maybe then some. To sprint down the court, to slash through the paint on a drive, to rain jumpers from the top of the key.

You go to the indoor basketball court at MIT, across the Charles River, with your friend and roommate Jeff, and get into pickup games. Most of the other players are collegians, too, all around your age, most your superiors at the sport.

Because you're young and guaranteed to live forever, you take no time to warm up. You're a decent outside shooter, quite reliable around the foul line, but you have nothing resembling an all-around game yet. You consider defense inconvenient and so seldom play any. You suffer intense anxiety and wish for nothing more than to avoid embarrassing yourself, hardly the attitude of a noble gladiator.

The other players seem to be having fun. Someday maybe you will, too.

On offense, you always go to one corner or the other, over near the baseline, and wait for someone to pass you the ball. Otherwise you have no idea where to position yourself on the court.

The other players may know you're there on the court, but show little evidence of caring. You never say a word during a game, much less call for the ball. If you get the ball at all, it's by default—nobody else is open—or a fluke.

Now you get the ball. You shoot. No surprise there: your first impulse is always to shoot. Why do otherwise? If you score, you've succeeded. It's just that simple. A basket instantly and irrefutably quantifies your prowess, and thus your right to exist.

That Wail In The Elevator

My Poppa lies in a bed at Mount Sinai Hospital, on Fifth Avenue at 105th Street. He's gone pale, his head tilted to the side on the pillow, the IV in his arm. He has cancer of the throat and he's dying.

I'm 29 years old and my grandfather Benjamin Sheft means the world to me. He took me to Yankee Stadium in 1960, my first trip there. I slept in a bed with him during Christmas vacations as a kid. He took me to his office across from Grand Central Terminal.

How can he die?

He always called me "Bobby boy," always cheerfully.

"Hello, Bobby boy!" he would boom.

He always seemed glad to see me. I could always count on his attention, depend on him to look me in the eye and lend me an ear. He saved me from my father, my absentee father, even became my father, my substitute father, doting on me, asking after me, worrying about me.

I would show him an article I wrote for a newspaper or a magazine and he might say, "Wow! Such a long article!" A long article always impressed him.

We would watch a basketball game and he might say, "They should be shooting better—that's why the Knicks are losing." To him, the game came down strictly to which team shot better.

He would come home from the office and call out hello and take off his suit jacket and loosen his tie and ease into his Eames chair with the evening news on TV and Nana would pour him a scotch on the rocks and he would take a sip and click his tongue and let out this long, deep sigh, exhaling all the tension from his day as an accountant keeping track of other people's money.

"So how goes it, Bobby boy?" he might then be ready to say.

He would ask me about school or my search for a job. I had trouble finding my first job after college. My problem was that I was particular about the kind of job I wanted, plus the city had gone into a serious economic slump and jobs were hard to come by.

"I'd like to see you situated," he would say, nodding his head with grave concern. He already understood something I learned only decades later: that a job was kind of everything. You had to make a living.

He would lean back in his chair, his legs opening and closing rapidly, a nervous habit of his, still charged up from his hours at the office. As he sipped his scotch—I noticed he always sipped it, gingerly, savoring it—his legs would be slower to open and close, meaning he was finally winding down.

He'd gone to college in the 1920s, Baruch at CUNY on East 23rd Street, the first in his family to reach higher education, and then he got married in 1927, and soon the Great Depression hit, and he went around to businesses in the Bronx—dry cleaners, auto-repair shops, anything—offering to do the books.

He'd eventually done well, well enough to drive a Cadillac, belong to a country club in Westchester, travel to Europe and Asia with friends.

But he always wanted to do better and seemed occasionally disappointed in himself. One time he told me about a residential property he bought along with some partners in the 1950s. As it happens, it was the very apartment complex in Fair Lawn where my mother eventually lived.

"I sold it too soon," he said. "I wanted fast money. If I had held onto it longer, I would be a millionaire now."

So that's how it went with my Poppa. He shared himself with me, his dreams, his life, his love. He gave me a glimpse of how a man should act, at the office, on the golf course, at home.

He also showed me, without ever saying as much, how much life could hurt you, how your wife could annoy you, how a client could cheat you. He took me to a deli for dinner once, and after we ate he lacked exact change at the cash register. "I'll owe you the penny," he said, but the cashier refused, and my grandfather, scowling, said, "I'll remember that."

He usually wore a frown, the result of a mouth that naturally turned down at the sides. He had a jaw like a bulldog—see our photos of him—and a chest thicker with hair than any you ever saw, and he could whack a golf ball 200 yards, and talked in a deep, gruff voice, and now he was dying of lung cancer and I'd never lost anyone I loved before.

One night I saw the frown erased from his face. My Uncle Leonard held a 65th birthday party for him, and my grandfather had more than a few drinks. His face grew red from all the scotch, and he laughed more than I ever saw him laugh and, surrounded mostly by friends but also family, he broke into song, "The Man On The Flying Trapeze." The only lyric I caught was, "He flies through the air with his balls hanging bare."

It had to be the happiest I ever saw him, and it made me happy to see him so happy, even if he had to get drunk to get there.

Weeks before he went into Mount Sinai, I visited him at home. The doctors had already diagnosed his cancer and I had no idea what would happen or how bad it might be.

"So did you hear about the Mets today?" I asked.

We had always talked baseball, he and I, which teams won and who hit a home run.

"Argh," he said, and waved his hand dismissively, a clearcut signal of resignation, maybe even disgust. It was then that I knew he might be far gone. If he had given up on baseball, he had given up on living.

And now a nurse came into his hospital room to say he had to go for tests and my grandfather said why more tests. He rolled over onto a gurney as instructed and the nurse wheeled him into an elevator and I went with him.

My grandfather—whose father was an illiterate peasant but who himself had sent his son to Yale Law school and bought his daughter a $21,000 house in 1954 and who could whack a golf ball 200 yards—then let out a wail, a wail keening and high-pitched and piercing, wailing his guts out, raging against the dying of the light. He could see the end coming now, just as I had when he stopped caring about baseball. I'll never forget how that wail sounded, and I never should.

And after he died, weeks or months later, I wrote him a poem, called "Letter to Poppa," imagining a conversation with him in heaven.

In his last days, my wife had visited him at the hospital. He grabbed her hand and asked in a fierce whisper for us to have a baby. And she said she would. And now my Poppa lives on in my heart, and in my son, whose middle name is "Benjamin."

Mating Season

Labor Issues

You took your time coming out, my dear son Michael. I think Mom was in labor for 36 hours.

Why you took so long I have no idea, nor do I figure you had any control over it. Maybe you really liked it in there—who could blame you?—and felt reluctant to leave. As we know, Mom is an excellent host.

Just the same, she probably found you to be an excellent house guest. And so we waited. After waiting, we then waited some more.

A nurse told us were going to have a girl, and for whatever reason, Mom and I both doubted her with all our hearts.

A pregnant woman came in and had her baby within an hour. Mom and I felt like complaining to the nurses, Hey, we got here first, how come she gets to cut in line.

I went out for breakfast at the Georgia Diner, assured I had time. As I ate my eggs, I knew my life—our lives—would soon change for good. Only I had no idea how, really, much less how much. No idea, either, how much I could love someone else, a child of my own, a son.

And let me tell you, Mom really had her work cut out delivering you. She huffed and she puffed, grunting and groaning, her brow shiny with sweat, all of us urging her on, Come on, Elvira, you can do it, keep pushing, push harder. I know she just wanted all of us to shut the fuck up.

But no, you were having none of it. In there you stayed, in your little amniotic domicile, probably watching a smackdown DVD or something.

It was tough. Mom tried the breathing exercises, but still she gasped. Finally, she asked to be medicated. It was enough already. You were running late. Mom was exhausted.

I wish I could remember it all better than I do. I should have captured it in a chronicle right then, rather than all these years later. But that much I remember. That, and the sense of something new coming, of discoveries and rewards in the offing.

And then, of course, now ready at last, out you came. And I saw it all, first the head, then the rest, as you emerged, bloody, crying, beautiful, absolutely perfect.

Welcome, Michael, I thought. Stay awhile.

Your Opening Act

You, my dear daughter Caroline, I worried about from the start, even before you were born. The doctor told us you were in there in an unusual position. Transverse breach, she called it.

Somehow you were upside down and slung across sideways. It was a form of occupancy less than ideal. It might even be dangerous, the doctor told us. The umbilical cord could get tangled up, even strangle you as you came out.

Hardly what Mom and I needed to hear eight months along. She took it pretty well, at least so it seemed. Me, I was another story I kept thinking about it day after day for those last weeks.

Please, I thought, let her be OK. We'd already had one perfect child. Was it too much for us to hope for a second? Go two for two?

The doctor kept close watch. Mom went to see her more often, just as a precaution, just to check on your position in the womb. Nothing changed. In transverse breach you remained.

Please, I kept thinking, let her be perfect. It was sort of a prayer, but sent out to the universe at large rather than to any god. I swore never to expect or ask for anything else again. I kept my concern to myself to avoid upsetting Mom.

The doctor showed us a sonogram of you so we could see your awkward position. It was decided that day that the safest course was for you to be delivered, at full term, by Caesarean. In those days, that meant I would have to stay out of the delivery room, unable to see you born, as I had our son, Michael.

When Mom went in the operating room at what was then St. John's Hospital on Queens Boulevard, I waited outside, more nervous than I'd ever felt. I needed to do something to keep my mind off my worries. So I wrote.

I had an assignment from *Omni* magazine. It had to do with either mummies or robots, I forget. A short piece. I tinkered away, trying to make it as perfect as I wanted you to be. An hour went by, maybe more. Then the doctor came out. She told me you had emerged fine, without a hint of a problem. I could go see you now.

Back I went to where all the new babies hung out, all in those little bassinets. I stood over you, your face so pink, your eyes closed, your mouth puckering, your fingers squirming, your hair matted. You cried.

I felt a rush of relief almost stunning in its force. You were OK. I could see that for myself. And then I felt my whole face wrinkle and flush and I broke down crying.

"Hello, Caroline," I said through tears. "I'm your Daddy. Glad you could make it."

Now you're an adult. You're pursuing a career as an entrepreneur. You're healthy, smart, beautiful -- in short, perfect.

For that, my baby, call me grateful beyond words.

Seamstress

The bare facts about Nettie are as follows.

Born in 1920, in Williamsburg, Brooklyn.

Mother Elvira, born in the U.S. Father Nicholas, from a town near Naples named Sala Consilina, a garbageman.

Brothers Michael and Nicholas and sister Carmela. Brother Anthony dies at the age of one from a rat bite.

Nettie drops out of the eighth grade at age 14 to be a seamstress at a sewing machine at a factory in Brooklyn. She sews collars onto shirts and buttons onto jackets, paid by the piece, all against a backdrop of dust and clatter. Makes sure the garments come out right and gives all her earnings to her family.

Sees Frank Sinatra debut at the Paramount in 1939 and is smitten for life.

In her early 30s meets a man with whom she will have a child but never marry.

Raises her daughter Elvira Ann, the father long gone, never to be spoken of, the man who never was.

Puts Elvira through Catholic school, takes her to mass, buys her beautiful red shoes she can barely afford.

Always celebrates Christmas to a fare-thee-well, trees, eats, gifts, the whole nine yards.

Sees her daughter study clothing design, enter the New York City garment industry and become an executive.

Retires in 1983, after 47 years hunched over a sewing machine, just in time to become a grandmother.

A Do-It-Yourself Kit

Slowly, my attitude about performing as a go-between for my mother changed. When I entered my thirties and she her fifties. I had pressing responsibilities—a wife, two children, my career. My mother would have to make an effort to be independent. Now, if she asked me to order a meal for her in a restaurant, I would tell her to order it herself. If the waitress asked me to translate for her, I would suggest that she ask my mother to repeat herself.

This came to a head at a family gathering. Once again, everyone around the table talked as my mother turned her head right and left, as if trying to follow a tennis match. My Uncle Leonard, her brother, was telling a story. Finally, she asked me the inevitable question: "What's Lenny saying?"

For years, I resented my relatives for all but shunning my mother and leaving me with the task of hearing for her by proxy. My mother, too, had resented that everyone else in the family rode this carousel of spoken language while she could only watch.

But as I sat there, I realized that she had never taken any initiative. She behaved as if she were helpless. By depending on me, she had assumed a power close to tyranny. Weakness served as her strength. I saw that even victims can be bullies, exploiting sympathy. How much was I really helping her as a go-between?

So I looked at my mother and pointed to my uncle. "Ask *him*," I said.

She lowered her eyebrows, puzzled and hurt, and again asked what Leonard has said.

I said, "Ask *him*! Go ahead. Ask your brother."

She asked him and, sure enough, he repeated the story.

"See?" I said. "You *can* speak for yourself."

I quit the job of being a bridge between two worlds. I still felt a duty toward my mother, but only because she's my mother, not because she's deaf. I distributed responsibility for her throughout the family, trying to gradually shed my lifelong sense of guilt and burden and pain. Yes, this slow pulling away left my mother feeling betrayed. Years later, she would still ask me, on occasion, to order for her in a restaurant. When I refused—as I always would—she looked baffled and turned on me with a scowl.

"Why not?" she would demand.

"Because you should do it yourself," I would say.

Even in her fifties and beyond, my mother struggled to survive without relying on her mother, her brother and the rest of us as crutches.

Maybe she had yet to get the message she should.

Maybe she never would.

Hooked On Hoops: Part 3

Welcome to age 30. You're married now and your wife has a job in Manhattan. You left your job as an editor at a magazine about a year ago to freelance as a writer out of the bedroom in your one-bedroom apartment. You live in the borough of Queens, in Forest Hills, and get by on modest incomes.

You've quit cigarettes and gained almost 20 pounds, apparently none of it muscle, courtesy of nightly vodka, a handy substitute for smoking. Your favorite grandfather is now gone from your life except in fond memory.

You're older than maybe half of the players now. You've started to notice a few mild clues to physical decline. Your waist threatens to thicken like so much béarnaise sauce and your hindquarters are yielding, if slightly, to the tug of gravity. You take longer to bounce back after a contest. You hurt myself often enough to wonder whether you should be accompanied to all contests by a paramedic.

You keep playing basketball, though, maybe three times a week -- outdoors during spring and summer, more like once a week, and indoors, in the fall and winter. Before you play now, you usually try to shoot around for five minutes, and take an insincere pass at some stretching—knee bends, toe touches—just to loosen your joints and circulate your blood. You talk to your teammates once in a while.

You're pretty good now, quick on your feet, better at fundamentals, usually among the best players out there. It's taken you more than 20 years to become a natural athlete. You play harder, take games more seriously, even defense. You're kind of a hothead, cursing yourself for mistakes, complaining about foul calls.

Your first thought on a given day is about shooting the ball. You shoot first and think later, like a trigger-happy gangster or a gunslinger in the Old West. You shoot anywhere, anytime, anyhow.

Your attitude is, your teammates should give you the ball. Period. You fancy yourself the go-to guy. You're always the star of your own drama, the other players merely your supporting cast. You keep track of shots you take and make. You shoot no matter what. You may shoot too much, but never too little, as least as far as you're concerned.

You borrow your philosophy about shooting from the compulsive gambler. If you're making shots now, you'll keep making your shots. But if you're missing your shots, you're bound to start hitting soon.

Who would dare disagree with such flawless logic?

So chances are, tonight you'll limp home sore and grunting from your latest act of masochism on the basketball courts. Yet no sooner will you climb into the steaming shower than you will promise yourself that next week you'll go easier and leave sooner. And just as surely as you make this vow, you're also going to break it.

In the shower you'll entertain theories about why you hurt so much. All this desperate speculation, you now realize, is an effort to escape the inescapable—that you're getting older.

As a boy, you played away your afternoons and summer evenings without ever seeming to get tired or hurt. You lived with the certainty that your body would always snap back, that you would remain forever lean and quick, that you'd never let age catch you.

Still, you hardly qualify to call yourself Methuselah; you're still years away from shopping around for a pacemaker. Besides, the longer you compete in sports, the better you understand how to capitalize on strengths and minimize weaknesses. I compensate for my leaden feet, for example by making sure to position myself well on defense in basketball.

And with experience you're bound to play smarter. In your youth, you disregard your brain and just play, often recklessly. But by now your muscles can draw on a long memory to pick out the right move for a situation. In the same vein, you cultivate a sense of how to move with economy.

With age, you also become your own best doctor. You get better at translating messages from your body. Even though you get hurt worse and more often, at least you now know how to take care of any injury, for example never rushing your recoveries.

The worst hazards for aging athletes originate in the head. Attitude is just about everything—almost a muscle in itself.

You play now mostly for the high, because on the most primitive level, sports are your benign addiction.

You have yet another motive for persisting at sports: ego. Your three-year-old son, Michael, may someday want to play baseball and basketball, soccer and tennis. You'd like to show him how to play, preferably without creaking too much.

Filibusters

As soon as I had a mother-in-law to call my own, I had some issues with her. For starters, Nettie talked too much. She would ask me a question and then give me the answer. I would interrupt her to get a word in edgewise, but then she would interrupt my interruption.

She talked to anyone and everyone, the clerk selling her the Lotto ticket and the stranger on the street with the cute schnauzer. She could talk to you for a half hour straight, only for you to leave to do laundry, and when you came back, she would still be going full-tilt. If she ever inhaled, I must have missed it.

It seemed no thought ever popped into her head that she deemed worthy of keeping to herself. Everything that came to her mind wound up destined, for better or worse, to come cascading straight into your ears.

Now, maybe you think this is all merely my opinion. But by even the most rigorously objective scientific standards, she was a human filibuster, her tongue equipped with everything except an "off" button.

But why take my word for it? Listen to this sample:

Oh I like that Peter Falk he's such a good actor I wonder what he's like in real life oh did you ever get me those tissues I like at Rite Aid oh guess what happened on Maspeth Avenue this morning right in front of the OTB yeah Mrs. Palumbo the librarian from your elementary school remember her she got hit by a bus I think it was the B-53 or maybe the B-59 and she's OK except she broke both legs and now she's in a wheelchair you know I love watching the clouds I really should write poetry oh I heard Payless is having a sale on sandals so maybe we should go next Saturday oh did you read in the Daily News today about the rats on the "L" line someone said they're growing big enough to wear saddles and speaking of rabies remember your friend Louise from St. Cecilia well she has diabetes now such a shame she always made such nice cannelloni.

See what I mean? Soon my mother-in-law started to feel like one big fat joke. On me.

Hey, let me tell you about some other traits I quickly discovered in Nettie. She talked too loud. Booming, bellowing, top-of-her-lungs loud. Operatically loud. Apparently she lacked volume control.

Nettie worried too much, too. Also loudly. Whatever she could worry about, she would worry about. She tended to see the world as a problem that defied solution, as a threat ever about to befall her, every event ripe with opportunity for martyrdom.

And all her loud worrying led to equally loud complaining.

Look, I'd like to tell you that I took all these little idiosyncrasies in stride, and that I even found such eccentricities charming. Really I would. But I never could. Her voice gave me such a headache that I often excused myself from any room she occupied.

Yet I took no action against her.

Working The Vice Squad

Sometimes nothing gets you going in the right direction better than quitting something.

I know. I speak as a longtime quitter. I've quit at least two major bad habits (though I still have several more to go).

Back in 1970, for example, away from home for the first time, in college in Boston, I started smoking cigarettes. A pack a day grew to two packs a day in short order. My life was designed around my smokes, or vice versa—hard to say which—with me smoking after every meal, smoking with a drink, and certainly smoking, always smoking, as I wrote, usually late into the night.

I loved it. Loved the whole routine, the ritual, the taste, the smell, but most of all the sight, the tendrils of smoke coiling under a reading light like some primordial fog. I went on like that for years, believing myself pretty cool, ever so much the writer, through college and into my first job. Knew it was bad for me, unhealthy, cancerous, yet I had no plans to quit.

Until I met Elvira. She hated my smoking. Hated it! She forbade me to smoke in her presence. Before we moved in together, she banned my smoking indoors near her. She also told me that kissing me was like licking the inside of an ashtray.

Ah, doomed romance!

Well, that was the deciding factor right there. If my kisses were going to disgust her, how could we ever live together?

So I quit. Oh, I tried a few times first. Once, I tried to quit by smoking nonstop, one cigarette right after another without interruption, in order to make the act so revolting I would stop out of protest. But I kept going back to my Salems.

Finally, on January, 1, 1977—about 14 months after meeting Elvira, 18 months before getting engaged to her and 26 months before our wedding—I quit cigarettes for good.

Same with hard liquor.

Now, I was never as much a drinker as I was a smoker. But make no mistake: I liked to drink. It had nothing to do with the flavor and everything to do with getting high. Vodka, mostly, but also gin, and once in a while, at least early on, scotch, too.

It never looked like it would ever evolve into a problem, except eventually, at the age of 35, I realized someday it very well could. So on August 6, 1987—8/6/87, as luck would have it—I quit hard liquor, too.

In both instances, it was really a matter of making the commitment, nothing more, no secret cure. Once I decided to quit, I quit, and never went back. No regrets.

In fact, I'm quite relieved. If I'd smoked over the last 40 years, how would I feel, what would I look like, how much different might our lives have turned out? Same with drinking. Almost certainly one vice or the other, or possibly the combination of the two, would have destroyed my health, or at least put a serious dent in it. And then maybe my career and our family.

But I stopped in time. Quitting gave me a fresh start. It's funny how it works out. No sooner do you get addicted to something than you grow addicted to going without it.

A Woman Of Ill Repute

Regarding my mother-in-law, then, I saw only trouble ahead.

Of course the mother-in-law is, above all else, a joke. Or at least widely regarded throughout popular culture as a big fat joke. That's just a straight historical fact.

You've probably even heard some of those jokes about the mother-in-law. Like the one about how the big reason Adam and Eve got along so well is that neither had one. Or how the definition of mixed emotion is watching your mother-in-law back off a cliff in your new Mercedes.

Funny, right? In the 1950s and 1960s, as I came of age, jokes about the mother-in-law practically ranked as a national pastime, right below hating Communists. Borscht Belt comedians riffed ad nauseum on "The Ed Sullivan Show" about the mother-in-law. Jackie Gleason, as Ralph Kramden on "The Honeymooners," bellowed about his blabbermouth mother-in-law.

The very term "mother-in-law" is the perfect punch line, a cheap laugh almost guaranteed. Go ahead, try it. Let's say someone is butting into your life, being a bossy, belittling busybody. All you really need to do in such a case is to ask, "What are you, my mother-in-law?"

Bingo!

Yet behind all the punch lines about the mother-in-law is evidently a real problem. Websites and blogs are dedicated to sharing horror stories about her. A husband and wife, suffering a double case of bad mother-in-law experiences, started a website, motherinlawstories.com, to grant others a public forum for venting frustrations. Of 16 websites about mothers-in-law, 12 are either negative about or openly hostile to the old dear.

Consider the research, too. Studies show that many men and women who divorce point to the mother-in-law as a factor in the split. An Iowa State University study concluded that the less conflict with in-in-laws, the more successful the marriage. Italy's Institute of Statistics found that the more physical distance between a married couple and a mother-in-law, the longer the marriage lasted. A program is actually now commercially available to treat pentharaphobia, or a "persistent, abnormal and unwarranted fear of mother-in-law."

In other words, having issues with your mother-in-law appears about par for the course. In 2006, a woman in England whose mother-in-law constantly bullied her -- permitting her only one phone call per week, banning her from leaving the house unaccompanied and forcing her to clean the toilet without a brush—sued her successfully. One man in France, so fed up with his mother-in-law, decided that rather than try to kill her with kindness, he would simply kill her. He stabbed her with a knife, claiming she had called him a loser and humiliated him.

Clearly, then, the mother-in-law occupies a unique status in society. Across all borders, she's often an object of scorn and derision, probably the most vilified family member in human history, the original woman of ill repute.

No, there's simply no other mother like this mother. Petty tyrant, castrating witch, *monster*-in-law -- pick your favorite pejorative. No wonder the concept of a good mother-in-law is generally considered an oxymoron. The term is practically a dirty word.

All your life, after all, you'd heard the rumors, the warnings, about the mother-in-law, and now you expected the worst. This woman was going to drop into your home unannounced at least twice a week, the better to step directly between you and your wife and block your view of each other and all radio contact. She'd start right in giving unsolicited, highly unwelcome advice about how to raise your children, handle your clients and, while she was at it, realign your investment portfolio. She'd watch your every move, absolute in the certainty that sooner or later you'll mess up, the only question being how badly.

Her main purpose—her holy calling, really—would be to second-guess you into an early grave. If you needed to know what to think about anything, she'd be quick to tell you. If you went left, she'd say you should have gone right. If you could collect a nickel for every compliment she paid you, you might eventually have a dime.

The only time a mother-in-law will ever give you, after all, is a tough time. She'll be your worst nightmare, compounded daily. She will loom over you, judge, jury and executioner all in one. Marry her daughter and you'll never be smart enough, good-looking enough, polite enough, or earn enough money to meet her standards. You'll have no chance of escaping your life alive.

Recall, if you will, that classic doo-wop song, "Mother-In-Law:"

Mother-in-law, mother-in-law
The worst person I know
If she leave us alone
We would have a happy home
Every time I open my mouth
Then she tries to put me out
I come home with my pay
She ask me what I made
She thinks her advice is a constitution
If she would leave that should be the solution

Except that when it came to Antoinette Chirichella, none of that turned out even remotely to be true.

Oh, I already know what you're thinking. Know exactly. You think I'm going to hand you some goody-goody story, all hearts-and-flowers, all too-sensitive-for-words, about how perfect my mother-in-law was. You think I'm going to get all Hallmark card on you and slobber schmaltz all over your shirt collar.

Well, forget that. Nobody ever accused Nettie of being perfect, least of all me. But as it happens, she came pretty close. So let me have my say.

Brother, Can You Cash A Check?

Last November, he told me about the check. He had tried to deposit it in several banks in the neighborhood. None would let him open a savings or checking account. The banks insisted on more proof of identity than his Social Security card.

He told me it was a big check.

Really, I said.

Yeah, he said. About $25,000.

Right, I thought. He slept in the doorway of the telephone building on Queens Boulevard, across from McDonald Park in Forest Hills. He sacked out on cardboard torn from large boxes and plastic bags stuffed with his belongings.

I'll show you, he said.

No, that's okay—I believe you, I said. The evening had turned chilly and his nose was running. No harm in humoring him, I decided.

He pulled from his back pocket a sheaf of tattered papers. Gingerly he handed the documents to me. I riffled through the fraying papers. Then I find the check. For a Theodore Campanella. From the United States Treasury. For $24,613.

The check, issued under the authority of the Social Security Administration and dated in August, warned: Void Within Three Months Of Issue Date. Two weeks left in the hourglass before he could kiss the money goodbye.

I had known Campanella for years. He seemed about 50. He had a swarthy skin and a salt-and-pepper beard. He hobbled along, a wooden crutch under his right shoulder. We would say hello to each other as I headed toward the Continental Avenue subway station. He would smile at my son and daughter if they happened to tag along.

I had given up on doing anything for the homeless. Every day on the E and F trains, some guy gave you a pitch. You wanted to come across. But you had your doubts. Where will my dollar go? Will it make a difference? I usually held onto my money.

But Campanella was different. He stayed clean. He never asked anyone for money. Besides, he smiled at my kids. He was okay. I would ask him if he were hungry or thirsty, and usually he said yes, and I would go to a coffee shop to get him some soup or a doughnut and coffee, to go.

Now I stared dumbfounded at the check. With this money Campanella could pull his life together. Hell, with that money *I* could pull *my* life together. He could rent an apartment. Take his right leg to the doctor. Stock his refrigerator with soup and doughnuts. Even look for a job.

But the banks wanted more i.d. Of course: Everyone who sleeps in a doorway has a Gold Card. This is ridiculous, I told Campanella. I'll open an account for you.

The next day I went to my bank and spoke with its president. No, she told me, without proper identification the bank could not accept the check. I suggested the bank verify the check with the Social Security Administration. Surely the bank could assign a bank officer to take an hour to run it down?

Sorry, she said.

So it went with several other banks. Then, with permission from Campanella, I called New York Newsday. I saw a human-interest feature about a homeless guy with a big check nobody wanted to cash. Straight out of Frank Capra. A civic-minded bank president would seize the opportunity to perform a humanitarian service, generate free publicity and turn a profit. Perfect.

A few days after a reporter came out to Forest Hills, an article appeared, with surprising details about Campanella. He grew up in an orphanage. He had a job in the shipping department of a plant in Long Island City. He had lived without a home for 17 years. He was 65 years old. The Social Security Check was a lump sum for disability payments that had never reached him because he had no address to reach.

Sure enough, a bank followed through on the check. Campanella obtained a letter from the Social Security Administration that verified the check as his. The article reported that Campanella had plans for the money. Find a home. Let a doctor examine his leg. Get his teeth fixed. Buy new glasses.

As I passed the telephone building on Thanksgiving Day, Campanella was nowhere in sight. Over the next few days, I looked for him on park benches and in the subways. Gone. I had saved a homeless guy from the cold streets. I felt heroic.

Then, on a freezing night in early December, I saw him in the doorway. Although swaddled against the cold—maroon parka, black hat with ear flaps, black scarf, brown gloves, thick blue socks, heavy black boots—he was shivering. From a foot away he showed no sign of recognizing me. Spittle had caked in the corners of his mouth.

What happened? I asked. What about the check? Wrong Campanella, he said.

How do you mean?

The check, he said. It was not mine. Another Theodore Campanella.

You must have known, I wanted to say. Usually you know if you have a $24,613 check coming to you. But I asked nothing, said nothing. And Campanella explained nothing. He had wanted the check to be his. I had wanted the check to be his. But it was not his check. Never would be.

I had wanted to do good. But sometimes, in reaching out to the helpless, we found ourselves helpless. Despite me, Campanella remained in his doorway. I had bought into his delusions about his identity. Given him hope for a home with walls. Harassed bank presidents to no effect. Unwittingly perpetrated a fraud on newspaper readers.

I had let Campanella down. I walked home to my wife and children.

In the days that followed, I passed Campanella in the doorway without looking at him, speaking to him or offering food. I sensed slowly swelling within me a tide of resentment toward him. He had crossed up my plans to be a Good Samaritan. I was gripped by suspicion that he had wronged me, that he had let me down—had ruined, with the wrong ending, a perfect Thanksgiving story.

Then I realized that all along I had had an inflated sense of myself in this evolving scenario. Campanella had existed only for my sake—I existed, therefore he did—or so I had believed, anyway. I needed to understand that he existed wholly independent of my acknowledgment of him. This story revolved around him, not me. As if to prove his independence, Campanella disappeared from his customary doorway for good.

As the new holiday season arrived, I began looking for another Theodore Campanella. But this time my attitude would be different. This time I would try to help someone without any strings attached.

The Full-Time Grandma

"Good morning," Antoinette Chirichella sang.

"Memah," said her two-year-old grandson Michael Benjamin. "Oooooo, Memah!"

Antoinette—known to family and friends as "Nettie"—closed the apartment door behind her. At 64, she was a handsome woman, clear-eyed and big boned.

"Hello Michael," she boomed operatically. "Are you happy to see me?"

Michael, olive-skinned and 32 inches tall, scooted across the living room to kiss her. She laughed and bent over to kiss him.

Nettie looked after Michael several days a week. She climbed on a city bus at about 7 a.m., transferred to another, and reached the Queens, N.Y., high-rise where Michael lived around 8:30. She would go home around 5:00 p.m. or, more often, stay for dinner. She always put in a full day.

Thanks to her retirement, Nettie was a full-time grandmother. As such, she saw Michael graduate from a gurgling, drooling, helpless human bean-bag to a running, talking, somewhat sufficient miniature man.

Until she retired, Nettie operated a sewing machine in a Brooklyn factory as a member of the International Ladies Garment Workers Union. For 47 years, day in and day out. In time, the job put blisters on her hands and gave her an ache in her back that lingered for decades.

She retired with the most modest of expectations. "I planned to do some volunteer work in hospitals, join the senior citizen center, maybe play some bingo," she said. "But deep down I was afraid retirement would be boring. After all, I had worked since I was 15. My whole life was sewing and bringing up my daughter Elvira."

A few months after Nettie's retirement, Elvira was pregnant and, in due time, Michael was born on July 11, 1983. Elvira could take only a six-week maternity leave from her job. Reluctant to turn Michael over to an unfamiliar baby sitter, she asked her mother if she would give her a hand.

For years, Nettie invested the same patience and perseverance in Michael that she once did in making sure the garments she sewed came out right.

On a typical morning she would watch "Sesame Street" with her grandson. Together, they would count aloud and run through the alphabet. She would offer him cereal in a bowl, a glass of orange juice, maybe a few slices of banana or some raisin bread.

"Eat, Michael," she would say. "Please eat."

She would then read to him or he would entertain himself with toy trucks or ride around the room on a tricycle. He often demonstrated a preference for doing exactly whatever he is not supposed to do, like seeking out the room's electrical outlets. Even for a two-year-old, he was uncommonly animated, with more physical energy than the average professional gymnast. Michael climbed onto tables with abandon, ran around in circles, danced to music on the radio.

"Oh, Michael," Nettie would say to him, "you're so funny!"

If the sun was out, Nettie would dress Michael and chauffeur him around the city sidewalks in a fraying blue stroller. They would visit the playground to play on the swings and the slide, or pass through the park around the corner.

"You're so lucky," the older women on the park benches often told Nettie. "We see our grandchildren only on holidays."

Once back in the apartment, Nettie would lay Michael in the crib for a nap. He rolled around under the quilt, bottle to mouth, until asleep. Nettie might rub her eyes and nod off for a few minutes, then peek in on him.

As often as not, Michael would wake up crying and cranky. Nettie would hold him, warm and small and soft, against her shoulder, feeling him breathe. She regarded his crying as an emergency, like a five-alarm fire that she knew should quickly be doused with an embrace and reassuring whispers. If Michael fell back asleep, she would let him stay on her shoulder.

The caretaking exacted its toll now and then, mainly because Nettie is less healthy than she once was. She usually awakened several times during the night. Her hands and feet ached from rheumatoid arthritis. She had cataracts and had to watch her blood pressure. On certain days, the buses were delayed and Michael whined virtually without end. Those nights Nettie would feel extra tired.

But the best medicine for whatever bothered her, she found, was Michael himself.

"I always look forward to being with him," she said. "I play with him, hold him, kiss him, squeeze him. I give him all the love I have. Michael is more important to me than anything in the world.

"He is everything.

"Taking care of him is the best opportunity I've had in my whole life. The older he gets, the younger I feel. All I want is to continue to watch him grow."

Nettie's example suggests that even if you plan your retirement right down to a decimal point, the biggest changes in your life may come about from just plain old luck.

Moreover, as Nettie discovered, retirement is a better time than most to get to know your grandchildren. The hours you once spent answering memos or working

in a plant you can now devote to walks in the park. Only through your grandchildren can you truly find out just who you are and how much nourishment in the form of love you can offer.

Nettie was lucky, and so was Michael, and so, for that matter, am I. You see, Antoinette Chirichella was my mother-in-law and Michael Benjamin is my son. I valued her role in raising Michael more than I can possibly say. I'm grateful she had so much love for Michael left over from her own hard life. She raised her daughter without a husband to help and never made more than $12,000 in a year. Nonetheless, I have never seen anyone love another human being so purely and without hesitation or question or doubt, a love that seemed ever-deepening and enriching.

In the early morning, Michael and I would go out on the terrace to look for Nettie coming along the sidewalk. I would point out to him the pigeons drinking from the fountain in the courtyard or, more likely, just kiss his neck. But I know he was only humoring me.

"Memah coming?" he would ask.

It always felt good to say, "Yes, Michael, she is."

Saved From Laziness

For most of my life I was hardly famous for working hard.

As a kid in school, I gave the least effort needed for me to get by, whether in class or in sports. In my first jobs, I never put in any extra energy unless I absolutely had to—neither came in early nor stayed late. When I freelanced at home, I would take breaks to shoot hoops or take a nap.

But then something happened that changed my work ethic for good, something momentous and marvelous.

You, Caroline. You were born.

It was 1988 and we had money problems. My income had shrunk because I'd decided, quite irresponsibly, to focus on writing my first novel. My family, especially my grandmother, until then usually ready to help support me, was growing disappointed with my professional pursuits.

And then you came along. You had such dark eyes and such animated features, always making faces, and we loved you so much, all three of us. And you made me want to do better.

Oh, make no mistake: I already had other incentives. But none inspired me as much as you. I would look at you in the crib, so small and needy and perfect, and I would think to myself, I really better get off my ass and start to make a decent living now.

Luckily, I landed a lucrative part-time job in New Jersey. I was doing the sort of work I never expected or wanted to do—editing and revising reports from management consultants to clients. Three days a week I drove an hour, put in about 10 hours, then drove more than an hour back, pulling down $50 an hour, for about $1,500 a week, much more than I'd ever earned. And my boss was picky to the point of psychotic.

But guess what? I never minded any of it. And you know why? Because I was finally doing what I needed to do. And that money came in really handy just then, really pulled us out of a hole, and even though the gig lasted only about eight weeks, it was just the quick fix needed.

And within the next year, I took another part-time job, also in New Jersey, this one for two days a week. And from then on—from then until now, really, the whole length of your life—I've finally worked hard, worked close to an average of six days a week. I discovered, at age 35, that you could go beyond the fatigue and make the extra effort and be rewarded.

And unless I'd run into financial trouble—and unless, most of all, you had come along—I question whether I would have made this leap. And this appetite for hard work has served me well over the years, especially the job at Ogilvy, and also with all the stuff I do on the side.

And I can trace that change directly back to you. It was you, little girl, who, more than anyone else—more than Mom or my parents or my grandparents—made me finally get serious about my responsibilities to my family and myself.

Mr. Too Cool For School: The Next Generation

You're seven years old, in second grade, and you've put on your standard outfit.

You wear pointy black cowboy boots, a brown leather aviator jacket and faded blue jeans, each knee with a rip of your own making. You have on black sunglasses and a black-and-white bandana wrapped expertly, by your own hand, around your brow. To top it off, dangling from your right ear, left over from a Halloween costume, is a gold-plated, clip-on hoop earring.

You're a four-foot tall, 45-pounder decked out like a rock star on a cross-country tour. Thus do you board the yellow bus for your daily trip to elementary school.

So it went with you then, my son Michael.

You would hang out in front of the bathroom mirror, combing your thick, wavy brown hair to mimic the styles you caught on MTV. You've begged us to let you grow your hair longer so you can sport a ponytail.

You're only seven, yet you've already mastered a second language: fluent backtalk. If I joke with you too freely or somehow upset you, you might tell me to give you a break or take a hike. You will propose, with growing frequency, that I either get out of town, get real, get a job or, more simply, get a life. Your mouth strikes me as a prematurely, precociously adult instrument.

Oh, you're the complete package all right: the funky uniform, the hipper-than-thou attitude, the up-to-the-minute idiom. Your purpose is clear. You want more than anything on the planet to be cool.

As you strut through our apartment, you lip sync to M.C. Hammer, fingering an air guitar. You now carry a comb to school and chase girls around the playground. You bop along with us on family outings—bandana, earrings and all—and draw gasps and surprised glances from passersby.

One time we all go out for pizza and the teenagers at the next table are so taken with your look that you're invited over for a cameo appearance.

You're Mr. Cool. Mr. Too Cool For School.

Just in case, just as a precaution, I had to stop you from turning into a kid I knew in junior high school named Tony. Tony had acted as if he had seen it all and done it all and nothing much mattered to him anymore.

You seemed at risk of becoming likewise indifferent. If you stopped caring, nothing would touch you, dulling your impulses for sympathy, compassion, love. If you acted like this at age seven—you seldom missed an opportunity, especially with an audience handy, to jut out your little jaw and tell me to cut you some slack—how might you then act at age 17?

So over the following weeks I tried to redefine cool for you. Now, cool, by overwhelming consensus, is based on your look, your image. But it seemed to me that your concept of cool should extend beyond mere aesthetics. So I took every opportunity to share my personal code for cool—to cooperate, to care and, better still, to be kind.

Well, something must have clicked. One day you went to school minus bandana and earrings. That afternoon you sat next to your sister on the living-room floor and, unbidden, read nursery rhymes to her.

The following weekend, when two boys traded punches in the schoolyard around the corner, you yelled so loud and for so long for the fight to stop that the kids felt too embarrassed to keep duking it out.

Then you went yourself one better. You watched a TV news segment showing how political upheaval somewhere, maybe Sarajevo, had left thousands of children orphaned and hungry. You turned to me to suggest we send some money.

Now that's cool, I thought.

The Hooky Express

We're riding on the R train, just the two of us, going from Forest Hills, Queens, to Times Square. It's a weekday morning, maybe 7 a.m. or so. You're headed to school, I to my job on Third Avenue in the 50s.

It's quiet on the subway, the only noise coming from the train itself. All the other riders are reading, staring or snoozing. It feels good to sit next to you like this, performing a fatherly duty for my little daughter Caroline. I'm there to make sure you get to school safe.

Sometimes you lean on my shoulder and close your eyes to catch a little extra sleep. Sometimes you tell me about a new song you like or a Chinese restaurant you want to try or what our family might do for fun that weekend. But usually you keep quiet, preferring to read or look out the window.

Those rides with you always felt to me like something of an expedition. Maybe a homeless man, talking to himself, would ask us for money. Maybe some kid would come on the train with his headset playing music too loudly. I played bodyguard, alert to every possible threat, ready to face down even the slightest attempt to violate your sense of security.

Once in a while, we entertained the possibility of playing hooky, you from school and me from my job. That tended to be the case more in June than any other month. That's when we really got the itch.

"Could we?" you would ask.

"We really should," I would say.

We would imagine how we might go out for pancakes at a coffee shop and, if it were Wednesday, even catch a matinee of "Phantom Of The Opera."

"Let's do it," you would say. "I'm serious. It would be so much fun."

"We really should," I would say again.

We would go on about all the wonderful places we could go, maybe the American Museum of Natural History or Sephora or Central Park or some Indian restaurant or the second-floor reading room in the main branch of the New York Public Library on Fifth Ave. You would go the day without teachers and tests and other students. I would get to skip meetings with clients and conference calls and hours in front of a computer shooting off e-mails to everyone and his brother.

In imagining our doing all this, and in listing all the options, we would get so excited, our voices louder, our pulses quickening. It came to feel almost as if we were already doing it.

But we never did play hooky. It all turned out to be just a game of make-believe, nothing but fantasy. I had a job to do and clients to serve and money to earn, and you had an education to acquire. My attitude was pretty set in stone. We each had responsibilities, and to do otherwise might be a disservice to ourselves and to others. That was that.

Too bad. As much as I tried to keep us on the straight and narrow, I might have shown a little flexibility. I regret it now—minor as regrets go, but still a regret. We really should have played hooky. Just once.

Now that you're 28 years old, I realize that even that small step away from our daily chores would be prized as a once-in-a-lifetime leap. I would always be able to say, "Remember that day we played hooky together? Remember how I said we could, and you said we should, and then we actually did?"

Then you would say, "Oh, yes, I'll never forget it. Never in a million years."

Dad, Overboard

Before we even pulled away from the port at Oak Bluffs, a wave surged high and broke over the ferry, briefly tipping the bow upwards. The sudden spray drenched the front deck. Some passengers cried out in alarm, but almost as if in awe at an amusement-park ride.

My wife, son, daughter and I were headed from Martha's Vineyard to Falmouth on Cape Cod. We'd just spent a few days in a house with our friends from Connecticut. It was to be the first leg of our trip home to New York City.

The show of oceanic force took us all by surprise, even though we really should have anticipated it. This was in 1995, in mid-August. We'd already gone through one big storm after another—seven in August alone, a record at the time—and felt duly battered. Now came Hurricane Felix.

Our family members were avowed landlubbers, no more nautical than your average native New Yorker. That left us unaccustomed to being buffeted by waves and lurching violently to and fro. Unsure what to expect we feared the worst, namely drowning at sea.

Our kids, then 12 and 7 years old, looked scared. My wife looked scared, too.

Hey, I thought, this could be good. I saw an opportunity to play an important role here. I would be the steady hand at the wheel, navigating my frightened family through this ordeal. After all, I was the father. If I'd learned anything from movies about families in dire straits, it was that the father might as well be the hero.

Except for just one little hitch: I immediately started to feel nauseous. Whatever sea legs I might once have possessed had long since disappeared.

The ferry plowed along its seven-mile route, listing up and down. The sea heaved all around us, the waves slapping the hull. Every few minutes, a surprised passenger let out a yell. Now, my stomach fluttering more insistently, I broke into a cold sweat and felt dizzy and wobbly.

Nothing about my condition should have caught me off-guard. I've long suffered from motion sickness. I get light-headed on airplanes and in buses and cabs. I once actually got quite woozy on a seesaw with my son.

And so, facing this predicament—and wishing only to prove myself equipped to handle the assignment of herding my family to safety—I promptly staggered to the railing, leaned over the side and barfed my brains out.

In short, instead of coming through in the clutch for my family, instead of fulfilling my fantasy as a stalwart seafaring old salt, I turned out to be unfit for duty. Out there in the throes of a wild, whipsawing storm, my son and daughter got to behold the spectacle of Dad losing his breakfast—mostly blueberries, as I recall—in the roiling Atlantic. A humbling moment indeed.

My wife huddled with the kids some distance away, on a bench at midship. "It's going to be all right," she kept saying, as if repeating the words enough would convince her to believe it. She took care of business, while I, of course, was no help at all.

Nearly an hour later, we reached our destination intact, but with me particularly the worse for wear. I came away feeling like a coward, even though my throwing up had nothing to do with cowardice. It was motion sickness, a common inner ear disturbance.

Even so, I've tormented myself for 20 years about the episode on that ferry. I've wondered how my kids perceived my inadequacy in that moment of need. Did they see me as a coward? I've calculated the likely damage to my reputation as a father.

As it turned out, that stormy ride would hardly be the last time I felt ashamed in front of my kids. I got laid off from a job. I've made bad career decisions and wasted money and had more than a few tantrums. And that's just for starters.

But I've also paid a lot more attention to my kids than my father ever had his. We've played sports together. I've rarely missed a chance to demonstrate my love. And yes, eventually I brought home the bacon. So maybe by now I've managed to redeem myself.

Then again, maybe the next time we all ride a ferry I should remember my Dramamine. And be grateful I have a wife—and our children a mother—who is, as ever, fully onboard.

Most fathers want to be heroes. And the more mythically noble our actions, the better. But we seldom measure up. For that maybe we can somehow forgive ourselves. Ideally our kids will, too.

The Clueless Coach

Some years back, I took a walk by myself around Cunningham Park in Queens, New York. And near a baseball field on the Union Turnpike side, I came across a man and a boy playing baseball.

The man held a bat and tapped out grounders to the boy. The kid, maybe all of 10 years old, had on a glove, but was having a tricky time of it, usually missing or at least bobbling the grounders.

"No," the man said. "That's wrong."

The boy listened.

"Get your glove down," the man said. "Get it down low."

The man hit the ball again, and again the boy flubbed the grounder.

"No," the man said. "You're doing it all wrong. Listen to me. Do as I showed you."

I stopped to watch. Apparently, the man and boy were father and son. At first I thought, how nice for a dad to teach his son to play ball. My father never did -- too busy working -- and I knew how good it felt hitting and catching with my own son.

"Good, Michael," I always told my son. "You're getting good. You're only going to get better."

But as I watched, I realized something was wrong.

The same dynamic kept repeating itself. This father criticized his son, belittling his performance, expressing disappointment and frustration, and doing so louder and more harshly. And the son, who struggled to apply the lessons and please his father, but to no avail, looked increasingly stricken with shame and embarrassment.

Maybe, I thought, I should say something. As a boy playing baseball, I had made the same mistakes. As a father, I believed in heavy doses of encouragement. Then again, I thought, maybe I should keep my mouth shut, mind my business.

I watched for a few more minutes, giving the scenario a chance to go right. I suspected the father, no doubt aware of my presence, believed I actually admired him for administering such discipline. I hoped the kid would demonstrate some improvement, or the father some tolerance for his imperfections.

Finally, I could take it no more.

"You're the one who's doing it all wrong," I said to the man.

"What?" the father said, looking at me in disbelief at my accusation.

"All you're doing is running him down, making him feel bad."

He looked at me, mouth open.

"Who asked you?" he said.

"Nobody had to ask me."

"Mind your own business."

"I've made it my business."

He took a few steps toward me. He was burly, broad in the shoulders, with meaty hands, maybe 10 years younger and 30 pounds heavier than I. He looked like a firefighter or construction worker.

"Look," I said as he came closer, "you're taking all the fun out of it. You're ruining baseball for your son. Is that what you want?"

I voiced this view more as a plea than in a tone of outrage. I wanted to reason with him, get him to understand. Competition is good medicine for kids, but so is a steady drip of encouragement.

"But you know what?" I said. "You're right. It's none of my business. It's yours."

And I turned to walk away. But as I left, I caught sight of the kid looking at me. He wore a little smile. Maybe he was letting me in on a secret. Maybe he already knew that no matter what, he was only going to get better.

He snagged the next grounder with ease. Who knows? He could be the next Derek Jeter.

No Holds Barred

You, Michael, had warned me—you, at age eight, weighing in at all of 48 pounds—that you intend to kick my butt. Now, Michael, the time has come.

It's Sunday, we're here at the gym, on a gray mat. I've dropped to my knees to approximate your height, and we're wrestling.

You charge at me, scowling and growling, and put all your moves on me. The clothesline. The pile driver. The suplex. You know plenty of moves.

Still, I slip one arm around your neck, the other between your thighs, and hoist you over my head for a full body slam.

Our match is make-believe, of course. Neither of us intends to hurt the other—we're just pretending to. I pull my punches, but still you go reeling. You attack me with a bogus face rake, and I snap my head back, yowling in feigned pain.

As we grapple, I ask myself, *Should I let him win?*

You had gotten interested in pro wrestling about a year earlier. You watched matches on TV, absorbed in the antics of Earthquake, Typhoon and the Nasty Boys. We bought you plastic models of your favorite figures, Hulk Hogan, The Macho Man, the Million Dollar Man. You subscribed to a monthly wrestling magazine, dipping deep into your allowance of $3 a week.

You begged us to take you to a tournament at Madison Square Garden. So we did. There, wrestlers with fire hydrant necks and arms like suspension-bridge cables strutted around the ring glowering. They leaped off the ropes and flung each other around with impunity, all in a carefully choreographed charade of combat.

But if the bout was a circus, the audience was a sideshow. Tattoos and biker jackets, cheering and jeering, nose rings, Goth makeup—the arena had more testosterone than a prison riot.

We took you to other tournaments, and your preoccupation grew into a full-fledged fixation. You collected wrestling cards. With your plastic action figures you enacted imaginary clashes between Ric Flair and Sid Justice. You scanned your wrestling magazine for news about the Undertaker and the Legion of Doom. Three nights a week you watched matches on TV, maybe between the Big Boss Man and the Ultimate Warrior.

Soon you knew all about every wrestler, right down to height, weight, age, ring record and best moves, and at the dinner table spared us no detail. All you ever wanted to talk about—any time, any place, with anyone—was wrestling. Our conversations addressed such pressing issues as, Who was better, Rowdy Roddy Piper or the Warlord?

OK, I figured, *no harm, no foul.* Pro wrestling gave you heroes to root for and villains to boo at. You could thrive on the imaginary inflicting of pain, on fantasies of dominance and submission. Wrestling would school you in the wages of conflict and competition, in the lessons of fair play and cheating, of right versus wrong.

Oh, make no mistake: I had my concerns. Pro wrestling sends certain unfortunate messages to its audience. If you're frustrated and angry, for example, your best bet is to bash someone in the kisser, or worse. The sport promotes a win-at-all-costs aggression. Of all the forms of cultural enrichment available, pro wrestling—with contestants who bring folding chairs into the ring to leverage as bludgeons—was never quite what your mother and I envisioned for you.

So now we're wrestling, you and I, and I have all of this on my mind.

Should I let you win?

You're all spindly limbs flailing. You rush me for a clothesline—right arm outstretched, the better to knock my head off. You fold your arms and ram me, and I spill backwards onto the mat. Your spunk surprises me. You clamber on top of me, your chest athwart mine, your palms pressed to the floor. I squirm under you, barely lifting my shoulder blades off the mat, as if unable to escape.

With your breath warm on my face, I lie still and let you pin me. For my money, you earned your victory.

Taking Her Best Shot

You had to be about 12 or so, Caroline, the first time you and I played tennis together. We went out on to the courts at the beach club where we were members for nine years. You must have had on a bathing suit and sneakers, maybe without socks. The tennis racquet looked so large in your hand. We each took our side of the net and began to hit the ball back and forth.

Right away I could see you could be a good player. You ran after every shot hit to you, and tried to return everything, too. You had a strong, smooth stroke, better on the forehand than the backhand. I was excited to be playing tennis with you, and to see how you took to it right away.

I love tennis, first played as a teenager, at maybe 18, but never gave it much time, too preoccupied with basketball, only to come back to the sport years later. And now I was out there on a warm summer day at the beach playing tennis with my daughter.

We played once in a while at the beach club, and then a few times a year at Cunningham Park, and you got better and better. You seemed to learn something new every time we played. You would get in front of the ball faster or bring your racquet back earlier or swing harder to smack a shot back at me.

That was no small skill right there, educating yourself as we played. It showed concern for craft, for performance.

But there was something else that impressed me the most, more than your natural abilities—your quick feet, your smart hands, your grace and your mobility—and even more than the close attention you paid to playing.

It was the effort you always made. You always tried your best. I never had to try to encourage you or motivate you, never had to call out and say, "Come on, Caroline." Oh, no. It came naturally to you, instinctively, to push yourself hard, to try to discover what you could accomplish.

That always made me so proud. Trying hard at anything was a reward I discovered late in life myself, probably in my 20s or so, and even then still none too well. I was just one of those kids who would do my homework or play softball and if I got tired and it felt too hard, I would quit. Just enough was good enough.

It was only much later that I realized there was never all that much need, when tired, to quit. You could keep going. And if you kept going, if you broke through that barrier of fatigue, you could find new strength, what athletes have called the second wind.

So to see you giving your best every minute at tennis brought me a double pleasure. Unlike me at that age, you had no quit in you. And I'm guessing now, seeing your dedication to everything you do, especially your singing, that you'll never have any quit in you.

Joining The Conversation

As my mother passed 50 and then 60, she finally, slowly, painfully came to terms with not only her first handicap, but also with her second.

After my sister and I left home to seek our own independence, my mother began to order meals for herself in restaurants and deal face-to-face with clerks and salesmen. She helped my father with his business affairs. She volunteered for social work in the deaf community. She began a clerical job with the Bergen County Department of Aging in New Jersey, the first job she ever got on her own. She came to wear a powerful hearing aid, through which she could faintly hear voices, music, noises.

Around the same time, the deaf embarked on a low-key crusade for rights and recognition that extended well beyond TTYs. They enrolled in regular high schools and colleges that offered the option of sign-language interpreters. They began to make economic headway and find employment as printers, plumbers, teachers, lawyers and corporate executives. They lobbied for captioned network TV and special-interest legislation for reducing TTY rates. More than ever, they were courted by political candidates of all stripes.

Even as the deaf were assimilated into the American mainstream, they still tried to preserve the integrity of deaf culture and its special sense of identity and community. Many still prayed at temples and churches for the deaf, studied and taught at schools for the deaf, attended festivals and conventions for the deaf, performed in theater and participated in sports for the deaf, and read Silent News and The Deaf American. They sought to straddle the worlds of the deaf and the hearing.

My mother straddled, too. She made TTY calls to friends. She even made a point to join conversations at holiday gatherings.

Nobody asked me anymore why she sounded so funny.

Best of all, she gradually began to rebuff suggestions from my grandmother about how to live her life. My grandmother, in turn—and to her credit—took the hint and started to back off. She learned that you *can* give a flower too much water, that we have to let people take care of themselves. I was thankful that my mother forgave her. I kept my fingers crossed that my grandmother, then 80, could someday forgive herself.

For a while, my mother came over once a week to visit our then three-year-old son, Michael. Yet another generation in my family thus came under the influence of her deafness. He was puzzled by her voice, but without fully understanding why, he would tap her on the shoulder to get her attention and look directly at her when speaking so she could read his lips. Before one of her visits, we taught him a vital phrase in sign language: hand raised, palm forward, with thumb, index finger and pinkie sticking up.

Translation: "I love you."

The Mystic Mystique

The first time we vacationed in Mystic, in August 1990, our son, Michael, was seven and our daughter, Caroline, only two, still drank milk from a bottle.

We spent our first day touring the seaport museum, admiring the Charles W. Morgan whaling ship moored to the wharf while a guide in beard and bandanna explained seafaring lore to all the landlubbers.

We returned to Mystic the next August, too, and wandered through its aquarium, marveling at the penguins toddling through simulated arctic habitats and 3,000-pound beluga whales corkscrewing through giant glass tanks.

We went back the August after that as well, and over dinner one night watched the drawbridge spanning the Mystic River yawn to a cantilevered opening to let a tall sailboat through.

By the following August, we knew just where to find the blacksmith and the apothecary at the seaport, and the dolphins and sting rays at the aquarium. A sense of deep familiarity had set in.

The next summer, I balked at the repetition and predictability of it all. Our choice to follow the same routine year in and year out started to feel reflective of a lack of enterprise, a failure of imagination. It seemed we owed ourselves a new, different destination, a dose of diversity, and should vacation elsewhere, maybe Boston or Washington or even New Orleans.

But my wife and kids preferred Mystic. After all, we'd always enjoyed ourselves there and knew exactly what we'd be getting, including the same modest motel. I knew better than to disagree.

So, back to Mystic we went, leaving New York City at six in the morning, our kids in the back seat, bagels and iced coffees in hand, for the ride along Interstate 95.

Once again, we ambled through the seaport, stopped in at the cooperage and the chandlery and heard the horse-drawn carriages clop along the dirt ways. Once again, we moseyed through the aquarium and checked out the baby alligators, the blue lobster -- a favorite! -- and the show with sea lions leaping on command out of an indoor pool. Yet again we witnessed the towering drawbridge admit passage to small craft and the occasional wayward swan.

Only now, the experiences felt somehow different. Our children, now 11 and 6, grew more curious about our country's illustrious maritime history. Caroline now took an all-consuming interest in trying new, preferably expensive restaurants to refine her taste buds. Michael now loved everything to do with movies and one night stopped near the Mystic River to behold in wonder the town silhouetted picturesquely against the moonlit sky. "It's pretty," he conceded, "but it would probably look better in letterbox."

So it went for 18 summers, our family heading to the same former shipbuilding center for vacation. Mystic has changed somewhat, with new hotels, new shops and new restaurants. The seaport introduced a life-size model of the notorious slave vessel Amistad and the ever-improving aquarium now offers a stirring exhibit about the Titanic. But much else, from the towering square-riggers to the hammerhead sharks, remains the same. Every day from May to September, the drawbridge still towers open at a quarter after the hour.

We've changed, too. As it turns out, our Mystic vacations are the equivalent of those pencil marks we used to put on our kitchen wall to measure how tall our kids had grown over the previous year. The trips give us a handy means of charting our progress, a basis for comparing ourselves and our shifting identities over the decades.

Michael, a new college student, completed a screenplay and started a blog about movies. Caroline performed in opera companies throughout New York and, as a bonus, can do 20 pushups in one fell swoop. My wife and I, once struggling rookie parents, are now married 38 years.

No longer do I ever dare suggest we go anywhere but Mystic for summer vacation. Ritual has its rewards, along with answering the call of continuity. We've forged a new tradition, no different, really, from turkey on Thanksgiving and presents on Christmas.

If we've proven anything, it's that even the same stuff can always somehow turn different. The old can somehow feel new again, the once-predictable, utterly surprising. Next summer, the four of us may go back to Mystic yet again, if only to find out who we all are now.

Setting Your Stage

"I like to sing," my daughter Caroline, then still three months shy of turning seven years old, tells my friend Don. "I like singing a lot."

"Oh, really?" he says.

"Yes," she says. "I'll sing something for you right now."

"Well, then," Don says, "by all means please do."

This is mid-August, 1995. We're on a beach, near the shoreline, vacationing in Martha's Vineyard. All of us, our family of four and his family of four, are wearing our bathing suits.

Caroline turns to look for a fitting venue. And right near her, as it happens, is a boulder. She clambers onto it as if onto an outdoor stage. The dunes are behind her, the reeds rustling in the summer breeze, the sky a sublime blue.

Caroline clears her throat, establishes her footing and settles in for her performance. Then she starts sing "Colors Of The Wind" from the then-new Disney movie "Pocahontas."

I'd heard my daughter sing the song all summer, ever since seeing the movie and buying the CD. It was her favorite song. She sang it in her room at home and wherever we went.

But I'd never seen her sing it like this, taking command of an audience. Her rendition is lovely, her pitch perfect, the emotion heartfelt.

Don and his wife and two sons listen raptly, mesmerized.

It's all well and good for me to admire her singing. But for me to see someone else appreciate it is something special.

Of course I had no inkling back then what would come next.

No idea that Caroline would decide to be a singer.

No idea she would beg her mother to get her singing lessons until she finally gave in.

No idea that before she turned 12 that we would, courtesy of recommendations from the Juilliard School, find her the right private singing coach, a longstanding professional willing to train a child, her youngest student ever to that point, the scheduled 15-minute interview going an hour, with the teacher saying afterwards that she rarely saw such focus even in her adult students.

No idea that for the next 10 years Elvira and I would schlep her, by subway or express bus or car, from our home in Queens to Manhattan as often as three times a week for lessons, rehearsals and performances—all those nights after a day of school, all those weekend afternoons, so she could be put through her paces, going through song after song.

No idea that she would learn every song from "Phantom of the Opera" backwards and forwards.

No idea she would be so deeply committed and disciplined, especially about caring for her voice and her overall health, that she studied the history of opera at every opportunity and practiced her scales in her room, wore a scarf around her neck on freezing days to protect her throat, even avoided cold foods and beverages, including her favorite, ice cream.

No idea that that before she turned 20, she would perform the lead in "Kismet" and "The Mikado" and "The Merry Widow," and with opera companies in Manhattan, Brooklyn and the Hamptons, and that she would even sing at a benefit with Marcello Giordani, a leading tenor from the Metropolitan Opera.

No idea, indeed, that she would actually get to do what we all knew she was always meant to do. Sing. On stage. In the spotlight.

But maybe Caroline already knew. Maybe she saw that boulder on the beach at Martha's Vineyard as a steppingstone. Maybe she was already looking for the next boulder to climb.

As it turned out, Caroline eventually turned away from singing to pursue a career as a chef. And she's already going strong on that front. But in both instances, we encouraged her from first to last.

You can never encourage your kids too much. You can only encourage your kids too little. Every parent has a choice.

Daring To Be Pretty Okay

From the start, first with Michael and then with you, Caroline, I wanted to be a perfect father. Whatever you needed from me, I promised myself you would get.

I had my reasons. You were both born perfect and deserved a perfect life, or at least as perfect as we could manage anyway. If I had to be perfect at anything, I figured, it might as well be as a father.

But here's what it probably all came down to: I expected to do better than my own parents had done. Much better.

My mother frequently yelled at me, often hysterically, over nothing—and so I pledged to myself to be quiet and even-tempered with you.

She often slapped me, sometimes swatted my backside with a big spoon, and once even punched me in the stomach, leaving an imprint of her fist there—and so I privately vowed never to lay a foul finger on my children.

My father often left the house before anyone else woke up, returning only after we went to bed, and on weekends, he would rather nap or putter in the garage—anything, really—than ask us about our day at school or play catch with us. And so I swore never to deprive my children of time with me.

But early on, it dawned on me that, like my own father, I'm imperfect, and decidedly imperfect at that, despite all the best intentions. All too often, I've lost my patience and yelled at you for creating a commotion. On some weekend mornings I've looked to escape the entanglements of family, if only for an hour, with some coffee and a newspaper over at Starbucks.

The list of everything I planned never to do with my children but found myself doing anyway is long. Memories of my father prey on my anxieties even now.

You're the same as he, goes the haunting refrain in my head. *No better, no worse.*

Then again, I've come to understand the struggles my father faced as a father. It took me years to appreciate the weight of the responsibility he must have felt, and the depth of his fatigue, too. I'd never sympathized in the least with him over his frequent absences or his degree of distraction in our company. But after working a long day, I feel as tired, as disoriented, as out to lunch, as he must have.

Now make no mistake here: as fathers go, he and I are more different than similar. It's probably fair to say, and my father might well agree, that fatherhood remained a concept he never quite seemed to grasp. I tend to believe I've had at least some idea of what I'm doing here.

But then I got to wondering about this whole business of being perfect.

What if I *were* a perfect father?

What if I never cursed, blew my top or lost a job?

Maybe a perfect father, by definition, is imperfect after all. The impossible ideal is an illusion.

Maybe I should grant myself the right to flaws—to exercise my prerogative, in short, to be imperfect.

Maybe if you see some of the chinks in my armor, that's a better, truer example for me to set.

Maybe the more imperfect I am, the more lessons I have to offer you.

Maybe being pretty okay is actually more than good enough.

Maybe, in the end, my imperfections make me some kind of perfect.

A Word Of Thanks

Thank you, Michael, my son. You made me a father for the first time.

Thank you, too, for respecting and trusting and loving your mother, and for recognizing inescapably how much she means to you, and to us all.

And for playing big brother with your little sister, the role of a lifetime, and for being ready to do anything to protect her.

And for dealing so well with being just like me, sensitive and introspective, bearing the blessing and the curse alike, because yes, it's both, but which more than the other might be hard to say.

And for never speaking ill of any of your friends, even though you could have, and of your girlfriends, too.

And for your wisecracks, especially that one time, when I asked you if you considered yourself short, and you said, "No, just undertall."

And for how your face looked in the moonlight in Southampton, your eyes beaming as you looked at the stars glittering in the sky, your mouth open in awe.

Thank you, too, Caroline, my daughter. Your brother showed me how deeply I could love someone new, and you've shown me I could love someone else new just as deeply. In a single stroke, you doubled everything.

Thanks for being so stubborn, once as a 2-year-old taking umbrage at me for daring to challenge you and jutting out your jaw and saying, "You think you're tough?"

But also for being so soft on the inside, talking to your dolls in your room, crying at all the classic Disney movies, growing your hair long so you could cut it and give it away to kids going through chemo.

Thank you, my girl, for climbing that boulder in Martha's Vineyard at the age of eight to sing in front of our friends. You're still every inch a songbird today.

Thank you, too, for how you looked that day I held you in the pool at the beach club, your face so gloriously gleaming with droplets of water in the summer sun.

And for those cherry-black eyes that can win me over or cut me to the quick, depending on your mood that day.

And for being so very alive, your nerves living so close to your skin.

You both came into the world as if from nothing and nowhere. But we know you came from the love your mother and I feel for each other, and our faith in the future. You are both rewards surpassing anything I might ever have imagined or, for that matter, ever felt I truly deserved.

I wish I could catalog every reason I'm thankful for both of you, but nothing I say could do justice to the gratitude I feel. It never ends, and it never will. You are my butterflies, my rainbows, my miracles.

Racing Your Old Man

Ever since you could run, Michael, we've raced each other. I always gave you a headstart and pretended to keep it close, but then of course I always won. I saw little point in ever letting you win because I wanted you to have an incentive to try harder.

We would race wherever we went, whether parks or playgrounds or backyards or the beach. I gave you as much of a headstart as I felt sure I could make up, maybe 10 yards or 20 or more. The only satisfaction I got from these races was the idea that I might be fueling you with a competitive spirit.

At no point did I ever expect you to feel shamed or belittled. And to your credit, you always agreed to race me, even though you knew you would always lose, and you tried your best, too.

Then, of course, you got older. You went from being eight, when I could literally run circles around you, to, say, 12 or 13 or 14. You were taller and stronger and faster. I gave you less of a head start now, and had to run a little harder, and our finishes kept getting closer. We kept racing all over, at least a few times a year, and I kept beating you, even as you hit 15 and 16 and 17, and I reached 50.

All that time, even though I took some pride in being pretty fast for my age, I was rooting for you to win. It was getting to be that time.

And then one Saturday morning in June we went to Long Beach, out on Long Island, and raced again. The sand was just starting to get hot and your mother and sister had settled into chaise lounges to listen to music and admire the surf. Naturally, I invited you to a sprinting contest and you accepted.

Now, maybe it's just my imagination operating in retrospect, but I recall a different look on your face. Your face suggested you knew something nobody else knew.

The time for head starts was long gone by now. The starting line was the same for both of us. We agreed on a finish line maybe 100 yards down the beach, near the breakers, where some rope lay.

And as Mom and Caroline watched, I called the start and off we went. We were neck and neck right away, and I tried to kick into a higher gear, but I had no higher gear. And then you slowly pulled away, a foot ahead now, then two feet, then more. You beat me and beat me clean.

I looked at you with a smile and you smiled back and I hugged you. It was one of my happiest moments ever. Nature had taken its course, the younger generation eclipsing the older, the son surpassing the father, just as it's meant to be. You were now the stronger and faster.

And it meant so much more than just running fast. It made me think you could do better than I in other respects, too. You would be smarter, too, and happier, and make more money, and generally be more fulfilled.

Of course we kept racing each other after that, even though the whole dynamic, including our expectations, had changed. You were going to win now. We both knew that. And it made it more fun for both of us.

Every year you beat me by a wider margin, more—I'm happy to say—because you got so much faster than because I got so much slower. You kill me out there and I have no prayer of ever winning again.

And that's exactly as it should be. It's as good a gift as a father could ever want. You're off and running, leaving me in the dust.

Look, Dad, No Hands

Piping plovers skitter over the dunes in the hot July sun. Offshore, a jet ski hums, tossing up a rooster tail of mist. A salty tang fills the nostrils.

Every summer for nine years, our family of four belonged to a beach club, with wooden cabanas propped on stilts along an Atlantic barrier island. For all nine of those summers I took my daughter, Caroline, out for walks along a jetty about half a mile from the cabana. The jetty jutted out at least 300 feet from the shore, a stretch of boulders no more than eight feet wide, the ocean on one side, a tidal inlet on the other.

"Let's go out on the rocks," I urged Caroline, who was six years old that first summer.

"No," she said.

"Michael does it," I coaxed, referring to her brother, five years her senior.

Off to the jetty we ventured, Caroline in her pink Little Mermaid bathing suit, barefoot, hair pulled back. We stepped up on the rocks, a steep rise for her, and she faltered, clutching my hand tight. I hoisted her aloft. We now stood some six feet above the sand, still inland.

I took short, slow steps, Caroline keeping pace alongside. The giant rocks clustered at cockeyed angles, some higher or lower, others tilted left or right, with ledges here and crevasses there. It felt like mountain climbing, only horizontally, and on a tightrope.

Caroline tugged on my hand, wanting to go back. I reassured her: This will be fun. You'll see.

As we headed farther out, the surf got louder and waves crashed against the rocks. Caroline, surprised at the sudden splashing, gasped. She hated it, she told me. "That's what Michael said, too," I assured her.

A sea gull landed and pecked at an overturned horseshoe crab. Caroline nearly slipped on the wet rocks, and though my grip on her hand kept her from falling, she cast me a scowl anyway.

We approached the tip of the jetty, thrust like a ship's prow out into the Atlantic. A few fishermen had settled there, surrounded by tackle boxes filled with all manner of hooks.

A few more steps, the rocks now angled sharply and slicker still, and we came to the end. Here, we were almost level with the ocean, and the surf splashed louder and higher around us. See, I said, we made it. Caroline looked around, her mouth open in amazement.

The next summer, Caroline joined me for weekly walks on the jetty without the slightest protest. She stepped faster than before across the rocks, her strides longer, more certain. She held my hand less tightly.

Summer after summer, I took my daughter out to that jetty. And summer after summer, she grew taller and stronger, ever ready for the challenge, now welcoming the ocean spray that once left her gasping.

In our sixth summer there, it was Caroline who invited me to join her on the jetty. No sooner had we clambered onto the rocks than she did something I never expected.

She let go of my hand.

I wanted to do nothing more in the world at that moment than to grab her hand again. After all, as her father I had to guide her and protect her from falling into the surging sea.

But off she strode, a few feet ahead of me now, clearly getting her sea legs. My eyes never leaving her, I asked if she was okay. Of course she was.

Caroline even took to wearing sneakers so she could bound from rock to rock like a mountain goat. Now it was I, heart in my throat, who felt tempted to gasp.

That's how it's supposed to be, really. The little girl, little no more, decides yes, she's ready to let go, ready to stake out her independence, to navigate any slippery rocks in her path. The father finds he is more onlooker than participant, given no choice but to leave the past behind, back there on the ever-receding shoreline.

Caroline let go. As for me, at least in my mind, I'm still holding on for dear life.

At Midpoint

That Other Day

You're at the World Trade Center at about noon on the Sunday before. You're with your wife and daughter. You're all sitting under blue skies at the fountain in the plaza between the towers.

People from all over the world surround the fountain. The spray glints in the sunlight, the sound almost a shushing. Dogs lap at the ripples. Little kids splash around.

It's a perfect day, the sort of day that makes you believe with all your heart that nothing bad could ever happen to any of us, that nothing could ever go wrong, least of all here. A glimpse of paradise—everyone feeling safe, at peace.

Later will be different. Later, everything will change.

Later, on that next Tuesday, you will leave your office in midtown Manhattan at dusk, more than 12 hours after everything changed. And as you walk home from the subway, along Queens Boulevard in Forest Hills, Queens, you will see a woman standing on the sidewalk in front of an apartment building holding a lit candle. Just standing there in public silently holding a lit candle aloft.

You will feel tempted to say something to the woman. You will want to ask her why, to ask if she lost someone that morning, to tell her you're sorry. But you wish to respect her right to grieve in privacy and decide to let her be.

Later, over the next few days, you will go to the roof of your 22-story building in Queens for a view southwest, toward lower Manhattan. And there, miles and miles away, across all the rooftops and the East River, you will see the massive ruins still smoldering.

Later, in the following weeks, you will hear about Michael Lomonaco, the executive chef at Windows on the World. You and your wife frequented the restaurant at the top of the World Trade Center a few times for special romantic dates in the early years of your marriage. You would get to know Lomonaco a little through your job and come to like him. He entered the World Trade Center about 30 minutes before the first airliner hit the north tower. But rather than take the elevator to his office on the 107th floor, his usual routine, he visited an optometrist in the ground-level mall to get his glasses fixed. That decision almost certainly saved his life.

Later, too, after everything changed, you will publicize a book titled "You Can Do It! The Merit Badge Handbook For Grown-Up Girls," authored by Lauren Catuzzi Grandcolas. Lauren planned an inspirational book that would teach girls and women new skills. But she happened to be a passenger on United Flight 93 that Tuesday, which was hijacked and then crashed in Pennsylvania, killing all aboard. She was pregnant with her first child. Her two sisters finished the book to honor her memory, and through your efforts appear on national TV to tell her story.

Later, more than two years after that Tuesday morning, you will get the privilege of promoting the newly created World Trade Center Health Registry. The goal will be to motivate survivors at or near the site of the attack to enlist in a 20-year study of physical and mental health effects. You team up with the Centers for Disease Control and Prevention and the New York City Department of Health And Mental Hygiene. You play a minor role in helping to draw more than 71,000 enrollees, making it the largest post-disaster public health registry in United States history.

Somehow, then, you stay connected to that Tuesday morning for the next 11 years, as if it's inescapable.

But all of that will be later. Right now it's still the Sunday before—that Other Day—and all of that has yet to happen. All you know is this moment, the tranquil hiss of the fountain, the giggling of toddlers and the yipping of puppies, the miracle of it all, of life here in New York City, in the United States Of America, with your wife and daughter. Safe. At peace.

That Other Day is the day you choose to remember. It's when you came to the fountain for the very first time, with no idea that it would be your last, no idea at all that innocence seldom remains intact, that perfect never lasts. It's when we all still had what we later lost. That Other Day is the day you refuse with all your being to forget.

From New Kid on the Job to Tribal Elder

I still have no clue how I became just about the oldest person in our office. Somehow, I must have missed the memo that was supposed to give me the heads-up. Today got here faster than I ever might have expected, and the time warp has given me whiplash. My term for this rite of passage, this occupational hazard? The flip side.

Of course, at 53, I'm hardly "old." But I'm older than all but maybe six of our 120 employees in the New York branch of our public-relations firm—slightly older than the few fortysomethings, somewhat older than the many thirtysomethings and much older than our ubiquitous twentysomethings.

It seems only yesterday I was still the new kid on the job, with no idea what I was doing and no one expecting me to know much of anything. When my colleagues gave instructions, I took plenty of notes, and nobody ever mistook me for anyone important. I worried about everything—performing up to snuff, getting chewed out by the boss, being fired—and lived in a state of low-grade paranoia.

Now, suddenly, I belong to that vaunted club known as senior management. I operate from the opposite end of the spectrum, a baby boomer plying my trade shoulder to shoulder with Generations X and Y. Now, when I share an observation, colleagues might take notes, and clients usually assume I know something. People at work are more inclined to listen to me, smile at me and laugh at my jokes—somewhere along the road I apparently became fascinating, charming and funny. I've graduated to the stature of tribal elder. It's practically an out-of-body experience.

Even so, being older than almost everyone on the premises has certain ... imperfections. Some of my younger colleagues have higher salaries, fancier titles and larger offices (luckily, I'm a stranger to envy), and I often report to those very folks. My age does create certain differences with my juniors, too—differences in priorities and points of reference.

For example, I now go to the dentist more frequently than I do parties. Most of my colleagues are getting married and having babies while I've just gone in for my first colonoscopy. I also find myself wondering how anyone could possibly care about Jessica Simpson when I still have a crush on Sophia Loren.

It's also strange occasionally being called "dude."

I perceive time differently, too. My younger colleagues typically talk much faster than I can listen—and, for that matter, often listen much faster than I can talk. Some co-workers will e-mail me a note, only to leave me a voice mail repeating the message five minutes later, then—still suffering from the lack of a response—pop into my office but moments afterward regarding the same thing. Like network television, I now evidently operate on some sort of a seven-second delay. It reminds me of the George Carlin joke about how the shortest interval of time in the known universe is that fraction of a second between a traffic light turning green and the guy behind you honking his horn.

The flip side definitely takes some getting used to. But get used to it I must, and for the most part have. I've realized that being an older employee has a larger meaning, an underlying purpose, special responsibilities: to pass along lessons learned, to influence and inspire. And to set an example as a case study in how to emerge from layoffs, recessions and other adversities all the stronger. Since I've already gone where my colleagues are still going, they can look at me and better see themselves tomorrow.

I'm also trying to "work young"—talking a little faster and listening faster, too. My comfort zone, previously only four square inches, has expanded to more like six. But above all, I've learned to respect my juniors. Only a few years ago, I never much cottoned to getting suggestions from anyone 10 or 20 years younger, and forget about following any orders.

Now I recognize that my juniors here often know better than I do—and keep me on my toes. And thanks to these "kids" teaching me how, I've finally emerged as a real team player. I also realize that after any serious discussion, the single most empowering question you can ever ask a younger staffer is "So, what do you think?" After all, even gurus can occasionally stand some advice.

The flip side has turned out to be both heartening and humbling. Little did I ever suspect that being older than almost everyone else at my job would give me a second chance to accomplish something long overdue. Namely, grow up.

Bargaining With My Father

In the dead of night, I tiptoe into my parents' bedroom. Only eight or nine years old, I'm a boy on a mission, about to commit a crime I still regret to this day. A floorboard creaks underfoot.

Even so, I have little reason to worry about being found out. My mother is deaf and my father severely hard-of-hearing. Neither is equipped to hear me, all four-foot-six and 75 pounds of me, least of all as I tread lightly around on the cushiony second-floor carpet.

My father is snoring, my mother silently asleep alongside him. My parents might awaken at any moment, only to discover me there, skulking in the dark. My ears are tuned to catch any signal warning me.

Still, I'm taking a chance here. My parents are sensitive to the faintest vibrations, trained by upbringing to be so. And also to the faintest aromas that might waft through. And, for all I know, superstitious as it sounds, to any changes in the molecular makeup of the air itself. So if right now I happen to graze a dresser or thump into a wall or plod just an ounce too heavily—or somehow give off a scent of quivering dread, a whiff of the scared, furtive, up-to-no-good little boy I am—I risk getting caught red-handed in the middle of my misadventure.

Yet I press on toward my objective.

With all the lights off, it's hard for me to see much of anything, just the outlines of furniture that somehow looks vaguely gray. I pause for a moment to let my eyes adjust to the dark. Slowly the room slightly brightens into clearer view, objects taking sharper shape. The two single beds joined together, the night tables, the lamps and, of course, sprawled under the blankets, my sleeping, unsuspecting parents.

My father snores louder now, his snorts coming rapidfire, punctuated with sighs and gasps. The snoring sounds thunderous in a house otherwise utterly silent, only the boiler in the basement audible, gas heat whooshing out from the vents. He might suddenly awaken, roused by his own noise. Might blink in the dark and sense my presence and there I would be, a skinny, curly-haired mischief-maker in my pajamas, trespassing. I would have to come up with some excuse to give him—I was having a nightmare, I heard an intruder—but of course it would be a lie.

His snoring subsides. I step past a closet and brush against a bureau and approach a coat rack. There hang the pants my father wore to work that day. I reach my hand out to feel along the pants and locate the pockets. My fingers catch an opening and I slide my hand down as deep as I can extend. My fingers feel my father's billfold. I pull out a clasp of crisp currency and flip gently through the bills. I bring my face close to the money, the better to make out the denominations and count. It's mostly tens and twenties, plus a few singles and fives, about $200 in all—a fortune by my reckoning, probably enough for a house and a car.

I ask myself how much money I can take without my father noticing anything missing.

I leave most of his billfold intact, but make off with a five and a ten. He'll never know. Impossible! How ever would he?

I repeat these late-night raids about once a week for the next two months or so, taking about $200 in all. I slide out of bed at 3 or 4 in the morning and take gingerly steps down the hallway. No one knows what I'm doing, much less has any cause to suspect it, and it thrills me, sneaking in there like that. I go back to my bedroom with the cash, a secret intruder within my own family, a triumphant suburban pickpocket, my temples still pulsing with a sense of danger averted.

I had no material need to steal from my father. We lived in a three-bedroom split-level colonial on a quarter-acre in an up-and-coming northern New Jersey suburb. My allowance of $5 a week, quite generous in 1960, easily paid for bubble gum, comic books and 25-cent cherry rickeys at the soda fountain counter.

But I wanted something from my father. A piece of him. Anything. He always worked, leaving early and staying out late to manage office and residential buildings. He came home mainly to eat and sleep, living among us like a lodger at an inn, his presence in my life defined largely by his absence. He went all but unseen and unheard but never unfelt.

My father never changed. Business always came first, family second, even after grandchildren arrived. He connected with everyone except his own family.

Still, as I gave the eulogy at his funeral, I remembered how I had picked his pockets. As a boy I had reconciled myself to my little adolescent crime spree. My old man had cheated me—of himself, mainly—and so I cheated him right back. Call it redress of grievance, or a quid pro quo.

Still, my guilt got the better of me. I schemed as a teenager about how I would return the money, secretly salting dollar bills back into his pants until I made good on my debt, my father none the wiser. As a young man, I even planned one day simply to hand him back the cash I stole, plus interest for good measure, and explain why, complete with abject apology.

But I never gave back a dime. My father never said a word about the missing money to me, nor, as far as I knew, to my mother or anyone else. Whether he ever even noticed I have no idea.

I like to imagine he knew all along. Knew and, what's more, understood. Now I do, too. It's the same for so many of us and our fathers. We strike our bargains. Mine gave me what he could. Finally, all these years later, I realize it has to be enough.

Learning How To Eat

By any objective scientific standard, my mother-in-law loved food. Loved the tastes and textures and sights and smells. Loved to sample every dish on the table, pressing her lips together and moaning with approval.

But Nettie loved more than merely eating. She loved everything about food itself. Shopping for it, preparing it, presenting it, even talking about it. No sooner would we sit down for a meal with Nettie than she would deliver play-by-play commentary as if she were an announcer at a baseball game. So it went at just about every meal my wife and children and I had with her for 23 years, including Thanksgiving at our home.

Mmmmmmm this turkey tastes so juicy . . . Michael, have some more . . . Oh, the cranberry sauce is so sweet . . . Caroline, sweetie, try some please . . . Do we have more gravy . . . Elvira, you need to get more gravy . . . You know how I like gravy . . . Mmmmmmm, the stuffing it has chestnuts . . . Bob, have the stuffing . . . Elvira, you told me Bob liked the stuffing . . . Do you think this will be enough? . . . Should we put out more?

All of which, I now admit, drove me nuts. Nettie always made a big deal about eating. You never had enough food on the table. You could never have too much, either, because even too much was never enough. And she fretted over every detail, her chatter never-ending and obsessive. I complained to my wife at every opportunity, ad nauseum. I suspected Nettie had a food fetish.

I, on the other hand, had exactly the right attitude toward food. Mature, practical. Eating was no big deal. If it tasted good, fine. A bonus, really. But basically I saw eating as eating. Food was fuel, intended mainly for function and performance. Why get carried away?

So we had a major issue about food, my mother-in-law and I, though I never told her so.

Then, in the fall of 1998, for the first time, I felt an urge to feed Nettie. More: to indulge her every gustatory whim. And so every Sunday afternoon around 5 I drove her to the restaurant of her choice for dinner. Voluntarily.

And as we all gathered around, I, too, made a big deal about it. I praised the picturesque meal displayed so amply before us. I identified each platter to her with a wandlike wave of my hand. I encouraged Nettie to try the veal piccata or some tandoori chicken. I inhaled deeply and theatrically the enticing fragrances that wafted forth. And as we dug in, downright convivial now, I went moan for moan with her.

That's how our Thanksgiving went that year, too, Nettie eating too much and talking too much and generally fussing too much. Everything stayed exactly the same as in decades past—except me. I had copped a new, more lenient attitude.

Only years later would I figure out why my view of eating with her changed. It must have hit me, finally, that her childhood had everything to do with it. Nettie grew up poor in Brooklyn during The Great Depression, her father a garbageman, with two brothers and a sister. I had imagined her life as a girl, her mother bringing macaroni to the table and Nettie asking herself the question she would ask in later years. Will this be enough?

I'd never connected this hardscrabble upbringing with how Nettie came to eat as an adult. No wonder: I'd grown up in an upper-middle-class suburb in northern New Jersey. I'd always had enough to eat, and known more could be had just for the asking, the cornucopia a given year-round. Because I never saw food as an issue, I could never understand why anyone else would.

Now I do. The 1930s left Nettie with a legacy impossible to erase: a famine sensibility. That's why she hoarded food in her cabinets, why she piled her plate so high at buffets, why she had to sample every dish. That's why she overate, why she talked so much about food, why she always saved scraps for later, even a smear of cream cheese. Better get my fill today, in case we run short tomorrow, she must have thought at every meal, never more so than at Thanksgiving. She had long since earned the right to regard food as a big deal.

As it happens, so many of us lately are shifting toward a food-as-fuel credo. We follow findings from the latest studies about nutrition like stockbrokers watching the Dow. We sit down to meals fretting about how many carbs we can consume, how much protein, and whether to allow ourselves seconds. We're turning into amateur dieticians, second-guessing our every finicky bite. We're the new Puritans, sugar and fat the new sins, all of us at risk of seeing food mainly as a hazard to our health, the primal pleasure of eating slowly evolving into a social stigma. Now we're the ones with the food fetish.

Thank goodness my mother-in-law at long last taught me how to eat. And that's why, in her honor every Thanksgiving, I plan to stuff my face. And you should do the same.

So please pass the gravy. Let's eat without guilt or anxiety. Let's heed the siren song of our senses, savoring every slice, and celebrate our plenty. In fact, let's give Eating Right a holiday. Let's feast as if it's going out of style (because someday it well might).

We came to this country to be free. Maybe it's time we once again ate freely.

Funny Valentines

In 38 years of marriage, my wife and I often joked about how deeply I'm in her debt. In debt, of course, more for her love, patience, wisdom and advice than for those six dollars she lent me in 1987 that I just never got around to paying back.

Luckily enough, I finally found the opportunity to bring this running joke home. As my wife sat at the desk in our bedroom paying bills, I noticed her calculator nearby. I stepped over and pecked in a few numbers, pretending to be doing some important figuring.

"Hey, guess what?" I said.

"What?" she asked.

"Hold on a second. Let me doublecheck." And I poked at the calculator again.

"Well, what do you know. It's true after all."

"What is?"

"It's just as you've always claimed. I really do owe you everything."

Every Valentine's Day the experts weigh in about how romance starts, and they offer the keys to keeping it going. Biologists cite pheromones and psychologists the whispering of sweet nothings into the ear. All well and good, but let's remember a sense of humor.

I happen to know this to be true. Years ago I met a young woman from Williamsburg named Elvira. Quickly I realized that, besides being cute, smart and kind, she was endowed with an excellent sense of humor.

Elvira invented nonsense words and did silly walks and made faces and mimicked Bette Davis in "All About Eve." I learned from her mother that once, as a teenager, she traipsed out in front of her family with a basket of artificial fruit propped on her head, imitating Carmen Miranda singing "The Lady in the Tutti-Frutti Hat."

As it turned out, her brand of humor suited me just fine. I, too, had certain tendencies in this direction. Thanks to my cracking wise and pretending to walk into doors, my fellow high school students elected me class clown (male division). I kept playing court jester well after college, too, and generally showed few signs that adulthood was even remotely imminent.

Elvira and I clicked, big-time. I asked for her hand and nuptials ensued.

Over the years, we've made fun of anything and everything, including the world, each other and ourselves. Our humor, mine and hers, is born of pain. Mine, because my mother became profoundly deaf in infancy and never heard my voice, hers because her mother slaved to make a living to raise her without much help from anyone.

We've gone through our share of crises as adults, too, from a daughter hospitalized at age 3 to my getting laid off twice. Our disappointment, frustration and anger seep out through our pores as jokes.

I'd ask you how you are, I once said to her, but I'm worried you'd tell me.

Hey, she retorted, did I ever let you know that meeting you back in 1976 was doubt at first sight?

You're the only person I know, I came back, who usually needs a second chance to make a good first impression. Listen, she concluded, look on the bright side: Nobody's killed you yet.

Once, after I misbehaved, she gave me a sympathy card. Inside, she had written, "Because you are so annoying, my heart goes out to you."

Through it all, such humor has promoted a sense of unity for us. You might almost say we married for funny.

Researchers, too, now recognize that a sense of humor can act as a kind of medicine for a couple. A dose of humor, taken regularly, can alleviate suffering of all sorts, everything from anxiety to grief, potent enough, even, to safeguard against alienation and divorce.

Studies show, for example, that the husbands and wives who are most satisfied with life together give each other high marks for humor, and that couples who share private jokes thereby enhance intimacy.

So here's my advice to couples: Humor each other. You know what they say: Laugh, and someone else may, too.

Take it from us. We're still kidding each other, still laughing together after 40 years. My wife and I have long since learned how best to settle an argument. We take a mature approach. We call each other stupidheads.

Why, just last week, during yet another domestic dispute, Elvira joked once again about how much she looks forward to the day she gets to collect on my life insurance policy. Seeking forgiveness, I asked her what I could do, right now, that would make her happy. "You mean," she said, "other than your immediate demise?"

Thus does humor remain the most valuable tool in our personal survival kit. And I think we know why. Our love for each other is much too serious for us to take too seriously.

My Sundays With Stanley

Toward the end, as he lay dying, pretty much all I wanted to do was make him laugh. I called him every week with a line or a joke or a story he might find funny. I plied him with levity. And laugh he often would. Even so, I suspected that as I tried to humor him, he was actually humoring me. Together, we whistled in the dark.

Somehow I got the idea that if I could just keep him laughing, maybe I could keep him alive. Scheherazade, the Persian queen who told tales for 1,001 nights to save herself from beheading, would have nothing on me. If I could just make him laugh often enough and hard enough and long enough, it would lengthen his life by 1,001 nights and maybe even save him from cancer. We would strike a deal. Just as I kept him going, he would keep me going, too.

But instead Stanley Siegelman, my friend, my editor and mentor, my surrogate father, my tribal elder, died anyway. Stanley, a father and grandfather, a World War II veteran, an award-winning editor with Hearst and Fairchild magazines and a long-time contributor of whimsical poetry to the Forward, had just turned 87 years old.

We knew each other for 34 years. Stanley hired me, then age 25, to write for *American Druggist*, the pharmacy magazine he ran. For four years he gave me heavy doses of the praise and encouragement I then most needed as a young writer. I invited him and his wife Shirley to our wedding two years later. After I left the magazine to freelance full-time, he referred business to me.

We stayed in particularly close touch over his last 10 years, after Shirley died. Right around then he started composing his poems for *The Forward*, perhaps to ease his grief. He loved to pun, compulsively so—years earlier he wrote an article about insect repellents that began, "Let us spray"—and saw the English language as a playpen for rhyme.

His whimsical poems addressed anything and everything Jewish that twanged his funny bone—the Eliot Spitzer debacle, a Brooklyn restaurant named Traif, you name it. He often told me of a poem in the works or just submitted and about to appear. Once in a while his editor would rejected a poem of his as perhaps off-limits, news Stanley shared with me with both disappointment and delight. At those times he reminded me of an otherwise polite boy who knew he was being a little naughty and mischievous. He caught a second wind late in life, publishing some 185 poems, humor his lifeline.

I visited him in Great Neck every few months, often on Sundays—my Sundays with Stanley. We went out to lunch at a diner and took walks in a nearby park near the water. Always we talked about writers and writing, about books and articles and essays, with special attention to Saul Bellow, Philip Roth and other literary heroes. We also discussed our own work. Even all these years later, I still showed him my materials, still addicted to his unstinting approval.

I've never had a talent for friendship, but luckily Stanley did. A friendship is a miracle and all miracles are to be treasured. He edited my copy, but never tried to edit my life. He remains the only person in my life I seem to have failed utterly to disappoint.

Toward the end, as he sensed his life coming to a close, he refused to let me see him, no matter how much I asked. "I have to confront this on my own," he explained. Still, he welcomed my phone calls and always asked me for news both personal and professional. "So tell me about your latest successes," he would say, and give me the floor. Years back I wrote a novel he had read that remained unpublished, yet he kept asking me, "Did someone accept your book?"

Eventually he would get around to telling me about his health. He always kept his accounts matter-of-fact, almost telegraphic. He took this test and that medication and the physician gave him the following prognosis. He conveyed such details with a scholarly detachment, ever the reporter, casting a cool clinical eye on his own mortality, perhaps the better to mask any apprehensions. "I'm terminal," he told me once. "There will be pain. That will be it."

Never once did he complain, nor seek sympathy, much less pity. That was just never his style. If his spirits sank, he never really let on. "It's a long haul and I'm getting tired of it," he admitted in an unwavering voice. "I'm tempted to close my eyes and let it be. The sooner the better." The last time we spoke, he wished me all the best. He said it almost officially, as if he already knew it would be the last time we spoke. I had run out of jokes and he had run out of laughter.

If Stanley was unwilling to complain even then, how can I ever? The man taught me how to die. He also taught me how to live.

Playing American

You're in New York City, outside Russell Sage Junior High School in Forest Hills, Queens, to be exact, and you've just hit the basketball courts. Here come Sanjit and Huan, in baggy shorts and tank tops, with Priel and Vloshko just behind, their Yankee caps on backwards. And now along lopes Yuri, hairless chest gleaming with sweat in the July heat.

Time to play three-on-three hoops. Only here, on this gray asphalt, as planes overhead fly toward nearby La Guardia Airport, we're going global, baby. Sanjit comes from Pakistan, Huan from Beijing, Priel from Tel Aviv, Vloshko from Ukraine and Yuri from Uzbekistan.

You're the only one born in the United States.

So you choose up sides, and the contest begins.

As it happens, you no longer remember quite when the basketball players in your neighborhood started to change. After playing on these very courts for 40 years, you've lost track. The only detail you recall for sure is that back in 1977, and even as recently as 1990, almost all the players came stamped Made in America. Jewish, Irish, German, Italian, occasionally black. This was neither good nor bad. That was who lived here, and that was who played here.

One day, though, a teenager joined in who spoke only Russian. A few months later, a Chinese kid who knew only broken English dropped by. The lineup started to change, piecemeal, without your even realizing anything had happened. The names of fellow contestants proved harder to learn, much less pronounce. The faces looked different, sometimes with skin darker or eyes narrower. Players from Tel Aviv might take to the courts wearing yarmulkes. New tongues were heard, too. Asian teammates could talk strategy among themselves in Mandarin without risking that opponents would understand.

Of course, Queens started going seriously ethnic back in the 1970's, when waves of Russian-Jewish immigrants, fleeing Soviet Communism, began settling in, mostly in Rego Park. But it took a while for the changes that followed to fully register—for you to realize, for example, that the players on your basketball court had gone from being largely native Caucasian to largely everything else.

These days, some games are made up entirely of players born on other shores. Now we aging children or grandchildren of Eastern European immigrants are vastly outnumbered, our monopoly over the courts long gone. For decades, it has been possible to play basketball with people from all over the world without ever leaving home.

The three-on-three starts off casually, the six of you looking to loosen up, to get a rhythm going. But you've been around the game long enough to realize that given human nature and the dynamics of combat, no honeymoon lasts forever. Eventually, the impulse to compete, to gain supremacy, will kick in.

So the shift goes in Parker Towers, your high-rise apartment complex off Yellowstone Boulevard, once heavily Jewish. Oh, sure, Molly and Bernie from the Forest Hills Jewish Center are still next door after all these years, but the Chirichellas are gone, and right down the hall are more families than ever from Hong Kong and Pakistan. The mailboxes show fewer Goldbergs and more Watanabes. The newest doorman is the first one hired from Guyana, improbably going by the name Ronald; his colleague Carlos, who arrived decades earlier, comes from Colombia.

So it goes, too, all along the spine of Queens Boulevard, from Long Island City and Sunnyside to Kew Gardens and Jamaica. Store signs have morphed from English into Russian and Greek and Korean. The corner delis now lay out newspapers in dozens of languages: the Chinese alone have no fewer than seven dailies. Suddenly it's harder to get good pastrami around here—Pastrami King and the Boulevard Deli are long gone, leaving behind only Ben's Best—but much easier to find baba ghanouj and palak paneer.

It's already widely known that no place in the United States, maybe no locale on the planet, is more ethnically diverse than Queens. What's a revelation is just how multicultural it has become.

It could almost be said that Archie Bunker doesn't live here anymore. In 1970, the year before the first season of "All in the Family," Queens was 86 percent white, with 80 percent of residents born here. Today, Queens is 44 percent white, with 46 percent of its residents foreign-born. The proportion of Asians grew the fastest in that span, to 18 percent from 1 percent. Main Street in downtown Flushing is now lined with more than 20 international banks, all financed with money from the Far East.

And changes keep coming. Recently store signs in Korean along Main Street have started to outnumber those in Chinese. Demographers predict that the most intense ethnic influx over the next five years will be in Astoria and Long Island City.

For proof, ride the subway from Manhattan out to Queens some workday during the evening rush. Every skin tone on the human palette is represented on those trains. Passengers may converse in Cantonese or Punjabi, may wear turbans or saris. Just for fun, try to guess who will get off at which stop, bound for which national enclave. The Koreans may step off in Flushing and the Colombians in Corona, while the Afghans leave at Jackson Heights and the Bukharians in Rego Park.

Or some Saturday, head out to Flushing Meadows Corona Park. Over on an emerald-green meadow, surrounded by families picnicking, Sri Lankans dressed all in white play cricket, the pitcher sprinting in the grass toward the batter, then hurling the ball on a bounce. Back beyond the Unisphere, on a makeshift field flanked by goal nets, Ecuadorians play soccer, dirt swirling into puffs with each kick. All across these acres—fittingly, the site of the original United Nations and two World's Fairs—with whiffs of barbecued lamb or pork in the air, people from everywhere are coming together to party.

Queens is like a conglomerate that keeps diversifying its portfolio, the better to profit from synergies. When it comes to being international, the Olympic Games have nothing on this borough. Unlike, say, the Iowa wheat fields, Queens is what this country is supposed to be all about, the true American heartland. It's every inch a symbol of the great experiment in freedom and democracy that is America itself. Still, tourists to New York would rather see the Empire State Building. So nobody ever comes out to Queens, only everyone, and seldom to visit, only to live here.

Quickly, your three-on-three turns what you'll charitably call tough.

Whenever Huan raises the ball to shoot, Sanjit tries for a block, hacking his arm in the process. Under the basket, Priel bumps hips with Yuri to box him out for a rebound, tripping him. Vloshko calls for the ball—"Here! Here! Here!"—and complains that you should pass more. Nobody gives an inch.

The game is sloppy; the players, new to one another, are out of sync. You consider the potential outcome here. If hostilities break out, no fewer than six nations will be involved. Nobody is singing "We Are the World." It may be a game, but each of you has a reputation to preserve. Still, it's more personal than political.

Some philosopher once said that to understand America, you have to understand the game of baseball. These days, let's make that basketball. The game is a welcome mat for the latest generation of arrivals, a Great Assimilator. The courts of Queens are the new Ellis Island.

The ground rules are still simple: if you live here, you get to play here. Where you come from is neither here nor there. Nobody ever says anything about the changes going on, and nobody has to. You could be from another dimension of time and space for all anyone cares, as long as you speak the universal language of basketball. Ethnicity dissolves into irrelevance if you have a good jump shot.

The names and faces are different from three decades ago, but the sport itself, how it's played, remains the same. Dribble. Pass. Shoot. Rebound. You have yet to see a style of play remotely identifiable as, say, Middle Eastern. The new arrivals may still observe Ramadan and eat paratha, but they all look to slash to the hoop like Kobe. They all aspire to play American.

So it is that when you bounce a pass down to Sanjit in the post, he dishes the ball off to a cutting Priel, and he hoists a jump hook that swishes through the hoop. Huan darts baseline, and just as he peels free from his defender, Yuri nails him with a pass and he banks in a layup.

At this point, you might be tempted to say something profound or patriotic about this little subculture. About how basketball, with its call for intricate independence among players, is the world as it ought to be, holding more potential than any other sport to unite us. About how anyone can join in a game at any time, players coming together at random to choose up sides on the spot.

And of course that's the game as viewed through prescription rose-colored glasses. Queens is no soda commercial with an international cast gathered atop a mountain teaching the world to sing in perfect harmony. Some Queens residents grumble about the new immigrants and would rather hear only English spoken here.

Even in famously liberal New York, not everyone wants the country's doors flung open to admit immigrants from everywhere in the world. You hear a refrain of doomsday warnings about neighborhoods being invaded and going downhill, of many longstanding residents ultimately leaving in dismay or even disgust. Given the close quarters in which New Yorkers live, ethnic tensions run as high here as anywhere.

Still, in four decades playing basketball here, you've never seen evidence on the courts of any issue over national differences. No name-calling, no arguments, no fistfights. In the occasional game involving Arabs and Israelis, you've actually seen peace break out. That's why the changing of the guard in Queens renews your faith in the future, and never more so than as a July Fourth approaches. Sappy as the sentiment sounds the moment it enters your brain, you think: if we can all play together, maybe someday we can all live together, too.

The other day, you're out there by yourself practicing some moves. Along come two tall, skinny teenagers wearing high-tops, dribbling a basketball. They're swarthy, with black hair and dark eyes, apparently from the Middle East.

Even though they obviously want to join you, they hang back, watching and waiting. It's as if they assume the court is private property and are reluctant to trespass unless given permission. You wonder if this hesitancy to cross borders without the proper papers was bred in some distant homeland.

So you look over, just to acknowledge that they're there, a payment of respect. Encouraged by this sign of interest, the older player asks, We can shoot, too?

Your answer, delivered with a smile, gives you a shiver of pride.

Hey, you say, it's a free country.

My Sweet Dilemma

It's New Year's Eve, I'm in a restaurant with friends and it's time to order dessert. Lemon meringue pie, says my pal Al. Chocolate mousse, says Georgia. Vanilla ice cream, says my wife. The waitress looks at me.

Nothing, I say. Nothing? she asks. No, thank you, I say. No dessert, Bob? asks Al. No, I say. Are you sure, Bob? Georgia asks. Yes, I'm sure, thanks. Oh, have some, she pleads. The waitress nods in agreement at all the coaxing. No, really, I say, I'm good.

This scenario repeats itself any time I go to a restaurant for dinner. Time for dessert rolls around, and everyone gets a strawberry cheesecake or a mascarpone tart.

Except me.

But my friends already knew my dirty little secret. I'd gone about 20 years virtually without ever having dessert.

Yes, you heard right.

Quite ugly as confessions go, I know. You should see how some people would look at me anytime I declined dessert—how high eyebrows arched, how quickly smirks materialized. Come on, they would say, you're kidding, right?

They consider me strange, a freak of nature, a genetic mutation. They figure I'm acting all healthier-than-thou, committing some kind of civil rights violation. Just who does he think he is, anyway, they think? They hate my guts.

Indeed, a business associate of mine actually called me to account on the whole dessert issue. You never get dessert, Bob, she observed, right in front of five other colleagues. How come? You must have a sweet tooth. How can you be so strict with yourself?

Why had I skipped dessert for almost my entire adult life? I dedicated considerable time in my childhood to consuming Ring Dings, Twinkies and whatnot. I like sweets well enough, especially anything chocolate—cake, cookies, doughnuts, ice cream.

I have no ax to grind against earthly rapture. So why always the thumbs down?

Okay, first, because my father, no stranger to sweets, got fat in his 40s, grew sedentary and later died of a heart attack. Second, because I'm looking to keep my weight right, stay sharp at basketball and live a long, full, active life, preferably with grandchildren and the whole nine yards. Three, an all-or-nothing policy on dessert simplifies my diet considerably—no need to calculate when I last had dessert or whether I was now entitled to another. Fourth, by the time dessert comes I'm usually full.

Unfortunately, my attitude toward dessert has endeared me to precisely no one. Everyone is supposed to get dessert. Dessert is a social custom, an all-but-sacred cornerstone of modern civilization. Apparently nobody trusts a person who always says no to dessert. It's regarded as just shy of rude, a sure sign of poor citizenship, an act of heresy.

I found myself stigmatized as a hopeless killjoy. Deserted, as it were. I felt singled out as a threat to common decency, guilty of a peculiar lifestyle preference. If you're ever looking to go directly and flagrantly against the grain of society, try turning down creme brulee in a public setting.

All of which I always found kind of . . . paradoxical. We talk about the pressure in our culture to be thin. But what about the pressure to be fat? The health-minded evidently have no right of first refusal. When it comes to how we eat, some of us are, in effect, talking out of both sides of our mouths.

Even so, after that dinner with friends, I felt haunted by the idea that maybe, just maybe, I was missing out on something essential. Would a little dessert now and then suddenly turn me morbidly obese?

So I promised myself to stop being such an extremist.

I would learn to live a little.

I would start to treat myself to dessert.

I've taken this big, bold adventure one step at a time, much like a castaway finally returning to the mainland, lest I lapse into shock.

First I'd nibble a fudge brownie, then graduate to going halfsies on a chocolate chip cookie. I even downed entire wedges of my daughter's delicious pumpkin-pecan pie. In such milestone moments, I've rediscovered the long-dormant ecstasy of the sugar rush.

You should see how people act around me at such watershed moments. Wow, they say, check out who's having dessert. Hey, Bob, what's the occasion? You had a religious vision? Doctor gave you only a year to live? You'd think I'd accomplished something epic, like inventing a pleasurable form of root canal.

Now that my diet calls for dessert, who knows what kind of random lunacy I might be capable of next? Maybe I'll skip my exercise once in a while, too, even sleep late this weekend. Maybe then I'll be fully welcomed back to society.

Let's call it the Reverse New Year's Resolution. It's the concept that our plans for self-improvement, however well intentioned, can work against us—that we should, at least once in a while, stop playing it so safe and let ourselves go a little. As it turns out, sometimes our sense of virtue can be our worst vice.

If we eat dessert, we might better taste life's other sweets, too.

Breakfast With Saint Peter

Two weeks after I turned 56, I was laid off after nine years at a company. The news came suddenly. One morning I got word, and by the end of the day I was gone from the premises.

I rode the subway from Manhattan back to Queens, thinking about how to tell my wife. I was the sole support of a family of four, including a son in college and a daughter studying music.

Within hours of getting home, I reached out to people I knew—friends, associates, recruiters, former colleagues and clients. Almost everyone lent some support: a lead, a reference, an offer of office space or a freelance gig, a kind word. Along the line, I reconnected with Peter. I'd known him for 15 years; we'd once worked closely together and over the years had stayed in touch, though mostly by phone.

Peter had gotten laid off a few times himself, so he knew how I felt. He'd always found new jobs. Over breakfast at a coffee shop just south of Central Park, he fed me advice and encouragement—and in the coming weeks never stopped. Though Peter had his own job, a wife and three kids, a long train commute and other, much closer friends, he made time for me.

Make a to-do list, Peter suggested, and then do it all. Call everyone important you know. Meet with anyone influential who will see you. You're going to be all right, he assured me. I tried to believe him. But no one, even the most confident, can be sure. Meanwhile, every day brought a new, unwelcome "first": the first family dinner jobless, the first supermarket trip jobless, the first rent bill jobless.

I knew full well how long it might take to find another job, especially at my age. The older you get, no matter how significant your accomplishments, the harder it can be. The looming recession and the tough job market gave me ample cause for anxiety.

But Peter would hear none of it. Day in and day out, he doled out pep talks laced with hard-won wisdom. Talent always rises, he said. Hold yourself accountable to your goals. After you've done all you can, do more.

On any job hunt, Peter said, the candidate always fears the "X" factor, the other guy. Make sure you're the "X" factor. Always be locked and loaded (he's big on military metaphors). Never get down on yourself, or let anyone see you sweat, or sell yourself short. Talk to so-and-so. Tell him I sent you.

Now, none of this might be all that unusual, except for this: Peter had cancer.

After suffering a massive heart attack, Peter was diagnosed with prostate cancer. Months of treatment, including external radiation and radioactive seed implantation, left him exhausted. It seemed his days were numbered.

The sight of him that morning at breakfast had taken me by surprise. Though still patrician handsome, he looked less than robust.

Peter had issues of his own, and could have told me so, and I would have understood. But he never did, and continued to help me. Thanks to him, I was better able to keep my own life in perspective. If Peter could face the end of life without complaint or a hint of self-pity, surely I could face my troubles. All I was missing was a job.

Eventually, by following his advice, I did land a new job. A better one, just as Peter had predicted.

And so I hereby raise a toast to Peter, and to all the Peters out there.

Peter remains my guardian angel. His strength gave me mine. Remember your value, he said. If you believe in yourself, most of the battle is already won. He taught me the most valuable lesson of all: How to keep my head up. Peter made me believe we might be a city of guardian angels. A country, even.

I have extra reason for such a belief. Peter's cancer just went into remission.

Lonnie's Deliverance

In a small town on Long Island more than 20 years ago, 17-year-old Martin Tankleff discovered his parents Arlene and Seymour at home slashed and bludgeoned to death. Martin wound up being charged with the double murder, then convicted, despite pleading innocent, and sentenced to life in prison.

More than 10 years ago, a private investigator decided to dig into the case. The PI had obtained evidence to suggest that others had committed the double homicide and framed Tankleff. But he needed help and looked to enlist my friend Lonnie Soury in the cause. Lonnie, a Manhattanite who runs a small public relations firm and often handles clients in legal matters, accepted the role pro bono.

Everyone does a good deed now and then. But Lonnie's actions were, to my mind, somewhat out of character for him. Love him though I do, I'd known him to be a slick, fast-talking operator who craved the limelight.

My next conversation with Lonnie quickly turned to Marty Tankleff. The push to reopen the case was rife with roadblocks, he told me, particularly a district attorney who faced apparent conflicts of interest and a media that remained indifferent. Lonnie went into the details at some length, his teeth clenched in frustration.

Every time Lonnie and I connected, the talk eventually came around to Tankleff. About a year later, Lonnie took me to lunch at the Harvard Club, then a client of his. Once again, it was Marty this and Marty that. The case was hard going: delays, depositions, a judge who was trying to throw it all out of court. Lonnie ranted filibuster-style over the lunchtime hush—"How can the judge be so blind?"—so loudly that heads turned to see the cause of the commotion.

As we left, I asked him, "Why are you doing this?"

"Because I have to," he said.

In the coming years, Lonnie was all-Marty-all-the-time. He conferred with lawyers, worked reporters, strategized next steps. He and his colleagues established a website about Tankleff, recruited supporters and garnered media attention.

The case became his grand obsession, and he paid a high price. He devoted so much time to the case that he lost clients and alienated friends, including me. His wife and children questioned his sanity, and he entered therapy.

Then, finally, came the unexpected. Even though the local court denied a retrial, public and private support kept growing. Two years later, new evidence and the ensuing newspaper headlines forced the case out of local courts. In December 2007, a state appellate court unanimously overturned the convictions. Suddenly, Marty Tankleff was out of prison and back with family and friends after 17 years behind bars.

Lonnie had proven instrumental in getting Tankleff released. In going the extra mile for someone else, in sustaining an act of altruism over five years, he transcended his own past—and personality—to deliver a humanitarian coup. In saving Marty, Lonnie saved himself.

After the Tankleff case, Lonnie promised his friends and family that he was obsessed no more and would resume a normal life.

But that never happened. He co-founded False Confessions, a public advocacy organization committed to bringing attention to wrongful convictions that result from false confessions in criminal prosecutions—and reforming the system responsible.

In short order, then, Lonnie found himself recruited to help free Damien Echols, an innocent man on death row in Arkansas. Echols was eventually released. More recently, Lonnie pushed to overturn the wrongful convictions of former Police Officer Richard DiGuglielmo and abuser Jesse Friedman. And he's somehow kept his personal life on an even keel, too.

Maybe we should all resolve to pull "a Lonnie"—a major good deed, or what we Jews call a mitzvah. Advocate for a cause beyond ourselves. Why would we do that? Maybe because, like my friend, we have to.

A Question Of Hostility

We are strolling, my wife and I, with our friends Don and Barbara along the sidewalks of Fairfield, Conn., where they live, on a Saturday afternoon in December. The only sounds are of birds twittering and squirrels scuffling through newly fallen leaves, the air tinged with the smoky fragrance of fireplaces. Just about everyone we see on the sidewalk looks us in the eye and smiles.

I'm reminded of the time I went, just for fun, to a place that sold fancy cars and, without intent to buy (much less the means), climbed into a Rolls-Royce. As soon as I closed the windows, I heard nothing but silence, as if the world outside had stopped.

That's how I feel now. All seems right with the world. I'm suffused with a feeling altogether foreign to me. A sense of serenity.

Barely a moment later, though, I find myself feeling jarred. Suddenly the peace around here actually seems rather ... violent.

"So," I say, turning to Don. "What do you do for hostility around here?"

I should explain. I'm a city guy at heart. For 40 years now, I've lived in Queens, in Forest Hills, and I've worked in Manhattan for a total of 19 years. In the process, I've forged an intimate history with hostility. I've gotten shoehorned into elevators in skyscrapers near Wall Street, sideswiped on the sidewalks of Times Square, and stampeded in the subways under Grand Central. If someone stares at me, I stare back. The same goes for shoving. I play pickup basketball in schoolyards, often with teenagers out to prove that they're tougher than I'll ever be.

The point is: Nobody has ever accused New York—or me, for that matter—of approximating serenity, at least to my knowledge. I doubt that New York City's tourism office pitches serenity as a selling point to out-of-towners.

Nevertheless, my delight at my clever question—What do you do for hostility around here?—is immediately tempered with dismay. What did I expect my friends to answer? "Well, Bob, truth be told, on slow days we usually just let a couple of mean hens go at it." Luckily for me, they laugh, a laugh that says, "That's just Bob being Bob."

Still, I know I've dropped a bombshell. I could have simply asked my friends where they got falafel around there. Instead, I've risked coming off as some hipper-than-thou tough guy from the big, bad city.

In asking this question, I've implicitly mocked the suburbs as a lake that never ripples. My wisecrack is more critique than passing comment, an act that can itself readily be construed as hostile. I'm a threat to the morale of unsuspecting municipalities across America.

In the days that followed, I reflected on the whole serenity-hostility equation. Was

I seeking basic tourist information? As in: "Excuse me, could you folks please direct me to the nearest outbreak of hostility?" Did my question imply that Fairfield might have to manufacture or import hostility in order to have any to call its own? Was I suggesting that other, like-minded New Yorkers, perhaps those looking to buy houses in this lovely setting, might regard hostility as an essential public service, as eagerly sought after as good elementary schools and functional sewage systems?

I soon came to a few conclusions. Though my question might have sounded silly, even deranged, I realized that I'd intended to be dead serious. I'd offered an innocent observation that had accidentally turned out to be true, and actually cut right to the center of my soul, circa 2006. It meant that hostility had somehow evolved into my idea of a pretty good time, or at least the benchmark of a normal state of being, and that when an element so essential to the environment suddenly is missing, it's worth worrying about.

The question defined me as a New Yorker. Sometimes, to recognize who you are and where you come from, you have to go someplace else. But my question also presented certain dark hints. Maybe I had lived in the city too long. Maybe I had grown hair-trigger combative, a chip on both shoulders. If the city gets into your blood, is it a tonic, a poison or both? Maybe I need to get out of town more often.

That Monday morning, as I was riding the R train to work, fellow passengers jostled and jockeyed for seats and spots to stand, as usual. Out on 49th Street, near Radio City Music Hall, fellow pedestrians cut me off and tailgated me, clipping my heels. Nobody caught my eye, much less smiled. Half the passers-by seemed to be spoiling for a fight.

New York throbs with impatience and aggression, suspicion and paranoia seething just below the surface, the hysteria and panic always latent. Ours is a city of confrontation, the rule of thumb to confront or be confronted. We're all competing here, for jobs, for money, for space. Competing, in this ecosystem so harsh yet fragile, to get through the day and live our lives and survive to the next. That vibe of hostility is inescapable, like the air and the light.

I crossed Eighth Avenue, going with the signal but, as I knew all too well by now, more or less taking my life into my hands. Sure enough, a cab making a hard right almost mowed me down. Ah, homesick no more.

The Layoff To End All Layoffs

Anyone ever laid off has a story to tell, and even those never let go have probably heard more than a few, too. In recent years, with more layoffs than we've seen in generations—3.5 million at last count—I've had occasion to hear plenty of such stories.

Take my friend Gloria. At a weekly executive-committee meeting, she heard the CEO discuss a restructuring, obviously code for layoffs. As a public affairs officer in the company, she was asked to draft a strategic plan about the impending changes, including some talking points, and submitted the memo.

Her company then invited Gloria to an annual offsite meeting. "Well, that's pretty reassuring," she said to a colleague. "My job seems safe after all." Why, she thought, would my employer fly me down, put me up in a hotel and feed me to a fare-thee-well unless I'm considered a keeper? "Well, of course," her co-worker replied. Why on earth would they let you handle all the media for the layoffs, only to chop your head off?"

Then came the big day. Each employee was herded into a conference room and given an envelope, but told to go back to his or her office before opening it. Gloria got an envelope, too. The note inside instructed her to go see her boss, then the HR person.

Her boss told her she was being laid off. Next, the HR person started to read a document to her. All about how the company needed to be better aligned to deliver on its new mission, and how these decisions came so hard.

"You can stop now," Gloria said. "I wrote that. Those are my talking points."

She returned to her office, only to find her colleague from the plane ride there crying. Spared the ax himself but in disbelief, he said, "They made you dig your grave and then kicked you into it."

As war stories go, that's pretty hard to top, if only in terms of irony bordering on the insane. Yet again and again over the years we've heard such dispatches from the front lines. Employees of long standing given the boot with little or no warning. Offered a pittance as severance. Asked to clear out that day. Heard of humiliations large and small.

Now, getting laid off is never pretty, and seldom even particularly humane. No big secret, that. But even though most companies are fair, others fail to demonstrate concern, much less generosity. In some quarters, layoffs have gotten downright ugly.

Imagine, for example, coming back to your desk from a break, only to find the IT guy shutting down your computer. Imagine being laid off over the phone while out on jury duty, or on your birthday. Imagine getting the news on a voicemail message or via a videotape mailed to your home. No need to imagine anything, folks: all these tales are true.

Hey, we're all adults here. We understand why employers lay us off. Business is business. But getting laid off is hard enough without your company compounding the fracture. Recruiters tell me that companies that lay employees off without a sense of decency will eventually suffer a backlash. For starters, those left behind will be less productive, with lower morale, and are highly unlikely to recommend that organization as an employer to anyone.

That's why bosses should try to show some respect. You never know about what could happen down the road, especially when the economic recovery truly kicks in. Come next year, showing a little heart might actually turn out to be good for business.

The Long Apology

So yes, Nettie talked too much, too loudly, and worried too much, too.

Every Thanksgiving at our Queens apartment, all these idiosyncrasies collided with combustible force. I'd like to say that I took them in stride and even found some charming. But that would be a lie. We were never going to get along, my mother-in-law and I—that much I could see from the start. The woman got under my skin more than acupuncture.

Still, I stifled my annoyance over my lot in life as her hostage, simmering instead. I never aimed a cross word at her, nor raised my voice to her, nor gave her anything like a dirty look. I bit my tongue and treated her with kid gloves. So it went for 23 years.

Then, in the fall of 1998, something strange and surprising happened. She suddenly stopped getting on my nerves—without acting any differently. Suddenly, all I wanted was to make Nettie happy.

After so long avoiding conversations, I started to talk with her. I asked about her life, listening as she reminisced about her childhood in the storied Brooklyn of yesteryear, about playing ringolevio and seeing Pee Wee Reese at Ebbets Field.

I took her for long drives. She told me how, as a girl, she had gained a reputation throughout the neighborhood for carrying herself like a lady at all times. *Look at Nettie,* everyone in school would say as she came down the street, her head held high, *she walks just like a queen.*

I never missed an opportunity to hug her.

I fantasized about someday bringing Frank Sinatra to her door so she could finally meet him.

Then, the following spring, Nettie, at the age of 78, went into the hospital for open-heart surgery. She suffered complications and sank into a coma.

She could no longer talk and now all I wanted was to hear her talk.

And only weeks later, on a sweltering June day, just as I had started to get the hang of getting along with her, she died.

Why my abrupt change of heart so late in the game?

Maybe it was because Nettie grew on me. Or maybe it was because I simply grew up.

Maybe it was because I'd seen her as a pain in the neck for all those years without realizing the pain in the neck was me.

Maybe I graduated from virtual intolerance to absolute acceptance because I realized she always came through when it counted.

Nettie had raised her daughter without a husband around, all on a pittance. When her grandson came along, while Elvira and I worked, Nettie took care of him, and when her granddaughter came along, she took care of her, too. What little money she had— she lived on Social Security and a flimsy pension—she spent on Michael and Caroline. Even when she took to a cane, she found the strength and dexterity to dress, change and feed Caroline all day long.

Nothing was ever easy for her, yet she never gave us an ounce less than her all. She never second-guessed me, never questioned my bad decisions or came down on me when I got fired from my first job; never stopped believing in me even when I almost stopped believing in myself.

Maybe, in those last months, I finally recognized how much I owed her.

Maybe Nettie talked so much because she grew up with three siblings and had to compete for attention at the dinner table. Maybe she had to be loud because only then could her sister seamstresses hear her over the sewing machines in the factory where she slaved for 47 years.

Maybe it dawned on me that even though she might never change, I certainly could.

So I made amends with an act of apology long overdue. My change of heart, my attempt to redeem myself and show her how much I treasured her -- coming just in time, before my long goodbye, before it got too late and we lost her forever—struck me as a miracle. It was as if, toward the end, I had somehow sensed she might be around only a little longer and we should roll out the red carpet and make the best of the few moments we had left together.

Nettie has been gone for 18 years now, and I would give most anything to get her back, even if only for an hour, just to keep my apology going. I would love to see her just once more with her grandchildren, both grown so smart, beautiful and talented. We keep her cane on display in our living room, leaning against a dresser, a symbol of all the support she gave us. Sometimes I hear her in my dreams, telling us, as she always would, that everything is going to be all right.

A single image is forever forged in my memory. One day Elvira and I went to pick up the kids from her in Williamsburg, and we saw all three coming down the block toward us, unaware we were there. It was a rare chance to see how they all looked together, from a distance, almost objectively, just a grandmother and her grandchildren unaware of anyone watching. All three holding hands, the kids looking up at her, sunning themselves in the warmth of her affection, Nettie beaming her high-beam grandma smile to the heavens.

If I ever forget how to feel grateful for anything, she's all the reminder I'll need.

No more easy punch lines, then. The mother-in-law has gotten a bum rap. Take it from me. My mother-in-law was no joke.

Confessions Of A Two-Timer

You're wheeling a shopping cart past the fresh mozzarella, your wife and teenage daughter in the lead, at the Fairway on Broadway and West 74th Street. The three of you troll the mazelike aisles, near collisions at every turn, for goodies to keep you all well fed for the next week or three.

Just a local family grocery shopping on a Saturday afternoon, right? Nothing unusual going on here. Except there is. Your family hardly qualifies as strictly local.

You live out there in Queens, in the distant hamlet of Forest Hills, 9.3 miles away according to your odometer. Your presence on the Upper West Side of Manhattan practically renders you an out-of-towner.

So why make the trek? Why set out from Yellowstone Boulevard, bounce over potholes in Elmhurst, brave cabby tailgaters in Sunnyside, swerve through the shadows cast by the el in Long Island City, cross over the East River on the 59th Street Bridge and spend 20 minutes hunting for a legal parking spot, all to do something most New Yorkers do simply by strolling around the corner?

The answer: Neighborhood Envy. Your family has come down with a strain of this peculiarly urban disorder. The three of you have visited the Upper West Side at least once every few weeks for more than a decade. You make these trips even though you know almost no one there except a few of your daughter's friends, her singing coach and a married couple you stopped hanging out with, for reasons you now forget, during the early Reagan years.

And while it's true that Fairway has sublime whitefish salad, you're about more than food. You're also drawn to the neighborhood for reasons sartorial, literary, architectural and pastoral. Your wife favors the Talbots here because she can buy a dress for her friend in the plus sizes unavailable at the store's counterpart on the Upper East Side. Your daughter is partial to the sidewalk vendors near Zabar's who hawk books new and used, including Broadway sheet music and operatic librettos.

You personally go for the forbidding Victorian grandeur of the Apthorp, the views from Riverside Park of barges and tugboats steaming down the Hudson, the benches on Broadway's malls, so hospitably positioned for people-watching. And, back to the culinary for a second, you savor the divine chopped liver at Artie's.

But more than consumerism and sightseeing lure you to the neighborhood. You dig the vibe. The babies and puppies, the graying beards and corduroy sports jackets, the smart conversations overheard, often laced with politics that still hang a Louie. It's all pretty easygoing, even civil, almost like a college campus circa 1972, back where you sometimes might want to be.

Still, you feel like a bit of a two-timer. Let's face it: you're cheating on your own neighborhood.

Now, Forest Hills has plenty of charms to call its own. Make no mistake about that. You can stroll through the cloistered enclave called Forest Hills Gardens, with Tudor masterpieces along its bucolic Greenway, their stone gazebos festooned with ivy. You can visit the justly fabled West Side Tennis Club, that hulking dinosaur landmark, where the U.S. Open used to be played, for so long so forlornly abandoned.

You can amble down Austin Street, the local Fifth Avenue, home to no fewer than four Zagat-rated restaurants along a single stretch. At least a dozen supermarkets can be found within a mile of Parker Towers, the apartment complex where you've lived since 1977. You like where you live, especially on summer evenings, when you can lounge on your terrace overlooking a courtyard green, a fountain spouting under lights.

Still, the stage is now clearly set for conflict. Your disloyalty leaves you feeling so guilty that your imagination runs amok. You dream of encountering an office colleague some Sunday afternoon on Columbus Avenue.

So, Bob, what brings you around here? Thought you lived in Queens.

I do. Just visiting.

Really? Just visiting?

Picked up some CDs at the Lincoln Center library.

Nothing else?

Had some noodles at Ollie's.

Aha!

But we're heading home now.

Come on, Bobbie boy, you can tell me. Looks like maybe you're getting a little on the side.

You get the idea.

Now let's fess up here. No New Yorker worth his salt is a complete stranger to Neighborhood Envy, even if he already lives on Beekman Place.

I have a friend in Park Slope who yearns to live on the Lower East Side, and a colleague from Staten Island who'd rather be in SoHo. Indeed, perhaps nowhere on the planet is neighborhood envy more prevalent than in New York.

That comes as no surprise, given our proximity to one another. We all live so cheek by jowl in this buzzing honeycomb: 23,700 people per square mile, topping even San Francisco at 15,500. Turn almost any corner, and suddenly another and altogether different neighborhood materializes. In the suburbs, you might have to drive a mile to notice sharp changes in demography. But in the city, you're intimately privy to—you can see, right up close—exactly how others live.

This shoulder-to-shoulder closeness can easily breed a grass-is-greener syndrome. Just as during childhood you always suspected that the family next door was happier than yours, so the next neighborhood over can come off as cooler, inherently more desirable than your own, and maybe even with better restaurants.

It's no wonder your family has fallen prey to weekending in Manhattan. It's no wonder you sometimes contemplate whether you would really rather live there.

Now the plot thickens. Your wife and daughter officially wish to move to the Upper West Side. They have started to lobby you, gently, citing numerous reasons, all practical. Your daughter studies music on Broadway and 86th Street. Your son goes to Hunter on Lexington Avenue and 68th Street, just across town. Your job is on Eighth Avenue and 49th Street, also pretty nearby.

Family negotiations proceed apace. Maybe a compromise would fit the bill: keep your three-bedroom apartment in Parker Towers but get some darling pied-à-terre just steps from Fairway.

Still, you're a conscientious objector. For one thing, you're seldom touched by any sensation approximating wanderlust; you believe that the advantages of staying put for long periods are woefully underestimated. For another, at heart you're a diehard resident of Queens. You savor your status as an outsider.

For now, these weekend jaunts are nothing serious, less secret affair than mere flirtation, innocent and harmless. You're just friends. Really.

Pancakes With Shirley

Even in the weeks just before he died of cancer, Stanley Siegelman kept writing poems. Already 87, the longtime Great Neck resident could hardly help himself. As he might have admitted, ever the incorrigible punster, he could always have done verse.

I knew Stanley for 34 years, first as my editor, then as my friend, always as my mentor. Through it all, he loved to indulge in wordplay, particularly the practice of punning. In a poem, he marked the 100th anniversary of the introduction of the bra. "This was a deed of some import," he wrote, "that over time won full support."

Ten years ago, he lost his wife of 47 years, Shirley. I began visiting Stanley every few months to keep him company. We always went to the Seven Seas diner on Northern Boulevard for scrambled eggs. We might then drive over to Steppingstone Park to converse and admire Long Island Sound. So went my Sundays with Stanley.

Around that time, he began contributing poems to the legendary *Jewish Daily Forward*. As a veteran journalist, he had published most everything—news articles and editorials, features and profiles—at first for Fairchild Publications, later for Hearst Magazines. But never poems. But then, he'd never lost Shirley before.

Over the next decade, Stanley waxed poetic about anything Jewish that would give voice to his keen sense of whimsy. From his manual typewriter poured some 185 ditties and limericks, along with quatrains, odes and sonnets. He satirized everything from politicians to Israel, Yiddish and circumcision. I suspect he crafted these rhymes as literary therapy, seeking to ease his grief over losing Shirley.

I marveled at his late-life creative resurgence, and offered to publicize his efforts. I could easily imagine *Newsday*, for example, profiling this prolific octogenarian. But however much I begged him to let me "pitch" him, ever-humble Stanley politely rebuffed my overtures. Clearly, he aimed more for private amusement than public acclaim. "Besides," he asked, "why would anyone ever want to do a story about me?"

The last time I visited Stanley, he asked to go out for pancakes. "It's too long since I've had any," he said. So out we went to a local pancake house. He quickly polished off a stack doused in maple syrup. I interpreted his request as a sign he wished to make this visit different, special, as if it might indeed be our last.

But his poetry never stopped. In one birthday card he sent me, he wrote, "Aging we cannot avoid, maybe it can be enjoyed?" In one of his last notes to me, he wrote, "I've just turned 86—no joke! Let's hope this ain't the year I croak."

Only the other day I found out while Stanley and Shirley first dated, he wrote poems for her. In a sense, Shirley inspired all of his poems over the last 10 years, too. No doubt his life with her was all pancakes.

Pulling His Punches

"Stand sideways," my father says. "Like this." He plants his feet, left in front of right, pointing toward me, and I imitate his stance. "That makes you a narrow target, harder to hit."

My father is teaching me to box. I'm 10 years old and he figures it must be time. We're in our kitchen in suburban New Jersey. My father, then 35 or so, is wearing a sleeveless T-shirt, his chest thick, his arms muscular, his belly flat. I'm a stringbean, maybe all of 80 pounds.

"Now bend your knees," my father says. "Like this." He demonstrates, and once again I ape his movements. "Crouch down. Stay on your toes. Keep your hands up, in front of your face."

He once boxed, he tells me. Golden Gloves, out of Newark, N.J., where he grew up Jewish in the then heavily Jewish Weequahic section. Tells me this matter-of-factly, same as he does everything else, with no hint of pride, much less bravado.

He shows me how to throw different punches—the left jab, the right cross, the one-two combination. He gives me tips on how to keep my punches short and compact, close to my body, with leverage from my legs for extra power. All along, he never even pretends to direct a punch at me.

I'm thrilled. My dad the ex-boxer from gritty Newark is educating me to fend for myself with my fists.

Then one day my boxing lessons stop. No explanation is offered, and I have no idea why.

I took up shadowboxing as a young man. Around our apartment, sweating and grunting, I copied the maneuvers of my favorite fighters, especially Muhammad Ali and Joe Frazier, often in front of a mirror, and always put into practice the few basics my father taught me.

My father died in 1997. But some 10 years after his death, I clicked onto Google to literally search for him, a random act of curiosity, quite out of the blue. I'd never known him, at least not as well as I'd wanted. Oh, he sometimes took me to work with him, and we once went to a doubleheader at Yankee Stadium, and a couple of times we shot hoops in our driveway. But I knew him mostly by his silences and disappearances and absences. He left early in the morning for work and came back late at night.

He kept his distance from all of us, even his own parents. A loner at heart, keeping his own counsel.

I missed him, and felt a sudden urge to find out something about him. Anything.

Right away the Internet yielded a surprise. A friend of his, the editor of a newspaper, had written a posthumous tribute to my father. The editor recalled interviewing him for a profile just a few months before he died. The piece was all about how my father, almost completely deaf from birth, had established a communications network, via teletypes, among the deaf community nationwide.

But now the editor shared a story behind the story. He had asked my father about his boxing career, only for him to go mum. Pressed for some history, though, my father reluctantly opened up. In the year he competed in the New York/New Jersey Golden Gloves, 1948, he had beaten every opponent he faced and reached the semi-finals. If he won one more fight, he would make the finals in Madison Square Garden.

My father dominated the semi-final match. His punches staggered the other fighter, and the referee stopped the bout, declaring a technical knockout. But whatever satisfaction my father might have felt was short-lived. His opponent collapsed in the ring and had to be taken out on a stretcher to the hospital. There he stayed overnight, kept under observation, his status touch and go. By morning he had recovered.

My father went on to compete for the championship in the Garden, he told the editor. I imagined my Dad fighting at the old Garden on Eighth Avenue and 50th Street. I'd gone there once as a kid and seen the Knicks play against Wilt Chamberlain. I sat high up in the stands, about as far back as you could go without leaving the building. The air was thick with clouds of cigar smoke and reeked of the cheap beer sold in the aisles. I pictured my father, representing Newark, going toe to toe with the best New York had to offer.

But as my father told the editor, he was unable to focus on the match at hand. All he could think about was the fighter he had sent to the hospital, almost killing him. He no longer had his heart in hitting anyone and he lost. He had put on boxing gloves for the last time.

My father called his friend after the interview to persuade him to leave out all reference to his boxing career. The editor readily obliged, and only after his death decided to go public, on the Internet, with my father's secret.

It's weird to discover your father's secret through the Worldwide Web, a medium available instantly almost to everyone on the planet.

As it happens, my father never wanted to spank me. My mother occasionally assigned him this job, probably to catch a breather from doing it herself. The first time he tried, he laid me over his lap and smoothed the spot on my backside where he planned to strike. But he swatted me only once and none too hard. He never tried again.

"Just never had his heart in it," I said, delivering the eulogy at his funeral from a synagogue pulpit. "My father was the gentlest person I ever knew. He never raised his voice and I never saw him angry with anyone."

Tears streamed down my face as I gasped out the words.

Now I know why. Why he stopped my boxing lessons. Why he never wanted to spank me. He'd witnessed the result of violence and saw no point in committing any more.

He simply preferred to pull his punches.

As for me, I still shadowbox in front of a mirror. I stand sideways, knees bent, hands up, keeping all my punches short and compact. I remember my lessons well. And nobody ever gets hurt.

Welcome To Camp New York City

'So what are your plans this summer?" my friend asked.

"We're going to stick around the city," I said.

"Really?"

"Sure, plenty of stuff to do here."

"Have you ever heard of a car?" he asked. "It's quite an invention. You get in it and when you come out, you're someplace else."

I got his point.

Come summer, especially on weekends, certain New Yorkers leave the city for vacation. They may head out to the Hamptons or the Berkshires or the Catskills or the Jersey shore. Off they all migrate, to roadside motels, seasonal rentals, and second homes, for a few days, a week-long break, or even the whole of August.

The rest of us stay put and summer in the city.

That's a real shame, because skipping town, while an opportunity exploited, is also an opportunity missed. Some Upper West Siders have seen Rome but never have seen Harlem, much less Queens.

This is bad for business, as restaurants and other merchants lose sales. It's also bad for the air, given all the gas consumed in driving longer distances and the pollution generated.

But this flocking instinct is also an issue of morale. Because weekending in, say, Provincetown carries a certain snob appeal, those of us left behind are relegated to feeling unhip, provincial, even vaguely stigmatized.

Make no mistake: The impulse to go away in hot weather, especially toward water, is human nature. The very ritual of hauling yourself off, along with the accompanying sense of movement, can feel liberating. Urbanites rightly feel a primal urge to break away from the sweltering subway stations and honking cabs for a change of scene, a place cooler, quieter, more rustic, just about anywhere as long as it's elsewhere.

Our family has gone on exoduses in summers past. Southampton. Martha's Vineyard. We belonged to a beach club in Long Beach, Long Island, for nine years. And we still visit Mystic, Conn. every August for a few days.

But in recent summers we've rediscovered all the advantages right in our own backyard. We've sampled local pleasures we seldom find time to see between September and May. The Bronx Zoo. The Brooklyn Heights Promenade. Arthur Avenue and Astoria. Just a few weeks ago, we rode the Staten Island Ferry.

Staying close to home on summer weekends, at least occasionally, comes highly recommended. Tourists cross oceans and spend fortunes just to visit our attractions. But we're already here. The city is vast, with 14 miles of beaches. Getting around town on a shoestring is easy. You benefit from the ultimate luxury: convenience.

Besides, the city on summer weekends is special, a different city, markedly so, from its other seasons. It has fewer people around, fewer cars, and thus more room to maneuver. It has more seats available in a sidewalk café for a leisurely espresso, more air to breathe, and it's quiet enough at night to hear the street lights change.

It's also in a more leisurely mood. You can witness the rare phenomenon of New Yorkers walking slowly. In sticking around, you feel a kinship with all the other diehard homebodies here. Suddenly, it's a city that feels smaller, more intimate, more hospitable, more *ours*.

Summer camp for adults.

Camp New York City.

Improvements in attitude are already underway. NYC & Company now prominently cites all five boroughs on its Web sites, touting the city to visitors and residents alike, currently via its "Summer Breaks" discounts.

The Bronx got into the act, too, with a new ad campaign called "We're Talking The Bronx." Brooklyn Borough President Marty Markowitz swore he himself summers in his home borough. But the city still needs to do more to market its virtues as a summer destination to its own constituencies. Our tourism industry still mainly targets outsiders in order to sell airline tickets and hotel rooms. Indeed, the Long Island Convention & Visitors Bureau no longer even tries to lure New Yorkers, so flush are its hotels with the likes of us, instead focusing on other nearby cities, such as Philadelphia and Baltimore.

We can do a better job stimulating inter- and intra-borough tourism. For starters, let's do some research, tracking the numbers on local visitor traffic that is now so hard to come by. Let's also convince all five boroughs to collaborate on a campaign to celebrate the city as ours.

So stay. Escape the urge to escape. Think of here as the new away. Stay, even if only on alternating weekends. Stay because you'll be going green and contributing to your local economy. Stay because, if you commit to this gesture of pride and loyalty toward your hometown, you'll truly earn your stripes as a citizen of the city.

Hooked On Hoops: Part 4

Say hello to 40. You take work more seriously now, and you'd better. You and your wife now have two children, a boy and a girl. You've graduated to a two-bedroom apartment. You've quit the slippery slope of freelancing for the sure footing of gainful employment, a job in public relations in Manhattan, and earn a decent salary. You've quit vodka, melting back to 160 pounds.

You're now about twice the age of the other players, and sometimes starting to feel it. Half your hair is gone, most likely with no intent to return. Your body has quietly begun its gradual betrayal. Your lower back has gone out on you a few times and you twist your ankles about once a year. You can still play hard for an hour or more, but now you try to give yourself more like 15 minutes to loosen up beforehand. After you play, you now have a marked tendency to flop onto the sofa for the next two hours without the faintest wish to get up again.

Still, you play two or three times a week, also running and lifting weights a little—as little as possible—to keep yourself tuned up. Somehow you're actually playing better than ever. This news comes as quite a surprise to you. It's no self-delusion either; others who've seen you play over the years tell you so. You're not only stronger, with more stamina, but also smarter, savvier. You make the most of your strengths, and you've finally discovered the relevance of playing defense. You're prouder, more competitive now. You never dog it out there. You're always looking to show the kids you still have a few moves left in you. You care so much about playing well you even curse yourself at the faintest hint of failure, and if the games get rough, you come close to getting into fights.

You still think about yourself first, last and always. You're still always looking to show how good you are, how much better. Your ego still requires more exercise than any other muscle you own.

For the first time, you really start to wonder how much longer you'll go on playing. You expect to quit within the next ten years or so. Maybe take up a sport that offers a dignity befitting a person with a half-century on his tires, something like tennis or—please, no—golf.

You're 50 years old now. Just saying that to yourself makes you feel the need to sit down for a spell. You have a big job with a big company that handles big clients. You finally make a more than respectable salary. You're still 160 pounds, but you may be half an inch shorter.

You're still playing basketball and, much to your surprise, often and well at that. You're now almost three times older than most of the other players. Some kids call you mister or sir, but none has yet to refer to you as Methuselah. You still get your shot off fast and accurately, your passing is still pinpoint, your dribbling assured. You harass opponents. You can still get it going pretty good out there, still have your moments.

On the other hand, your vertical leap, never exactly Olympian, may now hover in the single digits. Guys get around you more easily. The groaning you sometimes hear is you bending over for a loose ball. You just had a hernia operation that knocked you out of commission from basketball for four months, your longest layoff ever, and you're visiting the dentist more frequently than you do most of your family and friends. Your father is dead of heart disease, and so is your beloved mother-in-law. Age is ambushing you.

The game has stayed front and center in your life, seeing you through.

More and more, you ask yourself why you play. Sure, you have your reasons. Plenty, in fact. To stay healthy. To keep your mood on an even keel. To get out of your own head. Blah, blah, blah.

But why *this* sport? Why this obsession and no other? To keep your stomach flat? To enable you to sleep more soundly at night? Suppose you're now a terrific player. So what. Is that all there is? Is there any other there there? You've never really asked yourself before. By now you're supposed to have learned something out there, but sometimes you think you've learned nothing. You're supposed to have a bigger reason for playing.

Except you've finally realized something. You'd previously considered the ball your personal property and yours alone. But no. The ball actually belongs to everyone. It's supposed to be distributed, more or less equally, to any guy who's open.

And now, against all odds, perhaps even against your very nature, you're actually getting more generous with the ball. Once in a while, you make a point of passing the ball to kids who never get it, often to the worst players out there, or to the rare shooter who might be better than you, or to whichever teammate has a hot hand.

The Healthy Argument

"A good fight with your spouse may be good for your health, research suggests. ... Anger-suppressing couples were nearly five times more likely to both be dead 17 years later, the study found." ~ University of Michigan School of Public Health

For many years my wife and I never argued with each other. Only now do we see how keeping our grudges all bottled up probably cost us our health.

Precisely because we had failed to resolve our deeply rooted conflicts with each other, for example, I one day experienced my back suddenly falling off. We thus saw no choice but to take up a daily regimen of health-promoting arguing.

To start, we would get everything out on the table for at least 90 minutes a day, three days a week, arguing vigorously enough to get us aerobic. We would warm up first—loosening our vocal cords and facial muscles—lest we dislodge an ancient resentment too fast and twist a tendon.

Right away, though, we had some unforeseen issues. That first night we argued for at least an hour about what issue we should argue about in the first place. The next night we argued about which of us should be entitled to start our arguments.

Soon our new approach to connubial stability and longevity got on track. We disputed whether day was better than night. We were at loggerheads over how we would choose, if we had to, between air and water.

All this back and forth turned out to be exhilarating. Still, we always made sure never, under any circumstances, to argue immediately after a full meal.

Over the next few weeks we finally told each other everything we once suppressed as unsayable. At long last I came clean about how much I hated her habit of breathing during dinner. Likewise, she lashed into me for blinking while awake.

Within mere months our routine yielded impressive benefits. All the bickering left my wife too winded to inhale with any regularity, enabling her finally to quit smoking cigarettes. My jaw grew so sore I could now control my portions at meals. Before long a neighborhood orthopedist was able to reinstall my back.

With our health status now demonstrably improved, we decided to up the ante, figuring that arguing longer, harder and more often would mean better results. We argued in front of friends. After going hoarse, we argued in American Sign Language.

One day, though, we found ourselves arguing about whether we should argue less. The next day we even argued over whether to stop arguing for good. We questioned whether living longer would really be worth all the sacrifice.

Our long-term outlook had gradually turned bleak. Against all odds, we now faced a new risk. We had truly come to terms with each other.

The Lost Art Of Doing Nothing Well

As a boy growing up in Fair Lawn, New Jersey in the 1960s, I whiled away entire days at the municipal pool, stretched out on a blanket in the hot sand under the summer sun. I would get to my feet only to dip briefly in the cooling water or shuffle off to the snack stand for French fries fragrant in the shimmering heat.

If back then I could ever do anything at all well, it was nothing. Even as a teenager and then later as a young adult in Manhattan, I demonstrated a mastery of leisure. My near-genius for inertia wound up accurately reflected in my modest accomplishments academic, athletic and, later, occupational.

But right around my mid-30s, my attitude toward exerting myself suddenly changed. I developed something unprecedented—an operative work ethic. Now married, with two children to support, I grew a conscience. Feeling an acute case of responsibility, I got busy, even crazy busy, my commitment to indolence gone. I even vacuumed.

As it turns out, I have plenty of company: Americans are evidently doing nothing less frequently than before. According to a recent American Time Use Survey, from the U.S. Bureau of Labor Statistics, we devote only 13 minutes each day to "relaxing and thinking." That's three minutes fewer than in 2004, a drop of 18.8%. Most of our time goes toward either sleeping or working— that's 14 hours killed right there—followed by "TV and movies," "eating and drinking," and "washing, dressing and grooming."

A study published in Science in 2014 goes that one better: it showed that most people would rather engage in an activity, even if unpleasant, than do nothing. To find out, researchers at the University of Virginia and Harvard left people alone in a room for six to 15 minutes with nothing to do but think. The majority of participants, given a choice, actually preferred to administer themselves a mild electric shock than to do nothing at all.

The project calls to mind the comment from French philosopher Blaise Pascal that "All of man's troubles come from his inability to sit alone, quietly, in a room, for any length of time."

Surely the chief reason for keeping ourselves occupied is economic. We're all heirs to the Puritan ethic, the dictate that only the industrious are elected to heaven. We've believed nothing is what you do only if you're too old, too infirm, or too dead to do anything.

After World War II, the United States, flush with victory, prospered exuberantly. Labor unions helped legislate shorter hours, introducing a concept called the weekend. Our culture came to pride itself on exceling at a skill until then largely elusive for anyone but the privileged—namely, leisure.

But somewhere along the line, likely around the mid-1970s on, all that changed drastically, never to revert back to form. Inflation ran high and global competition stiffened. Upward mobility stalled, then reversed field. We could literally no longer afford to loaf around quite so much, our license to be lazy revoked.

In tandem with that shift, the baby boomer generation grew up—perhaps against all odds. In the process, we got serious. We got it into our heads that only if we aimed to be ever-more productive in ever-less time could we demonstrate our value as human beings and justify our existence.

With the Great Recession, our compulsions graduated into an epidemic. We kept to-do lists for our to-do lists. We outgrew our enthusiasm for lollygagging. We had no further use for introspection. Accomplishment morphed into the popular new high.

In the bargain, leisure took on the aura of a taboo. Just ask how a friend or colleague spent her weekend for proof. Nobody admits to hanging out or kicking back, let alone lying in a hammock gazing at butterflies.

The busier we are, the more important we feel. We're all so busy, in fact, we often talk about just how busy we are, sparing no details. Our ambitions hold us hostage. It's as if, anything is easy for us to do except to take it easy.

I find one trend alarming, especially during the summer, at the height of vacation season. Vacation means "to vacate," as in to vacate the premises and, for that matter, our regular state of mind. August in particular invites us to slow down, to attain what Italians call il dolce far niente, the sweetness of doing nothing.

I maintain that a little strenuous idleness can benefit us all. "Doing nothing," said Lao Tzu, the philosopher who founded Taoism, "is better than being busy doing nothing."

Accordingly, I pledged this summer to set aside a few minutes every day to daydream, to cut my thoughts loose like a kite catching a high wind. I unplugged in order to reconnect. Let me take my time, I decided, before someone takes it for me.

Toward that end, I took long walks in the woods, lounged on benches in parks to admire babies and puppies frolicking together, lingered on the boardwalk to marvel at the surf somersaulting toward shore, stared at the night sky overhead, the stars glinting away. In short, I stopped to take a breath, to savor silence and stillness and solitude.

Make no mistake: doing nothing takes some work. But if I'm lucky, summer will again come to mean what it once meant. My ventures into indolence will reacquaint me with that taste of carefree abandon that came with getting boyhood summers off.

In the best scenario, I'll just let myself be. I'll forget myself long enough to find myself all over again.

Sometimes doing nothing is pretty productive after all. Hey, if we're going to do nothing, we might as well get something out of it.

Hello, I'm From The Planet Queens

You're at a party a few years ago, chatting with a guest you just met. He tells you he lives in Manhattan—Tribeca, in fact—and now comes that question almost everyone inevitably asks. Where do you live?

"New York City," you answer.

"Ah, the city," he says.

"In Queens," you elaborate.

"Oh," he says.

"In Forest Hills," you specify.

"Aha. Cool."

That introductory conversation, all of 15 seconds long, contains a universe. It sums up how we Queens residents might see ourselves, how others might see us and, most telling, how we suspect others see us.

Let's take a minute to parse that dialogue and probe the attitude behind it, shall we? You designate yourself a New Yorker first, and in so doing, elicit an "ah," gaining community approval. Then, anticipating the usual follow-up question—"whereabouts?"—you pinpoint Queens. With this addendum, you come clean, as if offering a product disclaimer.

Your Queens reference draws an "oh," easily interpreted as quizzical and maybe even vaguely excommunicative. Queens? you imagine your Manhattan-centric interlocutor thinking. That's somewhere near Long Island, right? Home to a place actually named Flushing? Is that a U.S. commonwealth, like Puerto Rico?

Clearly, your fellow partygoer is now disoriented. You might as well have said, "Hello, I'm from the Planet Queens."

Unmistakably, you suffer from all the symptoms of Outer-Borough Syndrome, or OBS. It's a dirty little secret, this mental condition, the worst kept in the city a sense of inferiority by geography, an us-versus-them rivalry, shades of that famous Saul Steinberg illustration.

You've long felt self-conscious about being a Queens resident. You suspect that because you're a member of the bridge-and-tunnel brigade, complete with a "718" phone exchange, Manhattanites, by virtue of living in the true Big City, that sovereign principality, might regard you as somehow less smart, less sophisticated, less downright civilized that, indeed, you might be wearing the wrong clothes, reading the wrong books and somehow speaking the wrong language.

If you lived in Middle Village, you'd probably never be invited to that Soho party in the first place. It's almost a moot point.

Exactly how you identify where you live in the city outside Manhattan is an issue no doubt faced often by people from what might be termed The Other Four. This dilemma once emerged in bold relief as Mayor Bloomberg's plan for congestion pricing—the $8 a day charge for cars driving into Manhattan below 86th Street—met with accusations of a prejudice against the so-called outer boroughs that borders on conspiracy.

OBS has a long history. Back in 1969, Mayor John Lindsay famously delayed sending city plows to clean up Queens after a major snowstorm (and as a result, almost lost his re-election bid). Staten Island felt so desperately alienated from New York City that in 1993 its residents actually voted to secede. Just last year a Con Edison blackout lasting 10 days affected Western Queens, puzzling and infuriating many of its 100,000 residents.

Call it a tale of two cities. Indeed, Frank J. Macchiarola, former Chancellor of the New York City Public School System, once wrote that our city has essentially only two boroughs, Manhattan on one hand and then the other four, with citizens divided mainly into two classes, white collar and blue.

By most accounts, OBS manifests itself in attitude and action alike. It afflicts Staten Island the worst, followed by the Bronx, then Queens and, much less so, if at all anymore, Brooklyn. It's widespread and growing worse as income disparities widen, Manhattan drives out the middle class and the hipper émigrés are forced to settle in Manhattanesque annexes such as Williamsburg and Long Island City. It's a problem that needs to be solved.

Of course, Manhattanites are free to size up "the rest of us" however imperially they see fit. But why should we care? It is we who should change how we see ourselves, we who should see ourselves as equals in every respect, refusing to take a backseat.

After all, more than three-quarters of New Yorkers live "out here." We drive Manhattan's buses, build its buildings and fill its offices as doctors, lawyers and accountants. We're Manhattan's infrastructure. When you get right down to it, Manhattan is little or nothing without us. Maybe it's Manhattan that's really the outer borough.

Just recently you rode in an airplane and the passenger next to you, a young businessman from India, asked where you live.

"Queens," you said.

"I know Queens," he said. "My brother lives there. I hear it's cool."

He Tilted At Windmills

Some years ago, I was given the improbable assignment of ghostwriting the autobiography of Abraham Hirschfeld, the Manhattan parking-garage king who died at age 85.

Improbable, for starters, because I figured the world had already heard about his antics—how he campaigned compulsively for public office (Congress, Senate, dog-catcher) without any prayer of getting elected—no doubt more than enough. Improbable, too, because Hirschfeld often exaggerated his importance in society to a degree almost epic, and my challenge, as his would-be Boswell, would be to translate his tall tales, all starring him, into some semblance of truth.

Well, the Abe Hirschfeld I got to know over the three months of our project turned out to be just as advertised, yet different, too—a man few others ever saw. Oh, make no mistake: True to form, he never hesitated to rank himself as a leading figure of the 20th century. In our days huddled together in his co-op overlooking Central Park, he readily took credit for just about everything from the rebirth of the Democratic Party to unraveling the American tax code. "Is it bragging if it's the truth?" he once asked me, no doubt rhetorically.

Then again, his personal life showed true humility. He remained utterly loyal to his wife, Zipora, even as she drifted into distant dementia. Over dinner, as she tried to recall some detail from the conversation five minutes earlier, he would wait in patient silence, and only when she looked to him for guidance did he remind her.

One hot August night around 10, when Hirschfeld and I had just emerged from our long labors, Zipora declared a sudden craving for ice cream. "Of course," Abe said, despite looking tired. Soon the couple was strolling down Fifth Avenue, hand in hand, as if still youth in Israel.

We never finished the book, to be titled "Meshugga," Yiddish for "senseless, crazy, impractical." And so our hard-wrought chapters, still in my possession, remain unpublished. Even so, Hirschfeld delighted in seeing our chapters reflect him as he saw himself.

Here, captured for posterity, was Hirschfeld the rags-to-riches genius who invented the open-air garage, Hirschfeld the newspaper publisher, Hirschfeld the diehard yet doomed political candidate (comptroller, councilman, chief bottle-washer), Hirschfeld the visionary builder who would fix Yankee Stadium, Hirschfeld the humanitarian and crusader against injustice, Hirschfeld the friend and confidant of the powerful and influential.

He met Bobby Kennedy only once, then corresponded with him briefly, but somehow these encounters bloomed, in his florid imagination, into nothing short of a deep friendship.

Sure, he had his issues, and pulled some crazy stunts. After a jury failed to convict him for tax fraud, he offered to pay each juror $2,500 as a "reward." He single-handedly almost ran the New York Post into the ground. Worst of all, he apparently hired a hit man to kill his estranged business partner, landing him almost two years in jail. The public had every right to deride him as something of a fool.

Still, I loved the guy. So what if Hirschfeld lived a life all but unexamined, free of any second-guessing, with roughly the same fidelity to fact as P.T. Barnum? So what if he could never resist jumping all over any Big Idea that popped into his head, or that he serially deviated from even the simplest truth, or that his concept of himself as a hero never squared with public perception?

He brings to mind what my grandfather whispered to me, in frustration and apology, about my grandmother's zeal for control. "She means well," he would explain.

By my lights, you have to hand it to Hirschfeld. A Polish immigrant with a fifth-grade education and a thick-as-borscht accent, desperate for public acceptance and approval, he dared to dream about stamping his image on history, only to overreach—a classic tilter at windmills—and capture more notoriety than success.

He exercised his constitutional right to be a buffoon. Since when is it a crime to be blind to yourself and much around you, a victim of your own misguided reflexes? Hirschfeld deserves a legacy as a quintessential New Yorker—rough-hewn, Runyonesque, a character, ultimately unstoppable. Peculiarly American, too—self-made, even self-mythologizing.

His name might as well appear in the dictionary under the definition of "delusions of grandeur." For my money, if you're going to have any delusions, they might as well have some grandeur.

The Real New York City

Every holiday season without fail, tourists from all over the world pour into New York City. Visitors catch Broadway shows, admire the Christmas tree at Rockefeller Center and window-shop along Fifth Avenue. Hotels are booked and museums and restaurants are jammed. So it goes year-round too.

That's all well and good, at least for Midtown Manhattan, but Queens is missing from this equation. As someone who lives in Queens, I can tell you that almost no tourist ever comes here to visit. Indeed, most out-of-towners regard New York City as synonymous with Manhattan. All they're ever likely to see of Queens, both coming and going, are our airports. Once they hit Manhattan, they tend to stay put until it's time to cross a bridge and head home.

That's a shame, because Queens loses out to Manhattan on tourism dollars. More serious, by skipping Queens, tourists blow a chance to see the real New York City.

After all, Midtown Manhattan is more fantasy than reality. With its fabulous museums and fancy retailers, not to mention a white-collar work force that's largely Caucasian, it's practically a theme park.

Queens, on the other hand, though long stigmatized as an "outer borough," is infinitely more representative of the city as a whole and increasingly of other major American cities as well. About 46 percent of Queens residents are foreign-born. More than half of immigrants arriving in Queens within the last five years speak a language other than English at home. Indeed, Elmhurst has a high school where students come from 96 countries and speak 59 languages.

Yet for most tourists, Queens remains an unexplored frontier. That's in part because the city still regards promoting tourism to Queens as something of an afterthought. One recent year, the tourism budget for Queens, which is allocated by the city, was $33,000. (No, that's not a typo.) Nobody in charge even had statistics on how many tourists annually visit Queens, much less how much they spend, because nobody seemed to break out those numbers by borough. Not even New York City and Company, the city's official tourism marketing agency, had any idea.

No wonder; the agency's Web site listed 105 board and executive committee members, but only four lived in or ran businesses headquartered in Queens. Without a seat at the table where decisions are made, it's hard to see how Queens can have a true voice in the city's tourist trade.

New York City has to do a better job of getting Queens its due as a tourist destination. It could mean more jobs, and, frankly, the attention would improve our morale. So, with that in mind, here are some modest proposals to help put Queens on the map:

• Settle for second billing. Let's tout Queens not as an alternative competing directly with Manhattan—we'd never win, nor should we try to—but as an addition to it. It's the perfect place to spend the second day in town, the second week or the second visit to the city.

• Counter the perception that from Manhattan, Queens is out there. It's not. Queens is easy to reach. It's right across the East River. Play our underdog status as a trump card, even adding tongue-in-cheek signs on, say, the 59th Street Bridge that call Manhattan the gateway to Queens.

• Trumpet our novelties. Let's brag about how old Queens is (established in 1683), yet how new it all is, too (most of its buildings sprang up in the last 50 years); how populous it is (2.2 million people, larger than 16 states); and how, thanks to all its cemeteries, dead people here outnumber the living. And we're home to the Unisphere, which is the largest globe in the world; the New York Hall of Science and the American Museum of the Moving Image.

• Pitch the chance to witness life where New Yorkers actually live. After all, when you're in Midtown, you're more likely to rub shoulders with commuters and tourists than with real New Yorkers.

• Promote the international angle to lend a sense of solidarity to visitors. When it comes to ethnic diversity, Queens is hands down best in show. You can buy saris on Roosevelt Avenue in Jackson Heights, blini in Rego Park and empanadas in Corona. Any tourist interested in Asian cuisine should check out Flushing, home to more Chinese than you'll find in Manhattan's Chinatown.

All Americans, including city residents themselves, should consider a visit to Queens nothing less than a patriotic duty. More than reflecting America's past, Queens is a civics lesson in multiculturalism, a one-of-a-kind preview of our country's future.

My First Time

In 2010, I set up my first blog. I realize that made me about the two millionth person to do that. As it happened, though, I believed my blog had the potential to be something really special. Probably about two million people have said that, too.

Even so, the decision to blog represented a shift in attitude for me. Early on, I had dismissed blogs as a fad. How dare ordinary citizens presume to inflict themselves on an unsuspecting public? Besides, what self-respecting writer would ever write anything for free, much less do so for an audience of perhaps 14 readers? Anathema! Heresy!

At first blush, blogging struck me as rather an unnatural act, exhibitionism of the sort you expected on a reality-TV show, or in performance art, or at the circus. The very word "blogging" sounded to me vaguely like a gastrointestinal disorder. (Physician to patient: "Your colon appears to be clogged. It could be a blog.")

But slowly I came around. Some blogs, I noticed, actually maintained high editorial standards, even exerted considerable influence. Newspapers and magazines I respected started blogging like crazy. It dawned on me that the freewheeling give-and-take of the blogosphere, its inherent interactivity, could serve, much like the practice of voting, as democracy at its best.

Eventually, then, I came to entertain the once-unthinkable idea of doing my own blog. But about what? To what end? Soon I found my answer.

For more than 10 years, I had promised myself I would write something exclusively for our children, Michael and Caroline. It would be a family history, deeply personal, straight from me to my kids. After all, I'd already written for just about everyone else: newspapers, magazines, and whatnot. Surely I could manage such an assignment for my own children.

But for more than 10 years, I never got around to it. Somehow I just never found the time, only plenty of excuses. I had a full-time job. I had a part-time job. I freelanced. I needed to watch TV for several hours every night and play basketball on weekends. You've heard the song.

But then I resolved to do it. In 2008, I started a journal, one for each child. Every week I took an hour or so to capture a special memory about my kids and my own life—a vignette about the day Michael was born, for example, or about how Caroline started to sing so young, or about my mother, my father, and the other key players in my life. The journal wound up being equal parts celebration and confession, heavy on encouragement but light on advice.

That Christmas I presented the two handwritten booklets—with some 50 entries amounting to about 35,000 words—to my kids as gifts. The next year I completed a second set of journals about equal in size, also then given at Christmas.

My purpose was to show my kids how much they mean to me. I also intended to leave something behind—an heirloom, a legacy more heartfelt and tangible and valuable in its own right than any insurance policy.

Some months later—with permission from my kids, of course—I decided I would publish all the material on a blog to be called "Letters To My Kids" (letterstomykids. org). Once or twice a week I would post a "letter" addressed either to Michael or Caroline. Anyone and everyone would be able to see every word I wrote for my kids.

The blog would serve a higher purpose, too, a cause. It would urge other parents (or grandparents, for that matter) to start family history journals, too, and even to take a pledge online to follow suit. My tag line would be "Invest In Your Past."

I launched my blog on Father's Day. *The New York Times* "Motherlode" column covered its arrival. So did Womansday.com. Page views accumulated accordingly. Site visitors occasionally left comments. Subscriptions grew. Readers committed to my pledge.

So it was that I transformed from a blatant snob about blogging to a regular practitioner, converted from rearguard draft resister, adamantly averse to such self-publishing, to enthusiastic embrace. Only a few months in, I planned extensions to my blog, such as a how-to element—mini-tutorials on how readers themselves can get going on a family history. I even contemplated starting another blog or two (perhaps written on the fly, unlike this one, and thus more truly a blog).

When it comes to communicating, I now realize blogs are simply another medium, joining the quill pen, the town crier, and the BlackBerry. So let me praise this new vehicle, this cave wall painting, this soapbox, the once-lowly, now-mighty blog. We may owe it to ourselves, however strange a new tool might seem, to spread whatever stories live closest to our hearts for all to see.

A Mom In Full

She always knows.

Mom knew how to get you, Caroline, through your stay in the hospital as a little girl. She knew how to deal with the teachers and the principals to pull you through school. She knew, Michael, how to take care of all your earaches.

She knows how to take care of pretty much anything, even me, her third child.

She's always cooked the food and cleaned the clothes for all of us. She's kept the books and paid the bills. She even painted the walls of our bedroom, sponge-style, complete with perfect wallpaper trim.

She always knows what to do and how to do it. When we had troubles, she knew how to handle it. It made no difference what cropped up.

My grandparents, the Shefts, failed to disguise the displeasure they felt on hearing I was going to marry her. My father once gave me money, saying I had no obligation to repay him, only for my mother then to demand I pay it back. It bothered Mom, but she kept her cool.

She always knew how, almost as if she were born an adult. We had so many worries over the years, so many struggles, but she somehow kept herself together and took care of it, never complaining, never feeling sorry for herself, never making me feel anything toward her but pride.

And it's all because she always knows—knows how to say what has to be said, how to do what has to be done. In that sense, she's one in a million. In that sense, too, she's almost my exact opposite.

I almost never know. I almost never knew before, and seldom know now, what to say, how to act, about anything really. Some people have the gift of common sense, an internal compass that guides decisions, leads to good judgment, and she has it in spades.

It's among the reasons I've always respected her and trusted her and relied on her and certainly loved her.

Without her help, without her practicality and advice and loyalty, I shudder to imagine what might have become of me. It's a tricky project, trying to express everything she means to me, this special woman, this soulmate, this angel from heaven, this Elvira.

She saved my life.

And has made yours possible.

Passing It On

One summer afternoon, out on the basketball court in the schoolyard around the corner from our apartment in Forest Hills, I got into a game of three-on-three with some teenagers, including a kid on my team named Roy.

Roy, about 15 years old, all arms and legs, gangly and awkward, soon dropped a pass and missed an easy shot right under the basket.

Our opponents, all teenagers themselves, started to tease him. "Give the ball to Roy," they wisecracked. Roy frowned, competing harder, but to no avail.

"Come on, Roy," I said. "You'll hit your next shot. No sweat."

Still clearly new to the game, he struggled. "He's going to be the next Michael Jordan," our adversaries taunted.

Finally, I'd had enough.

"Guess what, guys?" I said. "See this kid you're making fun of? Someday he's going to be better than anyone here."

Roy looked at me quizzically, as if to ask, Is that true?

We lost that particular game.

About 10 years later, a guy in his mid-20s came out to the same courts. He looked familiar, only he was taller, taller than I, broad in the shoulders and deep in the chest, too. It was Roy.

We chose up sides for a pickup game, with Roy again on my team. Only now Roy could play. Boy, could he play. He hit his shots from all over the court. He passed the ball crisply to teammates, cutting to the basket. He snatched rebounds with authority.

But he was so much more than just the best player out there. He was also a perfect teammate. He set picks. He doubled up defensively if my opponent drove the lane. He called out encouragement to the third member of our team.

We won in a blowout. Afterward, Roy told me he now coached teenagers at basketball.

I left the court that day understanding yet another reason why I kept playing basketball. He was why. I had graduated to the role of mentor.

Let me propose we do more such mentoring -- ad hoc, grassroots mentoring, a guerrilla, drive-by sort of mentoring that happens in the moment. It can consist of nothing more than the right word from the right person at the right time.

As it happens, I had started playing basketball at age 8, and throughout my adolescence usually wound up chosen last for pickup games. I was always the worst player, the shortest, scrawniest, slowest and most timid. I knew all too well how Roy felt.

Today I'm 65 and I still hit the courts for pickup games around the corner. Yes, I like to stay in shape. Yes, the game is still fun. But through Roy I discovered a larger meaning.

At a certain stage of life, if we're lucky, we recognize that we're supposed to take on a special responsibility, that we should share the lessons we've learned and set an example for those who are younger. After all, we've already gone where they're still going.

Come summer, then, I venture out to the courts as a tribal elder to encounter the next generation. I never know what might happen. Tomorrow could bring me another chance to pass the ball. Tomorrow could bring me another Roy.

The True Olympics

Suddenly, one Sunday morning in spring, the players appear. They're pitching, hitting, running, catching. Is this baseball? No, it's cricket.

The asphalt playground at Russell Sage Junior High School in Forest Hills, Queens, has never hosted cricket before. Basketball, of course. Softball, you bet. Touch football, too. But only sports of domestic vintage.

You know because you've lived here since 1977. You're there to shoot hoops, but instead you watch cricket. It's the same as baseball, except different. The pitcher sprints before he hurls the ball, sometimes on a bounce. The batter swings his stick low, like a golfer. He then runs toward the pitcher, then pivots to head back toward home plate. The players are from India.

It's all so . . . *foreign*.

But then, you have no reason to be in the least surprised. You've long since noticed newcomers arriving in Queens from Pakistan and Hong Kong and Mexico City and Tel Aviv and the Ukraine. Queens is more ethnically diverse than any place in the United States (and possibly on the planet). So where else in this country but right here would you be more likely to see cricket played?

Indeed, the whole world is at play here in Queens. Go to vast Flushing Meadows-Corona Park some Sunday. Panamanians from Corona are playing soccer in sprays of dirt. Taiwanese from Flushing are swatting baseline groundstrokes on the tennis courts. Dominicans from Elmhurst are playing fast-pitch softball. And, of course, Sri Lankans from Jackson Heights are having a go at cricket. How fitting: this very park is the birthplace of the United Nations.

So goes the whole borough, singing the body ethnic. Sanjit and Huan and Yuri and Alfonso, speaking Punjabi and Korean and Russian and Spanish, playing in Cunningham Park and Forest Park and everywhere in between. When it comes to athletes representing the nations of the world, the Olympics once underway in Athens had nothing on Queens.

Slowly you realize more than ever now that Queens is home to the *other* Olympics, the *true* Olympics. Whereas the official Olympiad happens every four years, Queens holds its own ad hoc version every day. It's the same, almost a parallel universe, except completely different.

Here, contests are spontaneous instead of staged. Grassroots instead of corporate. Truly amateur instead of virtually professional. No going for gold, no sponsorship from Nike. Athletes here go unsung, much less televised, the games with more peasantry than pageantry. Individuals represent only themselves, not entire nations, and only personal philosophies, not political ideologies.

It's well known that New York City bid to bring the 2012 Olympics here, probably to Queens. But maybe that move might somehow have proven redundant.

Of course, some Queens residents grumble about the newly minted Americans. You hear doomsday warnings—from the direct descendants of immigrants, no less—about neighborhoods being invaded and going downhill. No doubt the ethnic ecosystem here remains in violent flux.

But in all your time playing basketball here, you've never seen solid proof of any problem over national differences. No name-calling, no arguments, no fistfights.

As far as you're concerned, nothing quite brings us together like sports. Granted, most newcomers in Queens play only among themselves, in tribal enclaves, the soccer games with all-Spanish lineups, the cricket contests exclusively Indian.

Only basketball, my favorite sport, has gone polyglot. Anyone can join in. Players come together at random, by chance, to choose up sides on the spot. Basketball is the world as it ought to be, with its open-door policy and insistence on teamwork—a perfect democracy, really. Some half-court games of three-on-three actually involve players from six different countries.

So just as we all ride the E train together, vote together, pay taxes together, we play b-ball together, too. How cool is this: you've played basketball for 40 years with people from all over the world without ever leaving your neighborhood. Here on these public courts, right in your own backyard, in this so-called "outer" borough, the real Olympic spirit—of unity, of global goodwill—lives and thrives.

Now you ask one of the cricket players on the sideline to explain the game to you a little. In halting English, he spells out some key details. The pitcher is actually called the "bowler," the batter the "striker." You can either run or stay put after you hit the ball. Anything that goes over the fence means six runs. You start to grasp the concept. Maybe next time you'll look to join in.

Grudge Matches

Some years ago, the neighbors who lived in the apartment above ours made certain noises every night—mainly thumping, galloping footsteps, as if baby elephants were competing in a race. I went upstairs one day to ask politely about it.

No, nobody's making any noise here, the husband and wife insisted, it must be coming from elsewhere in the building. Two children about five years old, each holding soccer balls, stood right there. Could the noises be your kids be running around, perhaps playing soccer? I asked.

Oh, no, they said, we never let the kids play in the house.

For weeks this pattern recurred, then months, the noise thundering through our ceiling, followed by our delicate check-in with our fellow citizens on the floor above and insistent denial of all wrongdoing. Every time I saw the couple, I glared without a word of greeting. Then, the minute they moved out of the building, the noises stopped.

Now, in my heart of hearts, I was probably supposed to forgive these neighbors this infraction. After all, forgiveness is catching on practically everywhere these days. Google references to the word "forgiveness" increased from 25.7 million in 2010 to 58.8 million in 2016, more than doubling. Someone established an International Forgiveness Institute, while others set up The Forgiveness Foundation and The Forgiveness Project. Websites inviting us to forgive and forget online abound. A cottage industry has emerged. Books such as "The Power Of Forgiveness" and "Total Forgiveness," all touting the virtues of forgiving others, are international best-sellers. Forgiving a perceived injustice is now regarded as the mother of all quick fixes, promoting understanding and acceptance and peace. Somewhere along the line, forgiveness graduated from option to obligation.

The concept has gone well beyond self-appointed spiritual advisors prescribing that forgiving those whom we feel have wronged us is good for the soul, that holding onto hard feelings will turn us bitter and hostile. Now, the medical community cites studies showing that forgiveness can prevent heart attacks, lower high blood pressure and ease depression.

I, on the other hand, have believed all my life in the healing power of the grudge. I've harbored grudges, with an almost equal-opportunity sense of fairness, against teachers and classmates, bosses and colleagues, even family and former friends. In exercising my Constitutional prerogative to bear grudges, I've stopped talking to certain people permanently. I've discovered that little feels quite so satisfying, so downright justified, as a grudge well nursed, preferably past infancy.

I'm neither proud nor ashamed of this.

For example, I once had a boss who, even though she hired me with much enthusiasm, somehow took a dislike to me from my very first day on the job. I had come to her highly recommended, complete with solid credentials, and none of my colleagues there found fault with my performance. Even so, this boss lied to everyone around me—inventing chores I had left undone and deadlines I had missed—and railroaded me into a layoff after only 10 weeks at the company. It happened just weeks before Thanksgiving, with me as the sole support of a wife and two children.

Was I to forgive her? Should I, under our new totalitarian regime calling for mercy toward others at all costs, likewise forgive the cousin who invited me and my wife to dinner at his home strictly on the pretext of making an Amway pitch? Or my long-time friend who sent me a client, presumably as a gesture of unalloyed goodwill, and then harassed me for months to collect a 10% finder's fee from me? Or the former colleague who brought me in for a job at his company, sent me through interviews with no fewer than a dozen individuals, then never bothered to let me know, even when repeatedly asked, that the powers that be had decided to go in another direction?

Forgiveness is hardly a new idea of course. I seem to recall a certain popular book calling it divine. And I have nothing against forgiveness per se. And indeed have forgiven people over the years.

What gets under my skin, though, is all the propaganda about forgiveness. Forgiveness has bloomed into a cult. The prevailing attitude is evidently that no matter what the sin, we must all be forgiven. The general public is suddenly expected to forgive every adulterous politician, defrauding CEO and celebrity gone wild, provided some apology is duly tendered. The case can be made that we're forgiving too liberally, too democratically, and thus guilty of doing so indiscriminately. Forgiveness can be nothing but a cheap shortcut to an unearned sense of nobility.

So is it ever forgivable to be unforgiving? Shall we now forgive every breach of etiquette, every atrocity? Should forgiveness be a reflex? Should everyone guilty of violating a cardinal sin or commandment be let off the hook? Surely people have done deeds so heinous, committed betrayals so egregious, they're beyond forgiveness. If we must always forgive, why then do we have laws and courts and prisons, all based largely on our society refusing to forgive?

Grudges, on the other hand, have recently acquired a bad name, and supposedly run the risk of turning us inhumane. But I say we should carve out a place in our lives for hard feelings. A well-earned grudge automatically suggests that we're still maintaining some standards about the actions others take and a reminder to draw the line somewhere between right and wrong. A grudge holds our feet to the fire and can teach us a lesson. Refusal to forgive, I submit, can be just as righteous, just as honorable, as forgiveness itself. Once again, the Bible weighed in on the matter, as I recall—something about an eye for an eye and a tooth for a tooth.

Unless someone sincerely apologizes, of course. An honest, heartfelt apology makes all the difference. Such apologies should be accepted—ungrudgingly—with forgiveness forthcoming.

Then again, I need to keep in mind those who for whatever reason have refused to forgive me. I had a close friend in high school who ditched me after college and has avoided me in all the decades ever since. At our 20th high school reunion I asked him why and he said, without going into specifics, that I had often mocked him and always made him feel inferior. And, in fact, looking back and thinking hard, I realized that even though I'd never intended to hurt his feelings, I had sometimes made fun of him. I apologized right then and there, truly sorry for any wrongdoing—but to no avail. He declined.

So I know how it feels to go unforgiven. And guess how it feels? Deserved.

Playing Catch With Strangers

I'm shooting hoops at the playground in the schoolyard around the corner from where I live when I see a young mother pitching a baseball to her son. He's probably about eight years old.

She lobs the ball toward him, but it goes nowhere near the strike zone. The boy frowns with serious purpose and swings wildly, missing. Again and again she pitches off-target and again and again he strikes out.

I amble over to the mother, as nonchalantly as I know how, to offer my services as a relief pitcher. Maybe because I'm a Dad I feel unable to resist a swell of temptation to do so.

"Yes," she says, radiating gratitude. "*Please.*"

My father played catch with me only once as far as I can remember. We went out onto the front lawn of our house and tossed a baseball back and forth, each throw smacking loudly into our mitts. That summer afternoon, I felt about as happy as I'd ever felt. That's just how it goes when you're eight years old and playing catch with your Dad.

But then my father got busy with work, too busy to play catch with me anymore, always leaving early in the morning and returning late at night, and that turned out to be that. He had to do what he had to do. He was also born deaf, creating an extra barrier between us, and tended to keep to himself.

I promised myself everything would go differently with my own son and daughter. We tried pretty much every major sport together—baseball, basketball, tennis, soccer, you name it. We flung around Frisbees. We raced in sprints. We saw who could swim underwater the longest. It went great.

But then our kids turned into teenagers and young adults. They outgrew athletics for physical pursuits presumably more mature, such as pushups and jogging. And once again, that turned out to be that.

Play has always meant the world to me, even as a so-called adult. So now, if I spot a kid who evidently needs to play, I try to oblige. That's just how I roll.

Once, my wife, son, daughter and I went to a Thanksgiving dinner our friends held in our neighborhood. Halfway through the feast, the oldest son of our hosts, in high school at the time, looked as if he had mingled quite enough with all the grown-ups at the table. As it happened, so had I.

Knowing him to be a serious athlete, I invited him to have a pass with a football in the street in front of the house. Out we went into the November night, shrugging on our overcoats to shield us from the chill. We flipped passes to each other for who knows how long.

"Better than turkey," the teenager later told me. "*Much* better."

Clearly, I suffer from an acute case of Peter Pan Syndrome. But just as clearly, I'm ever-ready to answer my calling as a Pied Piper of play.

So it went that recent August when my wife and daughter and I took our annual vacation in Mystic, Connecticut. One afternoon, as we sunned ourselves by the pool at the motel, a boy about 10 years old left the lounge chair next to his mother and slid into the water. Soon, clearly bored, he started to toss a tennis ball in the air to himself. Feeling equally bored and altogether simpatico, I joined him in the pool and held up my hand to signal for him to toss me the ball.

Whereupon the boy and I played catch for the next half hour, throwing the ball back and forth, the kid smiling the whole time. It perfectly fit my lifelong definition of fun—an activity spontaneous, absorbing, even therapeutic.

Afterwards, I said to my wife, "I swear, I could go through my whole life playing catch with strangers."

"Yes," she said, "I believe you could."

I could go through my whole life playing catch with strangers.

A short time later, I realized that in a sense I do. Playing catch, after all, is a dialogue, a conversation, a connection made. Every school had meant new classmates and new teachers, every job new colleagues and clients, every backyard barbeque new friends and acquaintances, every neighborhood new tenants and merchants, and every basketball court new teammates and opponents. I'd always, after a fashion, played catch with strangers.

Always would, too. Life, by definition, is strictly catch-as-catch can.

Playing catch with kids is a job I still covet, even though I'm now eligible for Social Security. Play is a language children speak fluently.

Every time I engage in a sport with kids, I'm in effect re-enacting that catch with my father on our front lawn and those games I played with my kids. I feel, if only for a few moments, restored to my roles as father and son, connected both to the boy I used to be and the father I'll always remain.

Back at the playground now, I pitch the baseball right down the pipe and the kid belts a shot into left field. His mother drops her jaw in disbelief. Then the kid clubs another blast even farther. He's walloping every pitch all over the playground, smiling now, proud of himself.

"Thank you," his Mom says as I start to leave. "*Thank you.*"

I go back to shooting hoops and hear a Mr. Softee truck pull up to the curb nearby, its familiar jingle a siren song drawing children and parents. And a minute later, the same kid, now probably feeling rather like a future Hall of Famer, walks over to me bearing an important message from his sponsor.

"My mom told me to ask you," he says, "if you want some ice cream."

I picture swirls of creamy chocolate piled on a cone and feel a twinge of earthly desire. But I decline. My reason is simple. I had already had my treat.

Closing Arguments

 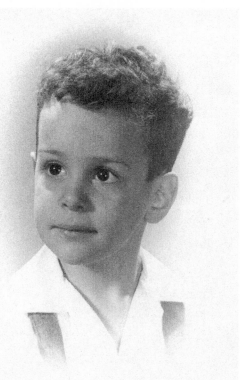

The Doorbell Rings Twice

I've arranged to come see my mother for the first time in 10 years, but the doorbell is going unanswered. She's unable to hear the bell because spinal meningitis in infancy left her profoundly deaf. But the signal is being translated into lights flashing throughout her home.

It's a Saturday morning in April, 2009. The birds surrounding her second-floor garden apartment in the northern New Jersey suburb where I grew up are chirping away as if in a Disney movie. I again press the button for the bell, only harder, but still nothing. The front door remains closed.

Ten years we've gone without our seeing each other. Maybe she's confused the date, I suspect, or simply decided to stand me up.

But no. The front door opens, and there stands my mother, now 80. She seems a little shorter, her hair all white, but still beautiful. We say hello and hug each other.

"You look good," I say.

"You look good, too," she says. "My handsome son."

We go up the carpeted steps to her living room and sit on a sofa facing each other. I mention how I waited a while for her to come down. Oh, the doorbell is broken, my mother explains. Perfect, I think. Ten years we go incommunicado on each other and, on the cusp of reconnecting, the doorbell comes unwired.

In 1999, I cut myself off from my mother. Why we fell out I will skip here. Why is almost besides the point. I decided enough was enough and she apparently decided the same.

I stopped calling her and she stopped calling me, too.

I lost track of my mother for 10 years—one-eighth of her life and almost one-sixth of mine. We had no contact—no visits, no letters, no messages delivered through third parties, much less a final confrontation.

I had no idea even whether she was still alive. I had no wish to hurt her, only to spare myself, along with my wife and children, any further hurt. But all the while, I struggled with my decision. Was I doing right? Was this helping?

Mother's Day is engraved in our hearts with warm images of families coming together to celebrate motherhood. In the classic holiday scenario, we give mom a card and a gift, take her out for dinner and snap a few photos. We honor her for doing a job—giving birth to us, caring for us, loving us—that no one else is nearly as fit to do.

But this American tradition, now more than a century old, has a flip side, seldom seen and little talked about and none too photogenic. For just as surely as some families today come together to celebrate, others remain apart, fractured by the ugly conundrum of estrangement.

Nobody has statistics on how many mothers and children are alienated from each other, nor whether such ruptures are on the increase—though some psychologists, based on anecdotal evidence, suspect that they are—much less why they happen in the first place.

Websites and support groups have cropped up to address mother-child estrangement, yet this phenomenon remains little-researched, little-discussed and much-misunderstood. Maybe that's because family estrangement remains a personal experience that defies psychological categorization.

So it goes for so many others. The causes are many—abuse, alcoholism and conflicts over everything from money and career choices to divorce, remarriage and sexual orientation. Estrangement can arise from a single incident, but it is also often cumulative.

The family itself has changed sharply over the last 40 years, too, possibly making estrangement more likely. Relaxed divorce laws and increasing geographic mobility—all in keeping with the never-ending American pursuit of happiness—have granted us a new freedom of choice. If anything bothers us, we want out.

That's why today someone somewhere has somehow gone missing, leaving a chair at the dinner table empty.

Estrangement remains largely a taboo topic in American life. It's a stigma, a dirty little secret, a silent epidemic. It flies in the face of all those homespun homilies about families sticking together through thick and thin. But as my own story suggests, such splits are rarely the answer. More likely, they're a stopgap that only creates new problems.

As it happens, I'm now an expert in estrangement.

Ten years earlier, my mother and I had sat across from each other in a booth in a Jewish deli on Seventh Avenue in Manhattan's Garment District. We would get together for dinner there every few weeks to catch up, usually over a hot dog and a knish.

My daughter had turned 11 a few weeks earlier, but my mother had sent her no birthday card. My mother had always sent birthday cards to both our children. So I asked her why.

"Why?" my mother asked, looking offended at the question.

Yes, I asked again, why?

"Well," my mother answered, "how come Caroline never sent *me* a card for *my* last birthday?"

I stared at her, dumbfounded at the remark.

"Because," I said, "she was only 10 years old."

"That's no excuse," my mother said in a huff. "She could have sent me a card. If she had, I would have sent her one, too."

I offered no reply, and we stayed silent. We shared the booth only for another few minutes. My mother paid the check, leaving half her food and a small tip.

We left the deli and stood on the sidewalk on Seventh Avenue. It was an early evening in mid-December, already dark, and pedestrians heading home from work swarmed all around us. I kissed my mother on the cheek and we said goodbye. I turned my back to her and walked away, toward the subway.

I looked back at her, just a glance, and waved.

She had failed me as a mother, often neglecting me. That I had long since accepted and somewhat forgiven. After all, she was young then, confused, a mess.

But then she neglected our children, too, failing as a grandmother. And now, as a case in point, she was begrudging our 11-year-old daughter a birthday card. My mother was older now, in her sixties, and she should have known better. Whatever excuses she had had about her actions before, she had none now.

She had used up all my sympathy. And so this proved to be the last straw.

I decided then and there never to see her again.

Eventually I stopped believing I could go the rest of my life without seeing my mother again—one of us could die, denying us the opportunity—and decided once again that enough was enough, only in reverse. Our rift no longer seemed to serve any purpose. We could start fresh.

I sent my mother an email out of the blue.

"I miss you," I wrote. "May we get together?"

In a few days, she replied, "I need more time."

I let some time pass and emailed her again.

"We should see each other before it's too late," I wrote. "Enough is enough."

She agreed, and we scheduled a reunion.

So on that Saturday afternoon I drive to the town where I grew up to reconnect with the person who'd once been the most important in my life.

In a little while, we walk to a nearby diner and order lunch. There, in a booth under a skylight, we try to catch up with each other on our lives over the last 10 years. Our conversation sticks to the basics. She has a boyfriend. I have a new job. My two kids have grown into adults.

I also explain my abrupt change of heart.

"I came today so we could see each other—nothing more, nothing less," I say.

"Everything that happened before no longer matters," I say. "Who did what to whom—it makes no difference. None of it means anything anymore."

My mother nods her understanding.

"We've both made mistakes," I said. "We've caused each other and ourselves enough pain. Nobody has to forget anything—or forgive anything, either. I'm here today so I can see you and you can see me. That's it. At this moment that's all I care about—that we're together now."

"Okay," my mother says. She reaches out across the table to pat my hand. "OK," she says again, nodding her head up and down.

It was all going according to plan. We were going to leave everything unspoken. All of it. It would be as if nothing bad had ever happened between us 10 years earlier. We would avoid the usual raised voices and finger-pointing and tears of apology and absolution. We were reconciled now, mother and son again. All would be forgotten and perhaps even forgiven. We would start fresh.

Except that my plan soon fell apart.

About a month later, my mother and I again met for lunch at the diner. And after we talk some more, my mother posed the question I most dreaded.

"Why did you stop calling me?" she asked. "What did I do wrong?"

I looked at her without a word, my lips pressed tightly together, my breath caught in my throat. I might have known an attempt to make amends after a decade of alienation would never come so easy. A clean getaway was going to be impossible.

"Please tell me," she pleaded.

"Are you sure you want to know?" I asked.

"Yes," she answered.

I'd had my reasons for breaking away, of course. I'd had 10 years to catalog every one, examining it, testing its legitimacy, justifying its existence.

"All right," I said. "I'll tell you. But next time. Next time I'll tell you everything."

And the next time we see each other, a few weeks later, I make good on my promise. I tell my mother everything. About Caroline's birthday card, too.

Enough is indeed enough.

The Miracle Of The Pies

Every spring, in the weeks leading up to Easter, in her apartment in Williamsburg, Brooklyn, my mother-in-law Antoinette made her Easter pies. "I'm making the pies," Nettie, as everyone called her, would announce. "Going to be busy, so nobody bother me."

The pie was an Italian specialty called pizza rustica. Her mother had once made the same pies from a recipe her family brought to America from Naples, Italy, so it was a tradition in the Chirichella family. Little Antoinette learned from watching her mother prepare the pies for Holy Saturday. She would slice the smoked ham and hot sausage into bits, fill the dish with fresh ricotta and romano cheeses, and brush the beaten egg wash onto the crust to give it a glaze.

In the early 1960s, with her aging mother no longer up to the task, Nettie took over the ritual.

Nettie made 15 or 20 pies every April for more than 40 years. Her mother had handed down her recipe on a sheet of paper, but Nettie never looked at the document, and so every spring made up the proportions in her head all over again. How many eggs should I get? she would ask. Such a fuss she made, I always thought. After all, they were just pies.

She stood in the kitchen pressing the dough with a rolling pin, her cheek smudged with flour, her fine hair in disarray. The pies came out looking like two-inch-thick omelettes—stuffed with cheese and flecked with meat, topped by a heavy, flaky, dimpled crust baked golden brown. She wrapped the pies in foil and labeled each one for the intended recipient (the size of the pie you got was a measure of her affection for you, the bigger pieces going to those she liked best).

The doorbell would start ringing at noon as our relatives came to collect this family dividend. Relatives came from all over Brooklyn and Long Island and Queens. No sooner were those disc-like shapes wrapped in aluminum foil dispersed far and wide than the buzz started. Were the pies as good as last year? Did Nettie still have her touch? Had she indeed used enough eggs?

Then Nettie, now 78, went for open-heart surgery, suffered complications and, only weeks later, died.

My wife and I drove from the cemetery to her one-bedroom apartment and started the sorry routine of going through her belongings. We scoured her drawers, cabinets and shelves, poring over clothes, photos and mementoes, to decide what to keep, give away or throw out. Nettie had lived on next to nothing her whole life, so we expected no hidden fortunes, and were almost done.

But oh, how mistaken we were. We opened the freezer and looked in, and there they were.

Nettie's pies.

She had saved a few wedges—including one actually labelled "Nettie," as if even in her own home, she had needed to earmark her handiwork as her own. My wife and I looked at each other in surprise and said nothing. Then we reached into the icy mist and took out the pies one by one. Gently, we placed each pie in a plastic bag to make sure they kept for the ride home.

In moments, we left her apartment for the last time and walked out into the hot, still afternoon, holding the residue of her life. Residents from her building, other elderly people, were parked on the sidewalk in front, settled into folding chairs in the shade. Her first cousin Mickey was outside, too. He looked at us with a frown, clearly sad. I reached into a bag and handed him a pie.

"Here you go, Mick," I said.

"Nettie's pizza guina," he whispered with awe, and smiled.

That Sunday night I gathered in our dining room with our 16-year-old son and 11-year-old daughter as my wife brought in one of the pies, steaming hot and giving off a savory aroma, and set it in the center of the table. She sliced a wedge for each of us, and we ate, chewing slowly, with long pauses between forkfuls, to make the meal last. We ate the pie silently, rolling our tongues around each morsel, scraping our plates for crumbs to make sure we left nothing to waste.

With each bite I recalled with fresh clarity everything Nettie had meant to me, had meant to all of us. How we had seen the pies as symbols of her kindness and generosity. How she had prepared the pies with her own hands as if her life depended on it. How she had raised her daughter without a husband around, all while toiling as a seamstress in a factory for 47 years. How she'd never second-guessed me, her son-in-law, even though I sometimes acted like a jerk. How she had lavished love and attention, from first to last, on her adoring grandchildren.

I'd eaten her pie every spring for more than 20 years, and they had always tasted good. But now, flavored with grief, the pie tasted better than it ever had. It was as if I could somehow taste the essence of its maker, her spirit, her soul. I'd never felt so deeply my love and gratitude for her.

Afterwards, my wife waved us all into the kitchen. She opened the door to our freezer and pointed toward the back. And there it was: the last of the slices, the one labeled "Nettie." "This piece I'm saving," she said.

And so she has. And there it remains, forever frozen, untouched, unseen, but never forgotten.

Other families leave behind insurance policies or jewelry. But Nettie left us a wedge of her pie. As heirlooms go, it's enough. Its presence will feed our hearts year-round.

Playing The Score

"I got him," the kid on the basketball court says, pointing at you. We're choosing sides for a pickup game of three-on-three and you're now on his team.

"Who?" asks another teenager, unsure where he pointed.

"Him," the kid says, jabbing his finger toward you. "The old guy."

Okay, he's got you pegged. You say nothing, even though you half want to thank him for the motivational speech. Oh, at 56 you're hardly "old," of course. But here on this asphalt playground, you're the oldest guy on the court. By a lot. You're at least twice as old as your fellow competitors, and three times as old as some.

As the teams are formed, you imagine how the other players see you. You're all of 5-foot-10 and 160 pounds, balding and bespectacled, nothing discernibly athletic about you. You're going to be a pushover, they'll be thinking, all slow motion and arthritic joints. You'll get your sorry ass schooled but fast, then be taken to the nearest museum for carbon dating.

No matter. You're here on this sunny late afternoon in April to play hoops for pretty much the same reasons you've played for the past 48 years. To dash around and take shots and grab a rebound or two. For the action, the spontaneity, the jolt of adrenaline.

Now the contest begins. Right away you hit a 15-foot jumper. Then you steal the ball and pass to a cutting teammate for an easy basket. Your team takes a fast lead. You smile over at the kid who called you old.

Damn, you think, it's good to be old.

But then the tide slowly turns. Your defender guards you closer, his forearm leveraged against your lower back, forcing you to throw away a pass. Now he gets the ball and starts to drive to the basket. Your feet adjust to his move a split second later than your brain so instructs, and he blows past you for a layup. The other side pulls ahead.

A small crack appears in your ego. Certain familiar questions suddenly plague you. Have other players gotten better over the years, or are you getting worse? Or could it be both?

Hey, you think, you're 56. You've racked up serious miles on those legs of yours. It takes you longer to warm up than it used to. These days, you head home from hard games feeling as if your body just went through a carwash, but without the car. So maybe you should cut yourself a little slack. You're still competing respectably—for 56.

Hold on, what's this now? Sounds suspiciously like a new attitude. And it dawns on you that it most certainly is. You're engaging in a ploy that athletes call "playing the score." If you're well ahead in a contest, confident of winning, you ease up. If, on the other hand, you're lagging behind, you push harder. You synchronize your effort with your competitive status at the moment.

Your version of playing the score is different, though. You're rating your performance according to your age. Grading yourself on a curve. And thereby lowering your standards.

So this is what you've come to. Falling prey to this handy excuse, this rationalization, for below-par performance.

So, addressing this dilemma, you reassert yourself. You flick a bounce pass that leads to a score. You smack away an attempted shot and run down the ball. You're breathing hard now, trying to catch a second wind, a twinge in your lower back threatening to grow into real pain. Still, sweating heavily, getting shoved around, you pull yourself together. You drive the base line, hard, for a reverse lefty layup that draws high-fives from your teammates. And soon your team comes out on top.

Why you hung in there, going head to head, refusing to settle for diminishing returns, is simple: Your ego still requires more exercise than any muscle you own. You prefer to live by certain standards, whatever your age. As Arnold Schwarzenegger—asked about lifting weights as he got older—once put it, "A hundred pounds is always a hundred pounds."

Maybe someday you'll concede an inch or two to getting older. Settle for playing a little slower, compete only against other old guys. Only practical, right? After all, golf has handicaps expressly to level the playing field. Playing the score is human nature, yes?

Well, no, actually. For now it's still too soon.

You're guided in this belief by a recent incident. Last summer, after a matchup in this very park, a kid paid you the best compliment about your game that you're ever going to hear. First, he said you played well. Thanking him, you made a rare confession: that sometimes you feel old out there. Oh, no, the kid protested. You play young.

That's it right there, what you want above all. To play young, without letting your age define you. To forget the score.

Now the three players who waited on the side for winners step onto the court to face your threesome. "Come on, old guy," your teammate says to you, "let's do it again."

And, despite your fast-stiffening joints, you're ready for a new game. Ready for another chance to show these kids old.

Why Father Knows Least

When it comes to being a parent, I would like to believe that my performance with both of you kids over the years has proven to be absolutely perfect.

Big mistake.

For however much I might prefer to regard myself as unfailingly attentive, infinitely patient, endlessly understanding and wise beyond measure—the father of all fathers, a future Hall of Famer—I've more than likely turned out to be selfish, distracted, temperamental and just plain dense.

And that's on a good day.

As fathers go, in other words, I'm no dream. Take that time I yelled at both of you over nothing whatsoever.

No, not that time, the other time.

Then again, I'm probably no great nightmare, either.

The upshot is this: I've practiced parenthood for 33 years now, and if practice makes perfect, maybe this year I can finally get it right.

So here, in the interest of achieving the massive self-improvement needed, are my top five resolutions along those lines:

Pay closer attention. It's widely rumored that I may once in a while miss certain key details in conversation—though in retrospect, I forget exactly what they are. So the claim may well be valid, and I promise to tune into your numbers on the dial.

Give you some space. About 800 square feet should do the trick, I figure. No more rapid-fire cross-examinations about your latest activities, and definitely no more enhanced interrogation techniques to ascertain your career plans. You might find the extra elbow room, not to mention the extra breathing room, comes in handy.

Stop interrupting. See "pay closer attention."

Watch my tone. You often accuse me of coming off as sounding harsh and condescending. The only reasonable explanation for such a charge is that I probably do. So I'm going to take voice lessons. I may even practice scales. Come tomorrow, look for my much-improved B-flat.

Share less. By this point, I suspect you both know as much about me—my background, my opinions, my philosophy—as you could ever possibly care to know, and possibly a good deal more. So, in the interest of full disclosure, I'm occasionally going to clam up.

I could go on, of course. But instead, let's conduct a forensic audit a year from now to see how these resolutions pan out. And please remember: the difficult may be doable, but perfection might take some time. Still, if I've learned anything, it's that every day the impossible becomes more probable.

The Strangers We Know

They're all around us, throughout our neighborhoods and elsewhere. Some we may see every day, heading home from work or getting on a bus or walking a dog. They show up at all hours wherever we go.

They're the strangers we know, all the people we recognize, day after day and year after year, without ever exchanging a hello, much less a smile or a wave. As we go about our business, these passersby become elements of our everyday environment, the scenery that surrounds us.

I see this one guy in our apartment complex who goes out almost every day to run errands. Because he is ubiquitous, my wife and I dubbed him Hugh Biquitous.

Hugh and I have passed each other on the sidewalks and streets umpteen times over the decades. He looks at me, I look at him. Obviously we can identify one another. Yet neither of us says a word, let alone stops to chat.

So it is with so many others I regularly see. The woman who flits around early in the morning sprinkling water on our shrubs. The old man who toddles to the office every weekday carrying his briefcase, even though his entire torso leans to the left almost a foot. The window-washer equipped with the extra-long squeegee who swabs away at storefronts along our commercial stretch.

We all "know" such strangers, what the social psychologist Stanley Milgram in 1972 called "familiar strangers." Live somewhere long enough, and pay close enough attention, and you're guaranteed to be familiar with plenty of strangers on sight.

That's life in the big city. Here we get to know more strangers—these fixtures, these human landmarks, in our ever-evolving cityscape—than we ever would outside a metropolis. "Familiar strangers" compromise a kind of community, almost a hidden network.

Among strangers most of us adopt certain attitudes and behaviors, if only to preserve our sense of privacy and anonymity. That's why strangers as a whole typically engage in the ritual of looking at each other, then sharply turning away. Sociologist Erving Goffman called this "civil inattention," the act of acknowledging the presence of others without wishing further contact.

This phenomenon of mutual disregard is hardly tragic. No one can know everyone, nor do any of us even remotely want to. Most of us may have all the acquaintances in our lives we can handle for now.

Then again, our choice to remain strangers to the strangers we know may do us a disservice. Some of us may be left to guess about the backstories of these people, filling in the blanks with our imaginations. Otherwise we might learn that the old man with the crooked back goes to the office every weekday to take his mind off his crooked back.

At worst, though, we may turn suspicious and paranoid about the strangers we know. We may sense enemies everywhere. We may wonder if our next-door neighbor is up to some evil and about to go to war with the world.

Years ago, my wife and I often saw a man and woman, evidently a couple, strolling around our neighborhood in Queens on weekends, just as we were doing. They saw us, too. But for months all we ever exchanged were glances. Then one day we said hello, and they said hello back, and the next time we encountered each other we started a conversation. From then on, they invited us over for dinner every New Year's Day for more than 10 years.

Every friend starts as a stranger.

Come next year, maybe I'll start a new habit regarding the strangers I know. Maybe the next time I see Hugh Biquitous, I'll greet him with a cheery hello, maybe even smile and wave. He'll hear my voice for the first time, and perhaps I his. That could be my big social experiment for the year.

Now this well-intentioned gesture of congeniality, violating our unwritten rules as grossly it does, may well accomplish precisely nothing. Hugh might wind up considering

186 ❖ Bob Brody

me presumptuous or delusional. He might wonder if I'm running for president and just scrounging for votes.

Hey, that will be okay with me. At least I will have tried.

Please feel free to make of all this what you will. But let's ask ourselves a question. What if, against all odds and contrary to current practices and goody-goody as it sounds, we all promised ourselves to do the same, at least with certain strangers? What would happen?

I'll tell you what. We'd all come together just a little. Some of the strangers we know would, once and for all, be strangers no more.

How to Be Taken Seriously at the Office

It's finally time for me to come clean about another reason why I've now gone 16 years, three months, two weeks, five days, 17 hours and 33 minutes without getting promoted.

Here's a hint: it has to do with gravitas. Gravitas is defined as seriousness or sobriety in conduct and speech, and as behaving with enough dignity to win trust and respect. Gravitas is that aura of take-no-prisoners authority so obvious in CEOs, bail bondsmen and 300-pound NFL linebackers. Abraham Lincoln had it. So do John Kerry and John Boehner. Russell Crowe oozes gravitas, so much so that he has to keep a handkerchief handy for blotting. Gravitas shows you mean business.

Now, make no mistake: by any standard, I'm a model employee. I have a pulse, for example. I've always walked the Straight and Narrow, now designated in our office with a white line drawn along our corridors. My attitude on our vision-and-values test has rated off the charts. My memos are extremely well paginated. And, just in case of an audit, I've always alphabetized my paper clips. All of which are surely key criteria to success in any self-respecting organization.

Yet I clearly have issues here. I have no gravitas whatsoever. Nobody in our company listens to me without immediately yawning, for instance. In my last performance review, my supervisor told me he felt a sudden urge to take a nap, even though he was doing all the talking at that particular moment. Nobody here, for that matter, ever gives me the time of day, even if I actually ask for it. Yes, I once supervised someone, but he happened to be dead, so we never really counted that. Because I have next to no gravitas, all I've ever inspired is indifference. Colleagues consider me invisible.

"How can we promote you?" my supervisor once told me. "We can hardly see you."

So yes, I've long known I lacked certain characteristics essential to being management material. But I always assumed I was missing something more basic, like a spleen.

So, with my annual performance review coming up, I took action. I hired a personal certified gravitas consultant. He would give me a gravitas makeover. First, he ordered me to undergo an MRI to measure my GQ or Gravitas Quotient. He then informed me my GQ was less than is found in most two-year-olds. Give me two weeks, he promised, and you'll have more gravitas than Hannibal Lecter.

Fast forward two weeks. My first day back in the cubicle I share with two others, newly equipped with key learnings, I put on moves that loudly bespoke gravitas. Walked with a slight swagger. Looked people in the eye, keeping my gaze steady. Spoke deliberately, pausing often. Deepened my voice, my words barely a whisper. Tented my hands meaningfully.

Right away, colleagues came to hang on my every word, even the punctuation marks. Some even recognized me on sight. Senior executives responded to my e-mails without my having to beg or whimper. To all within earshot, every one of my recommendations now reeked of strategic soundness. Co-workers, noticing my transformation, had difficulty pinpointing just what might be different about me. Have you lost weight? they asked. Experienced a spiritual awakening? Received a personality implant?

My consultant tested me again and found my GQ now ranked me somewhere between the Pope and Vladimir Putin. Advancing finally to senior assistant administrative account coordinator, I took on the special privilege of supervising someone still living.

For a short spell, I sort of missed feeling inconsequential.

Ah, but within two months it all went awry. Our market research had revealed a new trend afoot, and so our corporate culture would have to change to stay competitive. Gravitas was history, and so we would all have to do a 180. Turns out I'd become too serious by half. And maybe this rings true for us all.

I would have to learn to lighten up.

Life On The Line

My friend Stanley refused to let me come see him die. "Please, no," he said. "I have to confront this on my own."

I lived only about 25 miles away, so could easily have driven to his home. But he had cancer now, at age 87, and soon would enter hospice care. "Are you sure?" I asked.

"Yes," he said.

I respected his wishes, so we talked on the phone instead. "How are you today?" I asked him a few days later.

"Beyond repair," Stanley said. "But how are you?"

"Just checking in here," I said on my next call.

"I'm in a state of decline," he said. "No doubt about it. It will only worsen. But please. Tell me about your successes."

I called him about twice a week—our talks might go 15 minutes or so—and he always answered the phone himself. His wife, who used to answer the phone, had died 10 years earlier.

"Do you prefer I call at any particular times?" I asked him.

"No," he said. "Morning. Afternoon. Night. Always glad to hear from you."

"The nurses who come here are wonderful," he volunteered a month or so later. "Taking good care of me." I heard a quaver of gratitude in his voice. Pictured the nurses feeding him, bathing him, dressing him.

"My rabbi sees me every week," he later told me. "He prays for me to find peace." I envisioned the rabbi at his bedside somberly delivering spiritual comfort with Stanley smiling.

My own father had died 14 years earlier, at age 70. It happened suddenly, with a massive heart attack on the kitchen floor. I never got a chance to say goodbye to him, except at his funeral, when I bent over his coffin and kissed his cold forehead. In visiting Stanley in the years since, and now, in talking with him over the phone, he had become, in effect, my old man.

My father could hear only about 10% of all sound and later wore a hearing aid that helped a little. In conversation, I often needed to repeat myself and either speak more slowly or try to enunciate more clearly in order to be understood. Much wound up lost in translation. Compounding our difficulties in communicating, my Dad never much listened to anyone anyway, neither his parents nor his wife or his two sisters, much less his own son.

Too proud, too independent, too damn stubborn.

Stanley, on the other hand, could hear perfectly well. And, as a bonus, he listened avidly. He always proved responsive, always asked questions, always took an interest in me and my doings.

"Please tell me if I'm calling you too often," I pleaded to him after a few months of caregiving delivered remotely. "I never want to be a bother."

"You're no bother," Stanley insisted. "Call as often as you like. I want you to."

He usually sounded pretty happy. But I wondered. Was this how he chose to sound to avoid sounding as you expect a dying person to sound?

Soon I felt him changing. "I'm terminal," he admitted. "There will be pain. And then that will be it." With each call his voice sounded fainter, as if he were drifting away.

He often coughed to clear his throat. Our conversations grew shorter. After only a few minutes, he would say, "Please excuse me, I better get off the line now."

Despite his mild, professorial demeanor, Stanley knew how to hang tough. He'd served in World War II. He'd outlived his wife by 10 years, a rare feat among elderly men.

"Let me come see you," I begged. "Just once. I'll be brief."

"No," he said. "This is for the best. Let's face it. It's all just a matter of time now. It's been a long haul and I'm getting tired of it. I'm tempted to close my eyes and let it be."

Maybe he wanted to spare me from seeing him suffer. Maybe he wanted to spare himself from seeing me see him suffer. Maybe both.

His family gathered around him in those final days, mainly his two daughters, his brother from San Francisco and his grandchildren. Friends he'd known much longer than he knew me saw him, too. But I never again came face to face with Stanley. All I could go do on the phone was listen to him die, deducing clues about his appearance, attuned to his every word, literally playing it by ear. His voice served as my eyes. All I could do was imagine how he looked there in his bedroom, during his last days, his already skinny frame losing weight, lifting a cup of tea to his lips with his hand trembling.

So went our long goodbye.

I had no idea, of course, which call to Stanley would be our last. Always I tried to tell him something he might value as useful, even enable him, however briefly, to forget his pain. News about my son and daughter moving ahead in life. The scene from "Curb Your Enthusiasm" where the Larry David character learns from his father, belatedly, that his mother has died.

"I'm lucky to have you as my friend," I said. "I feel the same," he replied.

And then, one day in April, 2011, I dialed his number. Only this time his youngest daughter answered. So be it. By then Stanley and I had already said everything we had to say to each other.

Almost, anyway.

The Derek Jeter Of Queens

Derek Jeter has nothing on my pal Al, who has delivered packages for UPS now for 24 years, nine months, two weeks and three days, give or take. Al's counting down to retirement.

No disrespect to Jeter. His stats over the last 20 years are so consistent as to be spectacular. He tops the Yankees all-time in at-bats and games played, among other categories, leaving Ruth, DiMaggio and Mantle in his dust. He's the definition of solid and reliable.

But Al has put up serious numbers, too. He delivers an average of 200 packages a day. He racks up about 150 stops per shift, with his feet logging roughly 10 miles. All day he picks stuff up and puts it down, tons and tons of boxes, to bring goods ordered to customers on his route. Put his picture in the dictionary next to the words "busting your hump."

Jeter, now 40, is more than merely a baseball player, of course. He's the gold standard for behaving with modesty beyond reason. He's always treated his fans right, no less so off the field than on. He's the ultimate professional, long ago recognizing that his responsibilities extend far beyond driving in runs and getting his pegs to first base before the batter arrives there.

But Al, at 51, is more than a UPS delivery guy, too. He's taken the time to get to know everyone on his route in Forest Hills and everyone has gotten to know him, too. Walk with him along Queens Boulevard or Austin Street or Ascan Avenue for five minutes, whether he's in or out of uniform, and someone will come over to say hi. He's made a practice of going above and beyond the call of duty, ever ready with a smile and a big hello to talk with anyone at any time about anything, delivering good cheer along with most every package.

We look up to Jeter for a lot of reasons, of course. But now that he's sidelined himself from pinstripes for life, we fully appreciate his staying power. He's punched in at shortstop for two decades to take his cuts against the latest rookie with a 95-mile-an-hour fastball and snag line drives that appeared destined for left field. He's plain outworked everyone else and paid his dues 1,000 times over.

My pal Al's long-term performance deserves credit, too. He's driven his truck through rain and fog and snowstorms. He's put his back and legs into every lift and drop, pounding his feet flat and pulling muscles he probably never knew existed. He's carried those boxes to your door until he emptied his truck. He could have collected his paycheck every week without ever smiling, much less befriending so many of his customers. But he's treated his job as more than just a job.

By nature we marvel at anyone with the will and stamina and work ethic to get a job done over the long haul. Such exemplars serve as stand-ins for all the rest of us who, often against all odds, whether a recession or just hard luck, somehow manage to keep going.

Getting older ourselves invariably sharpens our appreciation for longevity. Ronald Reagan attained the presidency just shy of age 70, the oldest ever to occupy the Oval

Office, then served two terms. Pablo Picasso kept painting masterpieces into his 90s. Nolan Ryan pitched his seventh and last no-hitter at the improbably advanced age of 44.

So please do me a small favor. Just as you bade farewell to Jeter, take a moment to wish Al well on his final rounds. But let's also toast all the Als out there, all across the city, all across the country, all the graying teachers and firefighters and doctors and lawyers and accountants.

They, too, have stayed with it. They, too, are still going strong. As Jeter himself might be the first to acknowledge, they, too, have delivered.

A Phone Call To The Future

Back in 1964, my mother, father, sister and I drove from our split-level colonial house in suburban New Jersey to Flushing Meadows Park in Queens, New York, the site of the World's Fair, where we caught a glimpse of the future.

There, we entered the Bell Telephone pavilion at the northeast end of the site. We planned to witness the exhibit that would demonstrate a rumored-about revolutionary marvel. The Picturephone, also known as the Mod or Model 1—a telephone that enabled you, as if via television, to see the person taking your call at the other hand of the line.

My father and I stepped into one of the booths at the exhibit while my mother and sister went into another. We each sat in chairs placed in front of an oval device containing a small camera and a rectangular video screen. A cable connected the picture unit to a touch-tone telephone handset with buttons to control the screen.

To make the call, my father pressed a button marked "V" for video on a touch-tone telephone keypad, and my mother and sister appeared on the screen.

Our eyes wide and mouths agape in wonder, we waved in our excitement at one another. We then talked through a speakerphone for the next 10 minutes.

The device struck me, even then, at only age 12, as vastly more than merely a charming science-fiction novelty. If it ever became available in the homes of the general public, it would have far-reaching implications for all kinds of people, but especially for members of the deaf community.

Both my parents were profoundly deaf. My father had some residual hearing, enough so that he could, with a hearing aid, handle phone calls and other interactions, but he was generally out working. My mother could never use a standard telephone. And so she usually relied on me, her oldest child, to serve as her interpreter when she needed to call friends, relatives and neighbors and make arrangements by phone.

It was a service I often performed grudgingly, resentful at getting pulled away from playing with my toy soldiers or reading the sports pages or watching "Superman" on TV. Most often, the calls my mother asked me to make were to her mother in Manhattan. Since this was usually to schedule visits, I would have to navigate back and forth, conveying logistical information.

My mother always thanked me for the calls afterward, both vocally and in sign language. She would bring her palm flat near her lips and then toward me, as if blowing a kiss.

But after the World's Fair, all I could imagine was what a difference a Picturephone would make—to my mother and to me too. *If only such a creation could actually come to be,* I thought. With a videophone at her fingertips, my mother could just press "V" and call her mother, reading lips, as she was skilled at doing, to comprehend. She could connect with her younger brother in Long Island. She could ring up her friends throughout New Jersey any time she wanted, carrying on a conversation over the airwaves in fluent sign language. What's more, she could contact the police in case of an emergency. Or the fire department. Or a hospital.

Could such a miracle ever happen?

As it turned out, the Picturephone was impractical for home usage, and Bell never put it into widespread production.

Other, better solutions have come along, making the Picturephone seem hopelessly outdated. Deaf people are no longer anywhere near as isolated from each other and the hearing world anymore. Closed-captioning for television became widely available in the 1970s. So did teletypewriters adapted with a modem to run over phone lines. Cochlear implants have attuned those previously unable to hear to sound. And video chats via cellphones, tablets and computers are today simple and inexpensive.

As it has turned out, the future I wished for as a boy has arrived. My mother, now 87 and living in Thousand Oaks, California, relies on a phone that connects to her television and functions through a video-relay service available to those with hearing impairments. In effect, a Picturephone.

As a result, my mother converses in sign language regularly and easily with people thousands of miles away, hands slicing and swooping through the air. She stays in touch with her childhood friends, Ruth and Alice, both profoundly deaf and still living back in New Jersey. Smiling and laughing and blowing kisses to each other, they talk about growing up in the Bronx and bring one another up to date on grandchildren and other family news. People unable to sign can call her service, and an operator appears on the screen, signing what the caller says to her and relaying responses back to the caller.

Reality has finally caught up with fantasy.

"The videophone makes a big difference in my life," she recently told me. "Before, when you were a little boy, I always had to ask for your help. Now I feel independent, just like everyone else."

The Addict Next Door

About a year ago, barely awake after an afternoon nap, I heard a male voice call out. "Michael, get up, Michael. *Breathe.*"

Our son is named Michael. For a moment, while still in a fog, I imagined the worst. But I realized the voice had come from another apartment.

"Michael," the man pleaded. "Get up, Michael. *Breathe.*" The husky voice repeated the words, but with growing distress.

I opened our front door and stepped into the hallway and saw the door to the next apartment open. I knocked.

"Who is it?"

"Your neighbor. Can I help?"

"It's my son."

I entered, and in the living room I saw the father kneeling on the floor and leaning over his son, who lay sprawled on his back, his eyes closed and arms out to his side.

"What happened?"

"He just collapsed."

"Did you call an ambulance?"

"It should be here soon."

"What do you think is wrong with him?"

"Wish I knew."

With that, the father, about 55 or 60 years of age, bent back over his son, maybe 35 or so.

"Michael, wake up. *Wake up*, Michael."

He brought his face close to his son, clasping the sides of his head.

Then, without warning, the young man opened his eyes wide, as if surprised still to be alive. He glanced around the room in confusion, as if wondering what had happened to him, and recognized his father.

"Dad?"

"Michael," he gasped. "Oh, Michael." He clutched his son by the face with his hands, forehead pressed to forehead. "You're all right. "You're all right."

A few weeks later, I encountered the father in the hall. "I never thanked you," he said. "So thank you."

"How's your son doing?"

"Better."

I wanted to ask what had happened to him. But I decided against it. It was none of my business, I realized, even though my appearance weeks earlier had already made it my business. Besides, if the father had any interest in telling me, I reasoned, he would.

Some months later, heading down the hall to our apartment, I saw the son heading towards his door. He looked different, definitely thinner, almost unrecognizable.

"Glad to see you're doing okay," I said.

"Thanks," he said with a faint smile.

Again, I felt the impulse to ask what had happened to him. Again, I decided it was none of my business. Evidently father and son just wanted to be left alone.

Then came mid-September, a Tuesday at about two in the morning. From our living room, I heard a voice through the wall that adjoins our apartment to the neighbor next door. The voice sounded angry.

I went back to watching television, expecting the yelling to stop. But 15 minutes later, it was still going. I pressed my ear against the wall to hear better.

Something about a business deal.

Something about international travel.

Something about millions of dollars.

It was the son ranting, cursing, clearly anguished. Maybe some Wall Street merger had gone wrong. Someone tried to console him, probably his father.

I kept eavesdropping, remembering full well the son splayed unconscious on the floor a year before, alert for any sign of emergency. With the wall between us, his voice was muffled, and I could make out only a few words here and there. I felt strange spying, but felt I should just in case I might be needed.

Then I heard the word "Vicodin."

And then the word "methadone."

For a second I felt compelled to go next door again. But I had done no tangible good then—such gestures of concern are still only gestures—and doubted I could do any real good now either. So I stayed home. The son stopped screaming. I went to sleep.

From inside our apartment at about 11 the next morning I heard a walkie-talkie out in our hallway crackle and hiss. Through the peephole I saw a police officer pounding at the front door next to ours. Outside, in front of our building, the lights on an ambulance flashed red.

Through the peephole I saw the father come out.

"It's my son," he told the officer. "He's dead."

"An overdose?"

"Yes, an overdose."

The police officer went into the apartment. The father stood in the hallway alone and started to sob.

"My son is dead," he said to himself. "My son Michael is dead."

I could have stepped into the hall and tried to comfort him. He was roughly my age and his son, another Michael, about the same age as ours. But I stayed behind my closed door. This was now a matter for the police, I decided. It was none of my business.

From the window in our living room I saw the ambulance in front of our building, the technicians rolling out a gurney.

Afterwards I learned what had happened. Some weeks later, finally mustering the nerve, I went next door to offer the father my condolences and try to console him. I told him what I had seen and heard. The father then recounted the episode.

The son, who held an important position at a bank in midtown Manhattan, putting in long hours under heavy pressure to make big money on big projects, had gotten fired that morning. His addiction to opioids had hurt his performance and finally cost him his job. Security escorted him from his office building.

He was just then only a week away from finishing at a six-week detox program, where he received counseling and took drug treatment every day to counter his dependency, and recovery appeared likely.

He cried telling his father he had lost his job. He had once spent two years unemployed. "How am I ever going to start over again?" the son asked him the night I heard him raving.

That night, at about 3 a.m., the son told his father he needed to go get something he had left in his car. The father assured him plenty of good jobs out there awaited him and he would find something soon. They hugged and kissed and said good night to each other.

But while the father slept, his son went out to score heroin. The son got high—higher, the father told he believed, than he intended—and overdosed. At about 10 that morning the father found his son slumped in his bed, dead.

"I miss my son," the father told me, his words catching in his throat. "Every day I relive what happened. It never gets easier."

Maybe I could have saved him. Maybe I should have knocked on the door the night before to ask what was going on and how I might help. Maybe I should have noticed the warning signs.

But what could I have done? What *should* I have done? What can any of us do?

How are we supposed to know?

Sometimes, of course, our neighbors just want to be left alone. Sometimes what happens next door may just be none of our damn business.

Then again, we live in a city, a big city, the second most populous city on the planet, and even though we lead our private lives—so seldom looking each other in the eye as we pass on the street, so often acting as if we're all on our own and need no one else and would rather keep to ourselves, minding our own business, our instinct for self-preservation prevailing—sometimes we get involved and try to lend a hand to someone who might be in need.

And that's because, when you get right down to it, whether we're in our apartments or an office or a subway car, all our walls ultimately adjoin.

Getting Personal

Some years ago, I took long walks on the beach in Long Island with my daughter Caroline, then still only a little girl. We would climb onto the breakers and step gingerly across jagged rocks as surf splashed all around us. I would clutch her hand to prevent her from slipping into the ocean. But one day, because years had passed and she was suddenly old enough, she let go. She sought to establish her independence.

Naturally, I wrote an essay about the episode. I say "naturally" because I've long written personal essays. I started with my high school and college newspapers and kept going at my first real job, with a weekly community newspaper in Manhattan. One thrilling day, shortly after I turned 26, my firsthand account of getting stabbed in my East Village apartment appeared on the Op-Ed page of *The New York Times*.

Early on in my career, while freelancing full-time for 10 years, I turned out only a few essays. I needed to earn a paycheck, and that meant being practical, and practical meant pursuing assignments under contract. Essays are almost invariably done on spec, and so are anything but practical as business models go. Then, after I took a full-time job, in public relations, I focused all the more on making a living.

In recent years, though, I committed myself anew to the personal essay. Maybe it's because I found myself officially old enough to have a past, and also more inclined than ever to reflect on my life, and might even have figured I finally have something to say and now may even know how to say it.

I write personal essays because I tend to take life personally.

Doing personal essays is hardly easy, of course. First, I have to decide what to write. My key criterion: it should be singular, a song I alone can sing. I list my ideas, letting each one gestate, then deliberate to determine priority. I choose the one gnawing most persistently at my ankle.

Then my job is to craft an essay that excels. That's a given. Enough said about that—except that the process tends to involve burrowing around in my intestines, the better to sniff out a universal truth or two.

Only then do I encounter the anxieties of the marketplace. I submit my piece to an editor who never asked to see it in the first place, much less expected or necessarily desired it. I keep track of what I've submitted where and the reaction, if any.

Sometimes 10 publications will say "no," or offer only radio silence, before I happen across one that says "yes." Or pieces will miss the cut everywhere, doomed to languish unpublished for years, possibly for all time—even the ones I once presumed to regard among my best. Sometimes I feel discouraged, sure my most recent piece will be my last.

Because the genre has infinite flexibility, I enjoy creative carte blanche.

Chances are, I'll never be as skilled as E.B. White. Nor as rich as Warren Buffet. But you'll hear no whimpering from me. On those occasions when it all clicks—when I've addressed the right topic, adopted the right style, found the right editor—the rewards approach the sublime. I get my say about a matter close to my heart. I might also unearth a reality or two about my identity and what my life has meant.

If I'm really lucky, I might even inspire a response from one of those readers, as happened with the piece on Caroline letting go of my hand. Yes, a reader told me, I never realized it before, but that's how it was for me and my daughter, too. That's it exactly.

RIP: All The Stories I Never Wrote

One of these days I was going to write a serious essay about what I call the strangers we know. Those are the people we often see around our neighborhoods or offices, but never say hello to, much less learn the names of or get to be friendly with.

Eventually I was also going to do a serious piece about my pal Al. I would address how I've come to appreciate, rather belatedly, the true nature of friendship—all about how you really have to be a friend in order to make and keep a friend.

Deep, existential stuff, clearly Pulitzer material. Through the miracle of literary alchemy, I was going to turn ordinary everyday specifics into profound universal lessons.

Those stories might have turned out okay, too. But I decided against pursuing either one. Just ditched the concepts cold. And I may never change my mind either.

So it's gone in my 43-year career as a professional writer. I'll dream up an idea and get all giddy about carrying it out, only to see a "Stop" sign in my head and opt out instead.

History is strewn with examples of poets, playwrights, memoirists, essayists and short story writers pulling the plug. The list of authors who abandoned novels alone is notably long: John Updike, Stephen King, Truman Capote, Junot Diaz, Evelyn Waugh, Michael Chabon, Harper Lee, Richard Price, Saul Bellow, and Nikolai Gogol, among others. Works that never materialized could likely fill the Library of Congress.

By the way, FYI, I was always going to get around to writing some funny pieces, too. For example, an imaginary conversation between Chicken Little and The Boy Who Cried Wolf. They were going to be playing one-upmanship in the suspicion and paranoia departments.

I also felt destined, in due course, to do a satirical take on a distinguished U.S. senator who had long kept a dirty secret. He would decide to announce, after years of living in the closet and feeling abnormal and ashamed about his true identity, that he's finally coming out as bipartisan.

Truly hysterical material, the kind guaranteed to make Mark Twain envious. But no. I elected to nix those little conceits, too.

We writers have to go through this drastic weeding-out process, even if it means saying yes to an idea, then no and feeling as if we're two-timing ourselves. When it comes to excuses, otherwise known as explanations, we've got a million.

Maybe we've forgotten what originally infatuated us about it. Or suddenly doubt we can do justice to it. Or lack the time and energy needed. Or have higher priorities, such as eating and sleeping. After all, nobody can write everything.

In my case, the list of all the pieces I've decided against writing gets longer every decade. Let me now perform a sort of last rites.

I'm never going to write about all the major events that happened to take place in the world on the day I was born, or about how life is going for all the other guys out there also named Bob Brody, or about the inventor of the sound bite (who would turn out to be surprisingly long-winded), or about little-known voicemails in history (such as Romeo repeatedly leaving messages for Juliet). And that's just for starters.

Now, no doubt you've participated in brainstorms governed by the operating principle that no idea is a bad idea. That idea may in and of itself be the single worst idea of all time. Make no mistake: Bad ideas exist. Bad ideas abound. Bad ideas should be left to die aborning.

The trick, of course, is telling which ideas are which.

The upshot is this: No matter how much we expect to accomplish with our lives, however high we aim, it inevitably dawns on us that we're each given just so much time. So, if only in the interest of survival if not sanity, we must negotiate with ourselves, scale back our ambitions, accept our limitations and, yes, find peace. For a writer, this is no more and no less true than it is for anyone else.

And that's okay. Leaving certain business unfinished creates room for other, perhaps more promising projects. It's taken me a long time to learn this—that sometimes the best course of action is inaction, that even the best-intentioned projects can be misguided, and that a life well lived sometimes consists of mistakes you never gave yourself a chance to make.

So when you get right down to it, I'm probably never going to write all those pieces I just mentioned, as well as numerous others unmentioned.

Unless, of course, I should.

In which case, come to think of it, maybe I will.

The Party Of Yes

In the eight years I knew Jeffrey Zaslow, the best-selling author and *Wall Street Journal* columnist who died in a car accident in 2012, I gave him plenty of opportunities to demonstrate his tendency to say "yes."

Would you read an essay of mine about my mother? I would ask him.

Yes, he would say.

May we talk about a book idea I have in mind? I would ask.

Yes.

Almost two years ago, I told him about my plan to start my first blog. Would he be a member of my board of advisors? I asked him.

"Yes," he said. "Of course."

Just as I specialized in soliciting favors from him, Jeff, in turn, excelled at granting me those favors.

After I was laid off from a job in 2008, I asked Jeff and others I knew to keep an eye out for new opportunities for me. He immediately offered to give me job references and to steer me toward freelance assignments. But above and beyond almost everyone else I contacted, he also promised to make himself available to talk.

Throughout our relationship, Jeff encouraged me to pursue my ambitions as a writer. You should submit that piece about your father, he would say. You should definitely write that memoir about your family. "You're a great writer," he told me—and even though I never doubted his sincerity, somehow I could never quite believe him.

In his articles and books, Jeff wrote about what matters most. Love and loss. Family and friendship. All the personal stuff that happens while we're out there making a living and trying to earn enough and wondering which suit to wear to a presentation—or, for that matter, how to recruit someone for your blog's advisory board. He wrote about how we treat each other and also about how we feel, in our heart of hearts, about how we treat each other.

We never met face to face. I knew Jeff only through his writings and our frequent e-mail exchanges and occasional phone conversations. Ours was more a professional friendship than a deeply personal one. Yet his inherent compassion and generosity and humanity always came through loud and clear.

Still, as far as I could tell, Jeff Zaslow never stopped saying "yes." He said yes to my numerous, and often presumptuous, requests of him. He said yes to the singular responsibility of telling powerfully the stories of people with powerful stories to tell, whether it was Professor Randy Pausch in "The Last Lecture" or Gabrielle Giffords in "Gabby." He said yes to being a husband and a father and a son and a friend. He said yes to being alive.

If Jeff had ever become a political party, he would have qualified as the party of yes.

Only on one front did I ever have trouble getting him to say his favorite word. I invited him to contribute a guest column to my blog for Thanksgiving, all about his gratitude for his children. But he had just undergone minor surgery and was trying to finish writing his book about hero pilot Chesley "Sully" Sullenberger, *Highest Duty: My Search For What Really Matters*, so he begged off with an apology.

A few months later I asked him again, this time for Father's Day. Again, he took a pass, saying he was in over his head.

Then Jeff reverted back to form. He had let me know about his latest book, *The Magic Room: A Story About the Love We Wish for our Daughters*. Sensing yet another opportunity to advance my personal agenda, I sought for the third time to enlist him as a guest columnist for my blog. Maybe, I suggested, he could write a piece about why he wrote a book about daughters. He could cast it as a letter to his own three daughters.

"Yes," he said.

Giving Is The New Getting

A few years back, I caught wind of a pending newspaper article. A workplace reporter needed insights into finding employees who excel at customer service.

As it happened, I knew just the source, the manager of a diner I frequented in Queens, NY. I'd once complimented him on his ever-obliging staff and asked his secret. Hire people who genuinely like serving others, he informed me.

An interview I set up resulted in an article that ran, perchance, on USA Today's front page. The manager was quoted to good effect, with an accompanying photo of the diner. That piece hangs in a frame near the cashier to this day.

It's fun to do this sort of public relations—pro bono, of course, but also ad hoc, privately and independently—especially if it's unsolicited and thus unexpected, like a surprise birthday party.

In my 25-year career in PR, I've proven to be sort of incorrigible in this respect. I've promoted our local synagogue, whether for the cantor's retirement or for its annual book sale. I've represented an acquaintance who wound up imprisoned, in my mind wrongfully so, for selling apricot pits on the Internet as a cancer cure. I've championed the borough of Queens, the most ethnically diverse place on the planet.

Just last year, I pitched my long-time pal Al, a driver for UPS and, in the bargain, unofficial mayor of Forest Hills. Al had teamed up with his son Nicholas to handle deliveries from his truck during the year-end holiday season, forming possibly the only such father-son partnership in UPS history. *The New York Daily News* ran a full-page column.

None of which, by the way, qualifies me for the Nobel Peace Prize.

Still, I encourage you to resolve to do likewise. Take some time to conduct similar drive-by, grassroots advocacy. Of course, many of us are already committed to volunteering for Corporate Social Responsiblity initiatives and crusade for certain causes on behalf of our agencies and our clients. But I'm talking here about a different order of public affairs.

A lot of our neighbors and local institutions—cops, teachers, schools, libraries, parks, doormen, merchants—are unable to afford PR. But they're no less deserving of public attention and acclaim. In leveraging your talents, you'll keep your chops sharp and deliver good deeds to better your community.

As resolutions go, you could do worse.

Exit Lines

"I'm choking on a bitter pill/Quite terminally I am ill."

So wrote Stanley Siegelman, my friend of 30 years, as he lay dying at his home, a house in Great Neck, Long Island.

"In hospice now I am enrolled/My waning days with speed unfold," he went on. The 20-line poem is a thank-you to the health professionals caring for him: "They rescue me from the abysss/Bestowing kindness like a kiss."

Little wonder, then, that as cancer came to him, he kept at his poetry. No surprise, either, that as he struggled to stay alive, he also kept his tongue securely in his cheek.

"The metal stent was heaven-sent," he wrote in praise of his cardiologist, "Thanks to the stent/I'm still extant."

He also wrote, "My cancer, that villain, is planning to kill/One day, in its fury, it certainly will!/Its targeted victim I happen to be/The reason's elusive—but hey, c'est la vie!"

In 2009, in a poem formatted as a memo to his physicians, Stanley managed to make light of yet another surgery. With just one kidney left, he wrote, "Nonetheless I have derived/Great joy from having just survived!"

Even in the face of pain, even as he turned inward to contemplate his imminent demise, he gave in to gallows humor and stayed free of self-pity. At every turn, just as he always had among others, he deflected attention, by his own reckoning just a supporting player in the eternal drama of the universe.

But soon enough his poems reflected an attitude that grew understandably grave. He anticipated, for example, eventually being referred to as "the late" Stanley Siegelman. He mentioned his own funeral, but with his trademark modesty he cautioned his mourners-to-be, "No need to over-dramatize/or overlong to eulogize."

His levity, for so long his lifeline—the signature feature of birthday cards to family and friends, including me—is suddenly evident no more. A new poem opens declaring, "I mourn the loss of one whose heart still beats/I practice now bereavement in advance." It then goes on to contemplate his departure with the existential question, "Is ending a beginning, but disguised?"

The next year, still hanging in there, Stanley returned to this reality-versus-illusion theme. He likened himself to a runner who has "traveled far, at fully measured length," only to ask, "But what awaits him now, and in what guise? . . . The darkness/is it sunset or daybreak?"

In due course, my friend was too weak to type his efforts on the electric Smith Corona typewriter he used for decades, so he composed his poems by hand. His final verses, found by his family in a file folder, have remained unpublished until now.

The week after Stanley died, *The Forward* published the last poem he submitted there. "It will come, I know, as no surprise/(I speak, of course, of my demise)," he wrote. "The signs abound, for all to see/A curtailed life expectancy." He went on: "And if my reasoning is sound/ I'll soon be resting underground/ 'At times he made some people laugh'/ Might constitute my epitaph."

As it turned out, Stanley confronted his death as he had confronted his life—by writing about it. Writing was how he looked death in the eye, how he came to a what-will-be-will-be acceptance of his fate. In doing so, he shone a flashlight in his future, illuminating the darkness that may lay ahead for all of us.

PLAYING CATCH WITH STRANGERS ❖ 203

"Writing was his main mode of communication," his daughter Karen once told me. "It was his way of coping with his dire situation. . . He wanted to prepare all of us to accept the fact that he was going to die."

So many poets have delivered deathbed poetry, of course, from William Butler Yeats ("I lie awake night after night/And never get the answers right") and Alfred Lord Tennyson ("The stream will cease to flow/The wind will cease to blow/The clouds will cease to fleet/The heart will cease to beat") to Sylvia Plath ("Hooves, dolorous bells/All morning the/Morning has been blackening") and John Updike ("I see clear through to the ultimate page/the silence I dared break for my small time").

In showing us how to die, they also showed us how to live. What we say going out the door matters.

Stanley knew full well that in crafting his valedictories, a rhyme in his heart pulsing away right to the very end, he was honoring a long literary tradition. And so in one of his final acts, he implicitly acknowledged that his own contribution to this hallowed heritage would be forever humble at best.

He left behind a note that directed his two adult daughters to read only after his death. The note instructed that they go to the book shelves in his bedroom, locate a specific book and then turn to a certain page to read. There, they found Sonnet 71, courtesy of William Shakespeare.

"No longer mourn for me when I am dead," it begins. "Then you shall hear the surly sullen bell/Give warning to the world that I am fled." The author urges those left behind to forget him, even to stop saying his name and loving the life he led, "Lest the wise world should look into our moan/and mock you with me after I am gone."

Clearly Stanley felt Shakespeare had gotten death right, better than ever had and better than he ever would. And so he gave him the last word.

Requiem For A Bookstore

A girl about five years old sits splayed on the hardwood floor with Dr. Seuss. A teenage boy in a hoodie checks out the young-adult fiction. A white-haired man flips through a military history.

They're all visiting the Barnes & Noble on Austin Street in Forest Hills, Queens on a recent Saturday afternoon. And right now the joint is jumping. Awaiting attention from three cashiers are 11 customers standing on line. Ten more customers occupy solid wooden chairs near the escalator on the second floor, sampling the wares.

But seeing is deceiving, as James Joyce once wrote. For soon this book store, here at

204 ❖ Bob Brody

this location since 1995—across from the New York Sports Club, just down the block from a Chipotle, and all of three blocks from where I live—will close shop. The rent is going to triple, and Target will move in. A petition to save the 21,000-square-foot store, signed by 5,700 local residents, went for nought.

In 2015, Barnes & Noble closed its branch in Fresh Meadows, and did the same with its store in Bayside in 2016, leaving the chain unrepresented in Queens. The borough is home to 2.3 million residents, equivalent in population to the nation's fourth largest city after Los Angeles.

Just four years earlier, the Borders book store in Atlas Park Mall, in Glendale, Queens, announced its closing. I witnessed its last days, seeing everything marked down, even its fixtures for sale, its shelves now half empty, some aisles closed off with tape as if for a crime scene complete with chalk outline. The sight put me in mind of that scene in "The Time Machine," by H.G. Wells, when our intrepid inventor, who has traveled to the distant future, is thrilled to discover a library, a sign of culture preserved. He picks up a book, only for its pages, long unread, to crumble into dust in his hand.

Back in the 1980s, Forest Hills actually had two book stores, a rarity for any single neighborhood, especially in Queens. A Waldenbooks and a B. Dalton Books faced each other on Continental Avenue, just off Queens Boulevard.

Let me come clean about my bias here: I grew up kind of drunk on books. I once dreamt as a boy about bullies pursuing me with ill intent, only to find myself behind a glass wall in a room surrounded with books, now protected from harm. My grandparents had a den handsomely showcasing the hard-cover best-sellers of the day.

Back in the 1960s, my Nana took me by the hand to the cathedral-like Scribner book store on Fifth Avenue, with its Beaux Arts vaulted ceilings and magisterial black wrought-iron gates, and then, just yards away, to the Brentano's, too—landmarks gone since the 1980s and all too likely largely forgotten as well.

While a college student, I drove over the Washington Bridge from our home in New Jersey with my literary-minded friends expressly for trips to the fabled Gotham Book Mart, with its illustrious pedigree as a literary hangout, plus the Strand and Shakespeare & Company and all those other book stores scattered throughout Greenwich Village.

Call me sentimental, but every year I watch that "Twilight Zone" episode with Burgess Meredith as a meek bank teller smitten with books but doomed never to read all he wants. Occasionally I reread *Fahrenheight 451*, by Ray Bradbury, about a futuristic society intent on banning books. In my favorite scene, people who have secretly and illicitly committed whole books to memory go around in the woods reciting the texts.

Yes, bookstores are closing everywhere. But must this last bookstore close, too, leaving Queens virtually bookless? Forgive me if I take this personally.

Hey, business is business. Duly noted, fully understood, much appreciated. We all have to make a living.

The Barnes & Noble in Forest Hills has evolved over the years, heeding the call of the marketplace to cater to shifting demographics and tastes and new technologies. A section devoted to games and toys materialized. An outpost for promoting the Nook took root. Shelves set aside for all the major literary periodicals shrank by more than half, making room for lifestyle magazines.

Still, books are books. Books are different from toaster ovens. Books are meant to be cradled in your hand. To have pages you can turn with your fingertips. To have words printed in ink. To be opened in a delirium of anticipation and closed with a jolt of satisfaction. We often visit book stores with the best of motives, in a quest for stories, insights, the truth, meaning.

And right now the joint is jumping. Young and old, male and female, native New Yorkers and recent immigrants, even a police officer in full uniform—they amble among the genres and scan the shelves, heads tilted to read book titles sideways. Maybe the place will make a few dollars today.

But later everything here will change, and later is due to arrive soon. Within two weeks, some of the book shelves will turn bare and a few of the magazine racks will be gone. Books long since discounted will be marked down another 40%. Already the deathbed scenario is playing out. And by December 31, this book store will be no more than an image in my memory.

Later, maybe some bibliophile—civic-minded, entrepreneurial and well-capitalized—will see an opportunity to step into the breach and open an independent book store along Austin Street. That could be nothing but a pipedream. But if books teach us anything, it's that we should dream. After all, I recently learned that next June will bring about the first-ever Queens Book Festival.

For now, though, a girl of about six is tugging her father down an aisle. "I want the book with the elephant!" she calls out. "It will help me learn to read!" He follows her obligingly. "Oh, it's right here!" she cries out. "It's right here! We should buy it!"

The Big Thank You

I never thanked my 10th-grade English teacher for getting me interested in literature. I also never thanked my first boss for hiring me for my first job out of college. Nor have I gone back to thank my first girlfriend for granting me, at age 12, my first romantic kiss.

On Thanksgiving, of course, we're all on board with the tradition of expressing gratitude. We may clasp our hands in prayer and offer words of thanks to God. We may each take a turn at the dinner table to reveal the reasons why we're so thankful this year, praising our families, friends and colleagues while acknowledging appreciation for our health, our jobs and just being alive.

But seldom do any of us engage in directly thanking each other—the act of singling out a person expressly to say "Thank you, you made a difference in my life," complete with a detail or two about exactly why.

As in: Thank you for being my wife and the mother of our children, and especially for making our family your top priority.

As in: Thank you for being my friend, particularly for taking me out to lunch in 2007 because you knew I felt low and listening to me complain about my job for an hour.

We instinctively recognize gratitude to be a force for good. Ancient Greek and Roman philosophers cited gratitude as an important virtue. Studies at the universities of Utah and Michigan show it's healthy both to show and to receive gratitude—the heart and brain appear to function more harmoniously.

Yet all too many of us have limited our use of the words "thank you." We mistakenly assume all the people we care most about already know full well that we appreciate everything they've done. We suffer from a gratitude deficit.

As it happens, last Thanksgiving I launched a personal project to correct the record once and for all. I vowed to personally thank, at least once a week for the next year, someone to whom I felt I owed gratitude.

To start small, I approached my favorite doorman to thank him for taking such good care of our family over the decades. He placed his hand near his heart and thanked me right back for being among his favorite tenants. We hugged each other right there in the lobby.

More ambitiously, I called a former boss of mine to thank her for all her guidance over the years, but especially for refusing to hold a grudge against me after she gave me a big raise and I responded—with egregious ingratitude—"I thought we could do better." Unable to get her on the line, I left her a voice mail, but never heard back. I'm convinced she dismissed my well-intentioned overture as a misguided prank.

But quickly my little plan to acknowledge everyone deserving of thanks ran out of gas. Life intervened—job, family, television, sleep; you know the drill—and suddenly I lacked enough time to follow through. And so even though I got around to thanking some more people -- my Uncle Leonard, my pal Al, my colleague Brian—many more figures in my life, major and minor alike, wound up decidedly unthanked.

Today, however, I hereby renew my pledge. I'm going to track down all those special someones to deliver my special thank-yous. Once again my purpose is simply to do right by people who have meant the most to me—and yes, to clear my conscience over my previous failure to do so. After all, sometimes by going back, we can better move ahead.

Suppose everyone on the planet made a similar promise: a commitment to give people a heartfelt, highly specific thank-you. Parents and teachers would thus be duly honored. Friends and colleagues would feel forever connected. So would grandparents, coaches, customers and, for that matter, former girlfriends and boyfriends. This simple gesture—saying thank you, you matter to me—would promote a needed sense of belonging, a welcome spirit of unity.

And so I propose a public-service campaign. We could recruit celebrity spokespeople talented at expressing gratitude—Steven Spielberg comes to mind; his "Saving Private Ryan" and "Schindler's List" are strong in depicting gratitude. Enlist Miss Manners to issue guidelines about following the right etiquette. Stage thank-you free-for-alls in communities nationwide. Hold contests to determine who is thanked the most and who has thanked the best. We could call it all The Big Thank You.

Just imagine the ripple effect that would result. Think of how much it could mean to those doing the thanking and those getting thanked. With all that thanking going on, maybe we would learn to treat each other better, behaving more kindly and generously, than we do now.

Every day of the year should feel like Thanksgiving.

The Big Sorry

Before this year is over, before I forget and before I lose my nerve, let me check this item off my to-do list and just say what I have to say.

I'm sorry.

That's right. I'm hereby officially apologizing to everyone I ever wronged as a boy. It's a long list, but hey, you have to start somewhere.

To begin, I never apologized to that kid in the fifth grade I called fat, nor to all the Hebrew-school teachers in whose classes I seldom paid attention, nor to my sister for teasing her too much. So please let me do so now.

Sorry, all.

At age 15, while on duty as a salesman for a record retailer in a shopping mall, I regularly stole audiocassettes. The store detective told me he dubbed the thief "the phantom" and swore he would catch him in the act. Never happened.

Sorry about that.

I especially need to apologize to Larry, a kid a year older than I who lived in a house across the street from ours. One day some of us boys were roughhousing on our lawn, just rolling around in the grass and jostling each other. There lay Larry laughing and clearly enjoying the tussle with me standing over him. Then, for reasons I'll never understand, I kicked him in the face.

Larry clutched his jaw and howled in pain and shock and rolled from side to side. He ran home screaming. As it turned out, I had knocked out some of his teeth, and from then on he had to wear dentures.

As far as I can recall, Larry never told anyone. If he had, surely his parents would have talked to mine, and insisted we redress this grievance and pay his dental bills. But no. The incident remained our secret. Until now.

So I'm sorry, Larry. Sorrier than I can ever say. I never meant to hurt you. We were only playing, after all. Maybe you already know that. Still, I have no explanation and certainly no excuse.

Oh, I could go on about all the sins I committed as a youth. Throwing snowballs at cars and buses and trucks driving through the street, aiming at the windshields. Making prank phone calls to strangers to ask, "Is your refrigerator running? Maybe you better chase after it." Talking with my sister about my mother behind her back while in the same room because my mother is deaf and would never be the wiser. But the rap sheet would get encyclopedic.

The advent of a new year is as good a time as any for all of us who have any apologizing to do to clear our consciences and start fresh.

Of course, if I really meant business here, I would go one by one contacting anyone in my distant past to whom I owe an apology, rather than apologize en masse. The Big Sorry, I would call this personal campaign. But I have a day job, and it would take years.

If my youth proved unapologetic, though, my life as an adult has turned out to be anything but. Once I got married and we had children and I had to earn a living, I learned to apologize frequently. As a result, I'm what you might call an apologist— except for myself rather than, say, Big Tobacco or, for that matter, Congress. I would estimate, for example, that I've spent roughly half our marriage apologizing to my wife.

So accustomed am I to apologizing as an adult that somewhere along the line I developed the habit of apologizing in advance. I'll start a sentence with "Sorry if this offends anyone, but . . . " or "Forgive me if I'm being too negative here, but . . . " Apologizing pre-emptively eliminates the pressure to apologize after the fact.

Why I'm now looking to make amends has mainly to do with guilt. Guilt, despite its bad name, is actually good. Guilt is motivational. Guilt calls you out. Without guilt we might never feel sorry about anything, or even show up at our jobs. You could do a lot worse than to live a life governed by guilt. So feel free to consider me guilty as charged.

Shame and regret over wrongdoing can be highly instructive. You need the whole package in order to tender a heartfelt and full-blooded apology.

That's why I never quite understood the rationale for Yom Kippur, the Jewish Day of Atonement. Unlike some Jews, I believe setting aside a single day for penance is grossly insufficient. Who can possibly pack all the remorse we feel into only 24 hours? No, I believe in seeking redemption year-round.

And for this, by the way, I make no apology.

Hooked On Hoops: Part 5

You're 60 years old now. Go ahead, say something witty about that, hotshot. Like how often you get up at night to pee. Hysterical. Or about how it feels to suffer a detached retina. Twice.

So what have you learned? Here's what. Play the same game long enough, often enough, hard enough, attentively enough and you're bound to pick up a lesson or two, right? Experience translates into expertise, yes? In the bargain, you might get a pretty good read on yourself. It's like a longitudinal study—as with glaciers, you can see change only over a long time.

Basketball has great lessons to teach, more, you believe, than most any other sport. Reveals personality and character. Your decisions—whether you try hard, whether you shoot or pass, whether you play defense -- are instantly and unmistakably telling.

You pass even more now. Against your grain, in defiance of five utterly narcissistic decades and change, you pass the ball. When a teammate to whom you've passed the ball hits his shot, it feels like you've scored together. Good for him. Good for you. Good for us. Your teams actually score points without you shooting all that much. Imagine that. Sometimes win, too.

So *that's* why your teammates are out there.

Why, then, do you play? Because in a life that's almost exclusively mental, it feels good to get physical. Because in an existence that often feels premeditated, you need that jolt of spontaneity. Because even though you're eligible for Social Security, you're never too old to act young, never too much a man to try to stay a boy forever, never lacking enough in life to do your utmost to attempt to detain death.

Even at this stage, you keep discovering new reasons to keep playing. Even better ones. You've also learned the hardest of lessons, to try selflessness on for size. You're finally good enough at the game to set yourself aside, at least now and then anyway. To stop seeking your own glory and do some good for someone else. To connect with others, to teach, to help, to inspire, even. It's no longer how much you get, it's more how much you give. You've changed your attitude.

Congratulations, champ.

You even occasionally make jokes out there about your advanced age. About needing an oxygen mask or, better still, a paramedic. You might accuse a kid who scores on you of having no respect for his elders. You try to be a statesman out there. You pass out advice. Win or lose, you congratulate opponents. Your curse less and compliment more. You try to spread a little sunshine.

All this took you a long time, a *really* long time—sometimes stuff does. But then, you're a slow study, your evolution typically seismic. Now each time you play you look to commit a random and utterly thankless act of kindness with no desire for reciprocity whatsoever. Reaching this milestone, getting your head on straight, only took you about 50 years.

Now, at last, you know why you play. You get to be on a team.

Last Call For Unfinished Business

More than 15 years ago, I broke away from almost everyone in my family. My mother, my maternal grandmother, my sister, my uncles, my aunts, my cousins, my nieces and my nephews. Just stopped all communications—no letters, no phone calls, no e-mails, just resounding silence. It was like quitting a job, except I resigned, in effect, from my respective roles as son, grandson, brother, uncle, nephew and cousin.

Why I chose to do so is complicated. My father had died and some wrangling over his estate ensued. I had money problems and career issues. I believed my family had largely neglected me, my wife, and our children. Promises broken took a cumulative effect. I felt like an afterthought, cheated and hurt, and in turn, decided to spare our immediate family any further anguish. Bailing out seemed a simple solution.

But I often questioned my strategy of retreat. My commitment felt at once deeply right and deeply wrong, almost equally so.

By 2009, I realized I'd gone missing in action for too long. I'd grieved for my father and nursed my ego and pulled together my career and finances. I came to see that although the slights I suffered, emotional and financial alike, were more real than imagined, I was also probably a little too sensitive for my own good. Going through your life feeling always wronged is no life at all, especially if you then hurt others. The years had rendered much of my rationale for going AWOL largely irrelevant.

Suddenly, then, I stopped believing I could go the rest of my life without seeing my family again. Enough was enough. Hard feelings had softened. Besides, why doom myself to live—and die—leaving unfinished business? I was no kid anymore, and neither was anyone else, so if we family ever were to come to terms, it had better be sooner rather than later.

And so, hastened by a newfound sense of urgency, I resolved to start fresh. I would reconnect with my family, member by member.

My mother, then 80, came first. It was she with whom I had suffered the deepest rift. I felt she should have paid closer attention to me as I grew up, shown more concern, and spent more time with our children.

Our long-overdue reunion in my hometown in New Jersey went fine. We talked it all through. I told her about a song I remembered we schoolchildren sang when we went on a field trip and our bus arrived somewhere. "We're here because we're here because we're here because we're here," we sang. And so on, singsong, stanza after stanza the same. She nodded in understanding and patted my hand.

"I'm sorry," I said.

"I'm sorry, too," she said.

We held hands and hugged.

Since then, I've reconciled with other immediate family, too. In some cases, it turned out to be rough going. No campaign to make amends with family after falling out of touch is ever easy. Skepticism and suspicion may abound. For me it took phone calls, e-mails, and visits around the country.

One of my uncles, my mother's brother, still simmered with anger at me for "turning my back" on his sister and his mother, "the two women who loved you as a boy more than anyone." One of my aunts, the youngest of my father's sisters, asked me point-blank why I had disappeared in the first place and said she looked forward to hearing my explanation.

I made my case with my uncle and aunt as best I could. I acknowledged that going off the reservation seemed a good idea at the time, but less so in retrospect. In conversation with my uncle, I felt so bad about how all the misunderstandings had metasticized that I broke down crying.

On Thanksgiving in 2013, I patched together the final pieces to my family life. I came together with relatives, some now survivors of divorce and disease and loss of spouses, whom I had last seen at my father's funeral in 1997, almost 17 years earlier.

There, more than 1,000 miles from home, I reestablished my relationships with my father's two sisters, then 85 and 79, as well as three of my first cousins. No one cross-examined me or staged an intervention, much less expressed disappointment or bitterness.

"You're family," my Aunt Zelda told me. "You'll always be family," my Aunt Gayle said.

We each took turns at the table citing our causes for gratitude in 2013. "I'm just grateful to be welcomed back into the fold," I said.

"Well," one of my cousins responded, "nobody ever kicked you out."

Try though we do to catch up, we'll never get caught up. All the time lost, all the moments missed, will never be regained. However hard we try, nothing will be the same again. Bonds forged late may now run shallow.

This much I know for sure: together, at least for me, is better than apart, even if it comes late in the game. We're all running out of runway.

Maybe I expected too much from my family—too much attention, too much affection, too much advice. People with the narrowest gap between what they expect and the reality they get are supposedly the happiest. Expecting too much, much less much too much, can be a prescription for disappointment.

Then again, maybe they all delivered too little.

How much does it really matter anymore?

If life is both a hanging on and a letting go, then sometimes we have to do one in order to do the other. After all, we're here because we're here because we're here because we're here.

A Return To The Scene Of The Crime

Forty years ago, only five weeks after I'd moved into New York City, a stranger came at me with a knife and stabbed me in the chest.

Hello, Bob. Welcome to the big city.

As anniversaries go, this is hardly worth celebrating. But it's certainly worth remembering.

It happened around noon on a hot Saturday in Manhattan's East Village. I'd left behind my family's split-level in the suburbs of Northern New Jersey and, freshly graduated from college at age 23, moved into a $150-a-month studio, complete with roaches as roommates, on East 7th Street between Avenues A and B. Jobless, I figured it would only be a matter of time before I launched an illustrious literary career.

This was 1975, of course. A national recession had taken hold and hit New York

City especially hard. Mayor Abe Beame was considering defaulting on loans, declaring municipal bankruptcy and asking the federal government for a hand. Less than four months later, President Gerald Ford would tell the city, in effect, to drop dead, as unforgettably phrased in a legendary Daily News front page headline. Stuff had hit the fan.

Serious crime had gained a foothold, too. Tompkins Square Park, across the street, was overrun with drug dealers and drug addicts. Someone once climbed past my window on the fire escape in my building, followed by a cop with his gun out yelling for him to stop. Among my fellow tenants was a working prostitute and an aspiring arsonist, eight years old, with a nasty habit of setting fires in our incinerator room.

Whichever neighborhood you visited, but especially below 14th Street, you always dreaded the thug who might be lurking around the next corner. The whole city seethed with menace, seeming, even in daylight, somehow drowned in shadows.

Whoever had stabbed me got away with it. Only recently have I returned to the scene of the crime, at least in memory, and thought through how the experience shaped me.

To begin, I quickly grew more wary, more guarded. I'd come to the big city swaddled in suburban innocence. In the 20 years I grew up in Fair Lawn, New Jersey, our town saw exactly one murder, its first in decades.

Now I adopted a more confident walk, striding along with almost military erectness, affecting extra swagger at night for good measure, meant to convey that I would be no pushover. If I happened to pass a tough-looking guy on the street, I always looked him in the eyes. If anyone ever stared at me on the subway, I made a point to stare back. Though often afraid, I never acted it.

You could say I carried myself with a chip on both shoulders. Once, on an autumn stroll through Fairfield, Connecticut, with everything appearing almost cinematically idyllic, I turned to my boyhood friend and his wife. And, without even meaning to be a wise guy, I found myself asking him, "So what do you do for hostility around here?"

I turned more confrontational, too, even combative. I stepped in to break up fistfights between adolescents in the schoolyard around the corner from where I now live. If a car blocked a crosswalk on a red light, I slammed the hood in passing in protest.

A cab once swerved around a corner as I crossed a street near Third Avenue and almost clipped me, forcing me to leap clear. I chased the cab down the block almost 100 yards to the next stoplight. I pounded on the driver-side window, yelling at the cabbie that he could have killed me.

I took to watching movies where someone wronged wreaked revenge in the name of justice. The 1970s, of course, introduced us to the "Death Wish" series and Clint

Eastwood's Dirty Harry. Seeing payback doled out to bad guys, the more violently the better, took me back to my stabbing. Those narratives gave me a special voyeuristic thrill that has lasted even to this day.

For a few years, in my quest for redress of grievance, however oblique it might turn out to be, I played investigative journalist. I wrote magazine articles about how defense attorneys and police can rig lineups against either suspects or victims, about how physicians unfit to practice medicine by dint of drug addiction, alcoholism, psychiatric impairment or other compromising characteristic remained in good standing in the medical profession courtesy of whitewash-by-conspiracy, and how teachers who had no business teaching— either because they were abusive toward students or poorly trained or incompetent or barely literate or chronically absent—nevertheless kept collecting a paycheck.

I promised myself never again to let anyone physically get the best of me in case I faced another threat to survival. Recalling all too well a boyhood when bullies sometimes picked on me, I stayed fit, mostly through pick-up basketball in local playgrounds. If anyone ever fouled me too hard, I made a point to foul him right back, sometimes harder. I also shadowboxed, as if in training for a showdown, sometimes pretending to be pummeling my mugger.

In the case of my attack, the criminal justice system obviously let me down, whether by design or inadvertently. For all I know, my mugger went on to hurt others, even killed someone. Today, as a result, I'm averse to trusting the judicial process in general and lawyers in particular. All in all, I developed a serious problem with letting anyone get away with doing anything I considered unjust. For years I could nurse a grudge with the best, and my hardened attitude won me no fans. Unyielding in my self-righteousness, I dropped friends and shunned colleagues over slights. At one point I went 10 years without speaking to my mother.

New York City has never looked quite the same to me either since I was stabbed. Yes, I feel safer on the whole now, especially since the 1990s. But then, I moved to Queens in 1977, settling into a high-rise apartment complex right around the corner from a police precinct, and stopped commuting to a job in Manhattan in 2008. That's skewed my view.

Even so, much as I love it in the city, any time I venture into certain other neighborhoods—including Midtown, by the way—it feels as if some silent and sinister undercurrent is always simmering just beneath a thin surface of civility.

Oh, I could tell you that I suffered nightmares from the trauma for years, that I had to be heavily medicated to stay functional, that my personality was irreparably warped, that I wound up doomed to disappointment in the whole of humanity, and that I finally went rogue, stalking unsuspecting wrong-doers, an avenging angel wielding my own long knife.

But none of that would be true. Sure, the scar on my chest is still visible. Sure, getting mugged hardened me. But compared to other victims of violent crime, I got off easy.

Indeed, in the end—despite my heightened sensitivity, borderline paranoia, high-beam hypervigilance and hair-trigger indignation at injustice—the incident otherwise appears to have made little difference in how my life turned out. I married the right woman 38 years ago and we have two children, now fine young adults. I pursued a rewarding career, cultivated new friends and reunited with my mother.

Would my life have come out the same if no one had ever attacked me in my doorway that day? Maybe. I'll never know.

This much I do know. You can take precautions against danger—and make no mistake, by all means you should—but nothing in life is ever guaranteed, least of all your safety and peace of mind. You lose a job you love. Your father dies suddenly. Your three-year-old daughter is hospitalized, gravely ill.

Eventually we all get caught unawares. All of us get mugged. All that matters, really, is what you do afterwards.

Nothing Ends

My grandfather Benjamin Sheft and I walked side by side as the No. 4 IRT line rattled thunderously overhead. The afternoon sun cast a flickering crosshatch of shadows through the railway tracks onto 161st Street. Vendors lined the street selling baseball programs and pennants and photos. The aroma of beer and peanuts wafted from all the open bars onto the sidewalks.

The historic building loomed over us. We passed through the Gate 2 turnstile and took a winding ramp upwards. My Poppa kept his hand on the cusp of my shoulder to make sure I'd stay alongside him.

We reached the upper deck in left field and stepped out into the stands. I scanned the panorama under the Bronx sky. I'd come to Yankee Stadium on Sunday, Oct. 11, 1964, to see the New York Yankees play the St. Louis Cardinals in the fourth game of the 1964 World Series.

We sat as far away from home plate as humanly possible without actually leaving the premises. Nosebleed city. The players looked so small. All sounds from the field—the crack of the bat, a ball smacking into a mitt—were delayed a fraction of a second.

And so the game started. Leadoff hitter Phil Linz doubled. Bobby Richardson doubled, driving in Linz. Roger Maris singled, sending Richardson to third. Mickey Mantle singled, scoring Richardson. Elston Howard singled, bringing Maris home. Already, in the first inning, the Yankees led 3-0. All feels right with the world. The Yankee dynasty will yet again dominate baseball. Here, in the mother of all stadia, the Yanks will roll to World Series championship number 21.

I felt so giddy that I turned to my Poppa. "I wish this would never end," I said. And for a moment I expected him to tell me it never would.

Instead, he looked at me seriously, though with a smile. "Everything comes to an end," he said.

I had no idea what he meant. Certainly I doubted it to be true. How could it be? Everything will last forever. Of this I was quite confident. The Yankees will always be the Yankees and nobody you love will ever die.

The Cardinals came to bat in the sixth inning with the Yankees still up 3-0. Carl Warwick singled, and so did Curt Flood. Dick Groat hit a grounder to Bobby Richardson that looked like an automatic double play, only for the usually reliable second baseman to fumble the ball. Suddenly the bases were loaded. Third baseman Ken Boyer—older brother of Yankee third baseman Clete Boyer; the only brothers ever to face each other in the history of the World Series—stepped to the plate. Yankee pitcher Al Downing threw a high changeup.

Boyer swung and got all of it. He belted a shot that sailed out toward left field, heading straight for me personally. The ball climbed higher and higher, coming closer and closer. I held up the glove I brought to the game to catch it. Except now the ball dipped, sinking, and cleared the left-field wall, landing in the first deck below us. A grand slam home run.

With a single stroke, the St. Louis Cardinals took the lead, 4-3. Yankee Stadium went as quiet as you'll ever hear it with 66,312 ticketholders in the stands.

My own father had long since lost interest in baseball, too busy with work to pay attention to a sport that I ranked with breathing and eating. In any given October, he has no clue which teams competed in the World Series. He once took me to Yankee Stadium, a doubleheader against the Minnesota Twins, and there proved once and for all his utter indifference to baseball. Somewhere around the fourth inning, exhausted from his job, with cracked peanut shells littered in his lap and some 50,000 fans cheering all around, he actually dozed off, snoring away with Harmon Killebrew warming up in the on-deck circle.

My grandfather filled in for my father on the baseball front. In the very best of scenarios, a 12-year-old boy who loves baseball gets to share his love with someone older. He gets someone who will tell him about seeing Babe Ruth swat home runs and

Joe DiMaggio roam the outfield.

He took me to my first major-league baseball game at Yankee Stadium in 1960 and we saw Yankee pitcher Mel Stottlemyre hit an inside-the-park grand slam, the first pitcher to do so since 1910. We left the stands after the game and walked out onto the field, toward the exit near Monument Park in center field. One day, in one of his Friday visits to our home, Poppa brought me a surprise, an encyclopedia of baseball. The heavyweight volume was crammed with every statistic imaginable, and then some, and I devoured every page.

I could always count on Poppa's attention and never needed to court his affection. He always seemed glad to see me, asked after me, worried about me, doted on me. In this sense, he turned out to be the father I needed my father to be. All the more reason for me to adore my Poppa.

"Everything comes to an end," my Poppa said in 1964. And for a long time, I refused to believe him with all the brute will of an innocent who knows no better.

But after my Poppa died of cancer at age 70 in 1981, I finally believed him. The World Series game I saw with him came to an end (the Cardinals won the game and the Series). The Yankee streak of World Series appearances came to an end that very year, leading to a drought until 1976, by far the longest in team history. The team even fired manager Yogi Berra and announcer Mel Allen.

The original Yankee Stadium came to an end, too, the hallowed cathedral demolished before our eyes. The Bronx as we knew it -- the Bronx where I was born and lived my first 28 months -- came to an end by the mid-1960s. So, too, did my boyhood.

Then again, maybe my wish that everything will last forever has some truth to it, too. The Yankees are still the Yankees. Baseball is still baseball. And my Poppa will always be my Poppa.

After all, he loved me enough to take me to see baseball games when baseball meant the world to me. I still wear his Swiss watch and, come winter, his plaid woolen overcoat. I think of him often, all the more when baseball season rolls around.

Nothing you love ever really dies unless you let it.

How I Failed My Father

Dear Dad,

Inside the chapel, I stepped toward your coffin to gaze at you lying there, still and silent. I leaned over to kiss your forehead, now cold. It was February 1997, and you, age 70, were dead. You keeled over in the kitchen from a massive heart attack.

In the car on the drive over, I had expected to stay calm. But at the sight of the funeral home, I gasped in disbelief and sorrow.

Later, in the synagogue, I approached the podium to deliver the eulogy, only for my knees to buckle.

I told how you always acted so gently toward me, never expressing anger or raising your voice, and how you only once spanked me, but reluctantly, without force.

Tears streamed down my face. Sobs caught in my throat. I was a mess.

As we headed to the cemetery, I remembered how you, in reality, had failed me as a father.

You were hardly ever around. You left the house for work before anyone else woke up and usually stayed out until after we got to bed. You were always on the go, no sooner here than gone again, less here than gone.

Even on weekends, you came home mainly to eat and sleep. You remained remote from us, all but incommunicado, often napping in your recliner in the den downstairs.

I knew why. You sought asylum from the pressures of being a husband and father and brother and son. Sleep turned out to be the only neutral country that would take you in, the only territory you felt you could call all your own.

Yes, you brought me to work with you and took me fishing and once played catch with me on our front lawn. But otherwise you exempted yourself from asking about my friends and offering to help with my homework or otherwise participating in my life. I hardly knew you, nor you me. I often felt like an afterthought.

Back in the 1950s and 1960s, that's how most of our fathers acted—all business. It was how society expected breadwinning fathers to act.

You put work first and family second, even after your children and grandchildren arrived. Your dedication to the TTY dominated your life and mine and ours. You kept your distance from me and Mom and Linda and my own son and daughter. Maybe all you ever really grasped about family was the idea of distance.

Maybe, in a sense, you never really got off that train that took you away from home as a boy for 10 years.

We reached the cemetery and chanted Kaddish, a Hebrew prayer sad enough, I swear, to induce mourning even if no one has died. And then we laid you in the freshly dug winter soil.

After we buried you, about to leave you alone at last, much as you always wanted to be left alone, my Uncle Ward spoke to me and my sister.

"We all know he could have spent more time with his family," he said, "but he's a hero to the deaf community. So we should still think of him as a success."

It seemed too late for me to do anything more. The opportunity to reconcile appeared gone for good. We'd both blown it big-time.

Except that belief turned out to be mistaken.

In all the years since you died, I've kept searching for you. I've asked family and friends about you, about why you lived as you lived. And I've learned a lot I never suspected. And confronted the underlying facts.

Your sisters both told me how hard you tried to please your own father, but never successfully. A friend told me how you once stepped in to stop a bully in your neighborhood from picking on other kids. A former colleague told me how you served as an advocate for the deaf community for decades without ever expecting a dime in return.

So many fathers have always worked. They could have worked less. They could have spent more time being fathers. But maybe our fathers have done some good in the world. Maybe they influenced all of deaf culture for the better. What then? How much of a right do we have to feel wronged?

Maybe plenty. Then again, maybe none.

The decision your parents made to send you to school so far away at so young an age spelled your salvation in a society which otherwise might have given you a much smaller role to play. In the end, my grudge toward your parents about that decision wound up buried alongside you, where it belonged.

Because of your parents, that long train ride to the Midwest delivered you not only to your destination but also to your destiny. You then answered the calling only you could hear.

From the children of geniuses perhaps certain compromises are to be expected, and certain injustices accepted, especially if the genius is also a hero.

And so I came to feel closer to you in death than I ever had in life. Sometimes nothing brings people to life more than dying.

Now I understand this: You failed me, but I—if to a lesser extent—failed you, too.

I never acknowledged the hardships you faced being born deaf. I never paid much attention to anything you tried to teach me about the value of education, of hard work, of making money. I could hear perfectly, but tuned you out.

I must have disappointed you as much as you had me. I performed poorly in school. I took a while to get going in a career. I could have handled money better. I acted as if I needed no one, least of all my father, to tell me how to do anything.

Our fathers often fail us, just as I no doubt often fail my own two children. Wanting to get fatherhood exactly right renders our failures inevitable. But all of us, or at least some of us, could be better sons and daughters, too.

I'm haunted by how much we left undone. But you and I will never truly be done. I'll always see your face and hear your voice in my dreams.

Grudges nursed too long turn toxic. So of course I've long since forgiven you. But only recently have I begun to forgive myself, too.

Your loving son,

Bob

To Be Heard: Part 2

I started writing seriously at age 15, reporting for my junior high school and then high school newspapers. By 18, I decided with absolute certainty that I would someday write for a living. I served as editor-in-chief for my college newspaper. My first job turned out to be with a weekly community newspaper in Manhattan.

And I've made a living of sorts as a writer for 40-plus years now, logging 10 as a full-time freelancer. In a career marked by successes seldom more than modest, I've contributed to newspapers, magazines, corporations, nonprofit organizations, public relations firms.

In the process, I've written just about anything and everything you can write to earn your keep: how-to pieces, investigative articles, celebrity profiles, newsletters, brochures, two novels that went deservedly unpublished, a non-fiction book about athletes surviving cancer, white papers, market-research reports, issue-oriented op-eds, blog posts, web copy and, particularly over the last decade, personal essays about family and friends.

Of course every writer has certain reasons for writing. Maybe the incentive is literary self-expression or advocating for causes. Then again, maybe it's a quest for wealth and fame. For myself, though, I suspect an extra underlying motive.

I write, in a sense, to communicate with my mother, profoundly deaf since infancy. More specifically, I write to be heard.

Writing, after all, has unmistakable advantages over speaking. Writing is generally carried out in silence, much, for that matter, like reading. Nobody has to be able to hear your voice. Nobody has to come face to face with you, much less read your lips, see your facial expression or interpret your gestures. Nobody cares whether you talk too fast or move your mouth enough. You never have to repeat yourself. You minimize the probability of misunderstanding.

In writing, too, you have time to think about which words you're going to put down. You can go back over your first draft and revise—all conversation is a first draft—giving yourself second chances ad infinitum. And then, when you're finished, the words -- rather than floating in the air, only to evaporate—are right there, on page or screen, starkly laid out, with a stamp of permanence, in black and white.

When you write, then, even a deaf person can understand you. You can get through to your mother once and for all. She will now nod her head up and down to indicate comprehension. She will detect your cries from the crib. You will at long last be heard.

Still, even to this day, every time I write, it's as if I'm re-enacting those early attempts to communicate with my mother, now 87. I'm still struggling, still second-guessing myself, if only subconsciously, to get through to the one person on the planet I then most needed to understand me. If my writing ever fails -- as writers go, I'm pretty meticulous, tinkering, tweaking, polishing—I suspect I'm somehow failing my mother.

Only now, all these years later, do I realize that just as her deafness defined her, it also defined me. As it turned out, the very silence my mother heard almost all her life gave me my voice.

Taking A Bullet

We were halfway through lunch, my wife and I, when I saw a man running across the street toward us with a gun in his hand.

We were at a Cajun restaurant we used to like on Austin Street in Forest Hills, Queens. On this steamy Saturday afternoon in August, its shutters were flung open, leaving local passers-by in full view. Only two other tables in the place were occupied, both with couples. Fans spun overhead, and Delta blues played in the background. The air was fragrant with beer.

The bride and I, some 15 years into our marriage now, had gone by ourselves, our two kids still small and back at the apartment with their grandmother watching over them. We had ordered something suitably Creole, blackened catfish or crawdaddies rémoulade or some such. As best I can recall, we were probably talking about Michael and Caroline, parenting being always an emotional imperative but very much a managerial matter, too.

My seat faced the front door, Elvira across from me, her back to the outside, so she saw nothing of what was happening on the street behind her. But here he came now, maybe all of 30 yards away, running across the street right toward us, a stranger holding a pistol in the air.

I said nothing. No one else in the restaurant said anything or moved or seemed to notice. The event seemed to be happening exclusively to me.

After a second, I stood from our table and went around to the other side. The gunman came closer, looming larger against the building behind him. I could see him better now, tall and husky, his eyes wide and darting. I stepped between him and my wife without a word.

Then the man veered to the right, out of sight, and just as suddenly I saw why. A uniformed police officer came sprinting across the street after him, his gun out, too. The cop yelled something, it was hard to make out what, until he, too, swerved right, pursuing his prey.

Then, nothing. No more men running, no more guns held aloft. Just a lazy, sticky summer afternoon, shoppers still streaming all but obliviously along the Forest Hills version of Fifth Avenue, past the hair salon and the sushi place, maybe heading to the Midway Theater for that summer's blockbuster movie.

What are you doing? Elvira asked me as I stood behind her chair.

Uh … was going to the bathroom, I said, but … uh … changed my mind. I went back to my chair and sat down.

Nothing had changed, nothing except me, my heart still racing, my hands trembling, my throat suddenly dry. I tried to finish my lunch, but my appetite was gone. I sat and sipped my beer.

I kept the incident to myself. I knew that telling my wife just then would ruin her appetite, too. I also knew her well enough to realize that starting such a conversation would just get her going about life in this city, about the dangerous people out and about who should be put away for life without a second thought.

She had grown up in Williamsburg, Brooklyn, whereas I spent my childhood in the suburbs of Bergen County, N.J., so she knew a little more than I did about violence in the city. She had seen more of it, was much touchier about it, and certainly shared none of my romantic belief that there might be something cool about it.

I finally told her about the episode a week later, long enough to let her lunch go down.

You must really love me, Elvira said.

Must is right, I said.

And that was all we ever had to say about it.

Only years later have I reflected on why I did what I did that day. I'd lived in the city 20 years by then, leading a quiet, orderly, white-collar life, a deep groove worn in the route between my home and office. My comfort zone measured all of about four square inches; acts of daring were hardly my hallmark. I never stood too close to the subway tracks and usually stayed on the curb at red lights. So much did I watch my step, so safe did I play it, that if I went to a drive-in movie, I probably buckled my seat belt.

I was more or less a beta male in a city packed with alphas. As such, I've lived a life marked largely by anxiety and doubt and deliberation, by compromise and indecision and second-guessing, whether with family, friends or colleagues, my tongue curbed, my eyes averted and my punches pulled—in short, a life absolutely tattooed with certain characteristics of cowardice.

But in that moment in the Cajun restaurant, I acted completely out of character. Acted without thinking, without hesitating, without doing a risk-benefit analysis. Acted right on the edge of reflex, primal instinct my only guide, for once fearless. Acted, really, as we should act when our city threatens us, when some menace tests our courage as the suburbs seldom do, in order to protect what matters most to us.

I made my decision that day, a decision as unambiguous as any I ever made, the right decision. Maybe I'd just seen too many action movies. In any case, I did what needed to be done, and maybe doing it once will turn out to be enough to redeem me.

Nothing really happened that day—no shots were fired, no one was wounded—but in one respect something very much happened. For years I'd often asked myself that classic big question: Exactly how much do I love my wife, the mother of our children, the woman I always say has meant everything to me? Can such love be measured?

Would I, in fact, take a bullet for her?

Now I know.

Going, Going, Gone

Back in late June of 2011, my wife of 32 years left me. Elvira went to Rome and took our daughter Caroline with her, while I stayed in our apartment in New York City, in Forest Hills, Queens, with our son Michael.

Elvira and I had never spent more than about a week apart since our wedding, and I felt a loneliness that echoed my life before I met her. But three weeks later, she and Caroline returned home and our family of four resumed living together.

The next year, Elvira again left me for Rome, again with Caroline, and again I felt at a loss without her around. Again they stayed away for three weeks, and again they came back.

Right about here I probably should explain. Technically, nobody was abandoning anyone. Caroline intended to pursue a career in Italy as an opera singer, first to train on the island of Ischia and then to explore opportunities to perform with local opera companies. And Elvira, ever the devoted mother and trusted advisor, joined her on both trips to make sure everything went right.

Each time my wife left, I was of course sorry to see her go. But I also expected to fare okay, if only because I knew she would be back within weeks. The visits to Italy seemed rather a grand adventure, innocent and harmless, nothing more than Elvira and Caroline, always close to each other, off to the cradle of opera for purposes strictly professional.

It even pleased me as family breadwinner to finance these extended European excursions. Surely it was just a matter of time before Caroline, as she long dreamed of doing, starred as Mimi in "La Boheme" at the Teatro dell'Opera di Roma to standing ovations. I felt every inch a doting father, loyal husband and angel investor—essential to the enterprise and, for the first time in my life, even vaguely international.

Then the game plan changed. Caroline decided instead to become a chef. Elvira would return to Italy, only now to rent an apartment in Florence so Caroline could train at a nearby culinary school. This change in direction came as no whim. Our daughter, even as a little girl, felt drawn to fine food, cultivating her palate as Elvira cooked with style at home and took her to restaurants of every ethnicity.

So away Elvira went for yet a third time, in 2013, but now for two months. Again I regretted her departure, and felt incomplete throughout. But I sensed I could keep myself more or less together until she returned.

Except now Elvira and Caroline found themselves smitten to the marrow with everything Italian. None of which came as a big surprise. Elvira is a third-generation Italian-American, her grandfather from Salerno, and Caroline takes pride in her Italian heritage. With each visit to Italy they came more and more under the spell of *la dolce vita*—and of the art and architecture, the food, the language, the lifestyle, the Italians themselves.

And so Caroline made up her mind to live in Italy full-time. She would put her savings toward buying a house and open her own restaurant. Elvira planned to live there, too, settling in Florence or Puglia or Sala Consilina, where her maternal grandfather was born. So yet a fourth trip was booked. But then they discovered an ancient hillside town named Guardia Sanframondi, about 50 miles north of Naples, and that's where Caroline bought herself a house.

Quickly both came to know the community and made friends. Both applied for residency permits and dual citizenship.

To this point, I never questioned why Elvira would leave me repeatedly, nor felt any cause to. Surely she had the purest of motives at heart. But now an unmistakable pattern took shape. Her absences overseas assumed an unexpected—and, as far as I was concerned, certainly unwelcome—frequency.

A certain suspicion now dawned on me. Why was my wife really going away yet again? Did Caroline, by now 25 years old, still need her along? Were these visits a ruse to divert me from the underlying agenda at play here—namely, that Elvira planned, however gradually, to leave me for good?

That seemed highly improbable. After all, we had something close to a model marriage. From the start, we felt comfortable being ourselves with each other. We've always found plenty to talk about, laugh about, and enjoy our intimacies. She not only finishes my sentences, she also starts a few. And raising our children always took top priority.

Yet our marriage remained far from perfect, and that's largely, if not entirely, my fault. I grew up spoiled, seldom accepting responsibility for anything and expecting everything to be done for me. I tended, as a result, to think of myself first, not to mention last.

In our early years together, for example, I should have worked harder. Even after our children came along, I could be arrogant and sarcastic, and deployed tantrums and cold shoulders with impunity. I struggled until about the age of 35 to attain anything remotely approximating adulthood.

So Elvira and I suffered certain tensions—over my attitude, mostly, but also my actions—and argued more than we would have liked. My egotism and indulgences tested her patience to a degree beyond exasperating. She had serious doubts, justifiably so, about my competence to function as a grown-up.

Once, she even mailed me a card imprinted on the front with "Thinking of You With Sympathy." On the back she wrote, "Because you are so annoying, my heart goes out to you."

She meant it, and I saw her point.

Even so, I believed we could count on each other to be husband and wife for keeps. But maybe I had missed something important in this whole equation—some sign lurking just below the surface that we had reached the breaking point. And if she had resolved to leave me, who was I to blame her?

More and more now I missed Elvira—her face, her voice, the feel of the skin on her neck. At night, before I went to bed, I left the TV on QVC, her favorite shopping channel, just to simulate her presence. I listened on occasion to her voicemail from the airport months earlier, just to hear her leaving me a message. We emailed updates to each other across the Atlantic Ocean and talked about once a week by Skype.

And then Elvira told me last year that she, too, wished to shop for a house in Guardia, presumably just for the two of us. She had had her fill of living in New York City after a lifetime here. With both of us now in our 60s, she knew I planned never to retire. "You'll love it here," she told me. "You can always go back and forth."

Now, I'd never expressed the least desire to live anywhere but New York City, much less in a town in Southern Italy with homes five centuries old. Born in the Bronx and a city resident my entire adult life, I'm a diehard New Yorker. Why would I move given my lifelong feeling that I occupy, in effect, the center of the known universe? And, by the way, was this another ploy to break away from me? To call me conflicted over all this would be an understatement of the highest order.

But more than anything I wanted Elvira happy. And in short order, she found a house she liked, and together we decided she would buy it. She was living another life now, a second life, with friends I'd never met, in a town I'd never seen, speaking a language still alien to my ears and tongue. The love of my life, my one and only, was now more than 4,000 miles away for about half the year, often gone during our anniversary and our birthdays and on Thanksgiving and Christmas. And I got to witness her making her getaway in slow motion.

I grew anxious that my life as I knew it could go asunder, and suspicion hardened into paranoia. Certainly Elvira intended to part company with me, all without coming right out and saying so. As I'd learned from my own family, those closest to you often harbor the deepest secrets.

I also realized as never before, now that we were increasingly separated, just how inseparable we had become—realized how much I needed her and depended on her, how central she was to my life. I took every opportunity to confide in her how much I missed her and loved her—and to declare once and for all how much I wanted us to stay together.

Yet, reassuringly, Elvira kept coming back home. She never "left me left me." She was still the same woman, the mother our children adored, only more worldly now, and more fulfilled, too. Twice a year we got a chance to get to know each other all over again, to start fresh.

And so for months I left my doubts unspoken. I would see how it all played out, and cross my fingers that it would be in my favor.

But I had seen something, and now I had to say something. And when Elvira returned from Italy six months ago, I confronted her face to face. I finally asked her the question I'd dreaded asking in case she gave me the answer I dreaded hearing.

"Are you leaving me?" I asked.

"Of course not," she said.

"If you are, please tell me."

"That's a silly question."

"But you're moving to Italy without me."

"And you'll eventually be joining me there."

At this moment, she's here, packing her suitcase, plus clothes and dishes and books and DVDs to ship to Italy, 19 boxes in all. Next week she'll take a taxi to Kennedy Airport to board a flight on Alitalia for Rome, and then be driven by car to her new home, to be with our daughter in her new life. She'll stay longer than ever before, most likely six months or so, and then come back in the spring.

But this December I'll visit her there for two weeks. And next year I'll visit again. And then, over the next few years, with any luck, I'll stay there longer and more often. And we'll each lead a double life, one together and the other apart. I'll know she's there and she'll know I'm here. And maybe all that distance will ultimately bring us closer and make our reunions ever sweeter.

This much I know for sure: Elvira is my true home. Wherever she goes, I'll follow. That's just non-negotiable. And then maybe, just maybe, I'll be old and she'll be old and we'll stay put in that little Italian town with all the time we have left together.

Acknowledgments

If I tried to thank everyone I really should thank, it would probably take another book. And this book should already reflect the gratitude I feel to family, friends, colleagues, editors, mentors and others too numerous to name here. Truth be told, if I felt any luckier than I do, I would spontaneously combust. And no one wants to see that happen, least of all on a New York City sidewalk. So let me give special credit to my agent, Linda Konner; my editor and publisher, Naomi Rosenblatt; and my boss, Pam Jenkins. But let's be clear here. No one has mattered more to me in my life, nor ever will, than my son Michael, my daughter Caroline, and of course my wife Elvira, my one and only, my be-all and end-all. She is my north, my south, the whole damn compass.

CPSIA information can be obtained
at www.ICGtesting.com
Printed in the USA
BVOW09s1105150617
486953BV00001B/4/P